OECD
Economic Surveys

Japan

2008

OECD

ORGANISATION FOR ECONOMIC CO-OPERATION AND DEVELOPMENT

The OECD is a unique forum where the governments of 30 democracies work together to address the economic, social and environmental challenges of globalisation. The OECD is also at the forefront of efforts to understand and to help governments respond to new developments and concerns, such as corporate governance, the information economy and the challenges of an ageing population. The Organisation provides a setting where governments can compare policy experiences, seek answers to common problems, identify good practice and work to co-ordinate domestic and international policies.

The OECD member countries are: Australia, Austria, Belgium, Canada, the Czech Republic, Denmark, Finland, France, Germany, Greece, Hungary, Iceland, Ireland, Italy, Japan, Korea, Luxembourg, Mexico, the Netherlands, New Zealand, Norway, Poland, Portugal, the Slovak Republic, Spain, Sweden, Switzerland, Turkey, the United Kingdom and the United States. The Commission of the European Communities takes part in the work of the OECD.

OECD Publishing disseminates widely the results of the Organisation's statistics gathering and research on economic, social and environmental issues, as well as the conventions, guidelines and standards agreed by its members.

Also available in French

Table of contents

Executive summary 10

Assessment and recommendations 13

Chapter 1. **Key challenges to sustaining the expansion in Japan** 23
  Recent economic trends in Japan and the short-term economic outlook 26
  The polarisation of this economic expansion poses risks 32
  Key challenges facing the Japanese economy 33
  Conclusion 42

  Notes 43

  Annex 1.A1. Taking stock of structural reforms 44

Chapter 2. **Bringing an end to deflation under the new monetary policy framework** 49
  Monetary policy since the end of quantitative easing 50
  The direction of monetary policy 52
  Monetary policy in the light of longer-term risks 57
  Conclusion 59

  Notes 60
  Bibliography 61

Chapter 3. **Achieving progress on fiscal consolidation by controlling government
  expenditures** 63
  How much progress has Japan made in addressing its fiscal problem? 64
  The government's medium-term fiscal plan 66
  Continuing the downward trend in government spending 72
  Conclusion: additional revenues are needed to achieve Japan's medium-term
  fiscal objectives 80

  Notes 82
  Bibliography 83

  Annex 3.A1. "Growth scenario" and "risk scenario" of the 2008
    Reference Projection 85

Chapter 4. **Reforming the tax system to promote fiscal sustainability and economic
  growth** 87
  Major challenges facing the Japanese tax system 88
  Analysis of the major taxes in Japan 97
  Directions for tax reform 117

  Notes 120
  Bibliography 122

Chapter 5. **Enhancing the productivity of the service sector in Japan** 125
    The role of the service sector in the Japanese economy 126
    Factors hindering the growth of the service sector 128
    Polices to promote higher productivity in the service sector 133
    Selected issues at the sectoral level 145
    Conclusion 163

    Notes 164
    Bibliography 168

Chapter 6. **Reforming the labour market to cope with increasing dualism
    and population ageing** 171
    Falling wages and labour market dualism 172
    Ensuring adequate vocational training in Japan 182
    Coping with rapid population ageing 184
    Conclusion 186

    Notes 187
    Bibliography 188

Boxes
  1.1. The yen carry trade and its economic impact 29
  1.2. Population projections for Japan 34
  2.1. The new monetary policy framework 50
  2.2. How large is the bias in Japan's consumer price index? 54
  2.3. Summary of recommendations for monetary policy 59
  3.1. Long-term fiscal projections by the Japanese government and the CEFP 70
  3.2. Summary of recommendations for medium-term fiscal consolidation 81
  4.1. Major features of the Japanese tax system 90
  4.2. Principles to guide tax reform 94
  4.3. Recent progress in tax reform in Japan: a follow-up of the 1999 *Economic
      Survey of Japan* 98
  4.4. Earned Income Tax Credit systems in OECD countries 113
  4.5. A comparison of the OECD recommendations with those of the
      Tax Commission 119
  5.1. Government initiatives to boost productivity in the service sector 134
  5.2. Regulatory reform in public administration 137
  5.3. The privatisation of Japan Post and financial-sector reform 161
  5.4. Summary of recommendations 163
  6.1. Summary of recommendations to reform the labour market 187

Tables
  1.1. Japan's rebound from a decade of economic stagnation 24
  1.2. Short-term economic projections 27
  1.3. Population indicators and projections for Japan 34
  1.4. Potential economic growth in OECD countries 40
  2.1. A chronology of Japanese monetary policy issues 51
  2.2. The Bank of Japan's economic outlook 53
  3.1. The evolution of the fiscal situation in Japan between 2002 and 2007 65

3.2. Evolution of the medium-term plan of the government. 68
3.3. Long-term fiscal projections through 2025 70
3.4. Long-term fiscal projections through 2050 71
3.5. Projection of social spending to FY 2015 73
3.6. Long-run projections for the public pension system. 73
3.7. Comparison of the unit cost of public and private construction 77
4.1. Personal income tax and social security contributions. 91
4.2. Summary of OECD recommendations 117
5.1. Labour productivity growth in the service sector by industry 128
5.2. Product market regulations in the non-manufacturing sector in the OECD area. . 130
5.3. Time and cost of starting a new business. 131
5.4. Benefits of regulatory reform 136
5.5. The three-year Regulatory Reform Programme in 2007 138
5.6. The special zone initiative. 139
5.7. JFTC enforcement activity 141
5.8. Key structural features of the retail distribution sector 146
5.9. Comparison of major service charges in international ports. 155
6.1. Employed persons by status 176
6.2. Employment by industry and employee status. 177
6.3. A comparison of regular and non-regular workers 177
6.4. Reasons given by firms for hiring non-regular workers 179

Figures

1.1. Explaining differences in income 25
1.2. Factors supporting business investment. 28
1.3. Exports and exchange rate 28
1.4. Wage growth has turned negative 30
1.5. Japan remains in mild deflation 31
1.6. An unbalanced economic expansion in Japan 32
1.7. Population ageing in OECD countries. 35
1.8. The fiscal situation in Japan 37
1.9. Tax revenue in OECD countries 38
1.10. The share of non-regular workers is rising. 41
2.1. Interest rate developments in Japan 52
2.2. Projections by the Bank of Japan's Policy Board members 56
2.3. Bank lending is decelerating 57
2.4. Land prices in Japan 58
3.1. OECD countries with a large public debt ratio 66
3.2. Decomposition of debt dynamics 67
3.3. Projection of the social security fund balance 69
3.4. Public investment and level of income by prefecture 76
3.5. Renewal and maintenance costs of public infrastructure 77
3.6. Comparison of wages and employment in the private and public sectors 78
3.7. An international comparison of public-sector employment 79
3.8. Wage gap between private and public employees by prefecture. 80
4.1. Trends in Japanese tax revenue, 1990-2005 89
4.2. The tax mix in OECD countries. 90

4.3. Composition of sub-national government tax revenues. 92
4.4. The impact of taxes and the social security system on income distribution
in Japan. 95
4.5. The gap in tax revenue across prefectures 96
4.6. Value-added taxes in OECD countries 99
4.7. Statutory corporate income tax rates 101
4.8. Tax expenditures in the corporate tax system. 102
4.9. Tax treatment of R&D in OECD countries 102
4.10. Proportion of firms making losses according to the national tax code. 103
4.11. International comparison of corporate taxes 105
4.12. Personal income tax 106
4.13. International comparison of tax wedges. 108
4.14. International comparison of labour force participation rates and part-time
employment. 109
4.15. Annual income of female part-time workers 110
4.16. Indicators of progressivity in OECD countries 111
4.17. Tax and social security payments by income decile 112
4.18. Impact of abolishing personal income tax deductions 112
4.19. International comparison of immovable property taxes 116
5.1. Labour productivity by sector 127
5.2. Mark-ups in manufacturing and non-manufacturing. 129
5.3. Product market regulation and productivity growth. 130
5.4. The role of ICT-using services in labour productivity growth 132
5.5. Overall progress in regulatory reform in Japan 135
5.6. International competition in the service sector. 143
5.7. Contribution of foreign affiliates in the service sector in OECD countries. . . . 144
5.8. Turnover of foreign affiliates as a share of wholesale and retail trade 147
5.9. OECD indicators of regulation in retail distribution. 148
5.10. Trends in electricity prices in major OECD countries 149
5.11. Regulatory reform in key service industries 151
5.12. Electricity prices in OECD countries. 152
5.13. The OECD indicator of network policies 153
5.14. International comparison of harbour charges 155
5.15. International comparison of landing and departure charges. 157
5.16. Regulations in professional services 158
5.17. Regulatory reform in public services 160
6.1. Unemployment in Japan 173
6.2. Wage developments in this expansion compared to past upturns. 173
6.3. Productivity, wages and the labour income share. 174
6.4. Employee compensation by component 175
6.5. The link between wage growth and part-time employment 179
6.6. An international comparison of long-term unemployment. 183
6.7. Long-term projections of the labour force. 184

This book has...

StatLinks

A service that delivers Excel® files from the printed page!

Look for the *StatLinks* at the bottom right-hand corner of the tables or graphs in this book. To download the matching Excel® spreadsheet, just type the link into your Internet browser, starting with the *http://dx.doi.org* prefix.
If you're reading the PDF e-book edition, and your PC is connected to the Internet, simply click on the link. You'll find *StatLinks* appearing in more OECD books.

BASIC STATISTICS OF JAPAN

THE LAND

Area (1 000 sq. km), 2006	377.9	Major cities, 2006 Population census
Cultivated agricultural land (1 000 sq. km), 2004	47.3	(million inhabitants):
Forest (1 000 sq. km) 2004	250.9	Tokyo (23 wards) 8.5
Densely inhabited districts[1] (1 000 sq. km), 2005	12.6	Yokohama 3.6
		Osaka 2.6
		Nagoya 2.2
		Sapporo 1.9
		Kobe 1.5
		Kyoto 1.5

THE PEOPLE

Population, August 2007 estimate (1 000)	127 785	Labour force in per cent of total population, 2007	52.2
Number of persons per sq. km in 2005	342.7	Percentage distribution of workers, 2007	
Percentage of population living in densely		Agriculture and forestry	3.9
inhabited districts in 2005[1]	66.0	Manufacturing	18.2
Net annual rate of population increase		Service	64.2
(2000-2005)	0.1	Other	13.7

PRODUCTION

Nominal gross domestic product in 2007		Share of agriculture, forestry and fishery in gross	
(trillion yen)	515.7	domestic product, at producer prices in 2006	
Growth of real GDP, 2007	2.1	(per cent)	1.5
Gross fixed investment in 2007		Share of manufacturing in gross domestic	
(per cent of GDP)	22.3	product, at producer prices in 2006 (per cent)	21.6
Growth of real gross fixed investment, 2007	–0.3	Growth of industrial production, per cent 2007	2.7

THE GOVERNMENT

			House of Representatives	House of Councillors
Public consumption in 2007 (in per cent of GDP)	17.6	Composition of Parliament,		
Current public revenue in 2006		January 2008:		
(in per cent of GDP)	34.5	Liberal Democratic Party	304	84
Government employees in per cent of total		Democratic Party	113	120
employment, 2007	9.7	Peace and Reform (*Komei*)	31	21
		Communist Party	9	7
		Others	22	10
		Vacancy	1	0
		Total	480	242
		Last elections	September 2005	July 2007

FOREIGN TRADE AND PAYMENTS
(2007, trillion yen)

			Exports	Imports
Commodity exports (fob)	79.7			
Commodity imports (fob)	67.3	By country (per cent)		
Services	–2.3	USA	20.1	11.4
Investment income	16.3	EU	14.7	11.3
Current balance	25.0	Asia	48.1	40.2
Exports of goods and services		Other	17.0	42.6
(in per cent of GDP)	17.6			
Imports of goods and services		By commodity (per cent)		
(in per cent of GDP)	15.9	Foodstuff	0.5	8.2
		Mineral fuels	1.2	27.8
		Machinery and transport		
		equipment	64.8	25.1
		Other	33.5	38.9

THE CURRENCY

Monetary unit: Yen	Currency unit per US$, average of daily figures	
	Year 2007	117.8
	January 2008	107.7

1. Areas whose population density exceeds 5 000 persons per sq. km.

Executive summary

T he Japanese economy is experiencing the longest expansion in its post-war history, and growth is projected to continue at a 1½ to 2% rate over the next two years. This expansion has been largely driven by buoyant business investment and strong export growth, especially to other Asian countries. Moving forward, Japan faces a number of challenges to sustained growth, most notably persistent deflation, a large and growing public debt and widening disparities between different segments of the economy. While large manufacturing firms have benefitted from buoyant export growth, the non-manufacturing sector – dominated by smaller firms – has been lagging in profitability, confidence, investment and wages. Dualism has also increased in the labour market, with a further rise in the share of non-regular workers, with lower wages and weaker social protection. Addressing these challenges requires a comprehensive package that includes sound macroeconomic policies and structural reforms to raise labour force participation and productivity while also tackling disparities in the economy.

Ensuring a definitive end to deflation. After raising the policy interest rate twice under the new monetary policy framework introduced in 2006, the Bank of Japan has appropriately left the rate unchanged since early 2007. Further hikes would not be warranted until inflation is firmly positive and the risk of renewed deflation is negligible, hence avoiding the risk of derailing the expansion. Given the need for an adequate buffer against deflation, the Bank's Policy Board should raise the lower bound of its understanding of price stability, which is now set at zero.

Achieving progress in fiscal consolidation. Japan has reduced its fiscal deficit from 8.2% of GDP in 2002 to around 4% in 2007 (excluding one-off factors). But government debt has continued to rise, reaching around 180% of GDP in 2007. It is essential to achieve the target of a primary surplus for central and local governments combined by FY 2011 as a first step towards reducing the government debt ratio in the 2010s. While the first priority is to further cut spending, measures to raise revenue are also needed.

Implementing a comprehensive tax reform. Tax reform should aim at promoting growth, addressing the widening of income inequality and improving the local tax system, in addition to raising additional revenue. Meeting these goals will require wide-ranging reforms, including an increase in the consumption tax rate and the broadening of the direct tax bases. With only a third of firms paying taxes and more than half of wage income exempted from taxes, there is significant scope for base broadening. Base broadening would facilitate a cut in the corporate tax rate to promote economic growth. Aspects of the tax system that discourage labour force participation and distort the allocation of capital should be removed, thereby accelerating growth. An Earned Income Tax Credit could be introduced to improve income distribution. The complicated local tax system should be simplified.

Enhancing the productivity of the service sector. Labour productivity in Japan is 30% below the US level. Closing this gap largely depends on reversing the significant slowdown in productivity growth in the service sector in recent years. This requires a comprehensive strategy aimed at promoting competition by accelerating regulatory reform, strengthening competition policy *and increasing international openness to trade and inflows of foreign direct investment. The special zone initiative should also be revitalised with more focus on nationwide regulatory reform. It is also essential to address regulatory problems in key service industries, such as the retail sector, energy, transport and business services.*

Tackling growing dualism in the labour market while promoting higher labour force participation. *The share of non-regular workers has reached about a third of employees, raising serious equity and efficiency concerns. Increasing dualism is creating a large segment of the population with lower wages, short-term job experience and limited opportunities to enhance their human capital. A broad strategy is required, including enhancing employment flexibility for regular workers and expanding social security coverage and training programmes for non-regular workers. Encouraging female labour participation is essential in the face of a rapidly ageing population.*

ISBN 978-92-64-04306-0
OECD Economic Surveys: Japan
© OECD 2008

Assessment and recommendations

*The expansion that began in 2002 remains
on track despite slower growth in 2007…*

The economic expansion, the longest in Japan's post-war history, continued through 2007, although at a slower pace of around 2%. This protracted upturn has reversed a decade of economic stagnation that reduced Japan's rank in per capita income from the fifth highest in the OECD area in 1992 to nineteenth in 2002. Business investment and exports have been the main drivers of growth, accounting for about three-quarters of increased output since 2002. Corporate restructuring to reduce excessive levels of debt, production capacity and employment laid the foundation for a rebound in business investment, while buoyant export growth boosted corporate profitability and demand for additional capacity. Closer trade links with Asia, which now accounts for one-half of Japanese exports, have sustained export growth during this expansion. In 2007, exports expanded almost 9% despite weak demand from the United States. With exports growing strongly and corporate profits at record levels, the expansion is projected to continue through 2009, with growth rates of between 1½ and 2%.

… and the uneven nature of the economic upturn…

Uncertainty about the world economy in the context of increased turbulence in international financial markets since mid-2007, coupled with the uneven pattern of growth in Japan, pose risks to continued growth. In contrast to buoyant exports and business investment, other components of domestic demand have decelerated since 2005. While strong export growth has favoured manufacturing, the non-manufacturing sector, which is more dependent on domestic demand, has been lagging in terms of profitability, confidence, investment and wage growth. With 90% of small and medium-sized enterprises in the non-manufacturing sector, the unbalanced recovery has also created a significant gap between large and small firms. In addition, regional inequality has increased, as areas specialising in manufacturing have benefited the most from this expansion. A more balanced economic expansion, with stronger growth in services, would ease these disparities.

*… in part due to falling construction activity
and wages*

Domestic demand has been further weakened by the disruption of construction activity after the revision of the Building Standards Law in June 2007, which resulted in a 40% drop in housing and corporate construction starts in the third quarter of the year. In addition, a 0.7% decline in wages during 2007, which reduced labour's share of national income to its lowest point since 1990, has limited private consumption. The persistent weakness of wages despite the marked fall in the unemployment rate is due in part to structural factors, notably the increasing portion of lower-paid non-regular workers in the labour force. Given weak domestic demand and falling wages, deflation continues with the core consumer price index (excluding food and energy) declining by about 0.2% in 2007, the ninth consecutive annual decline. The fall in the price deflators for GDP and private consumption was larger at around ½ per cent.

The central bank's decision to leave interest rates unchanged since early 2007…

Given slower output growth, increased uncertainty about the economic outlook and continued deflation, the Bank of Japan has appropriately kept its short-term policy interest rate unchanged at ½ per cent since February 2007. Under the new monetary policy framework introduced in 2006, the central bank sets the policy interest rate to achieve a path of sustainable growth under price stability. As part of the framework, the Bank of Japan's Policy Board announced that 0 to 2% is its understanding of price stability in the medium to long term, the first time that it has specified an inflation range. In addition, the central bank examines risk factors that may significantly impact economic activity and prices in the longer term.

… should be maintained, while reforming the new monetary policy framework introduced in 2006

The Bank of Japan should not raise the short-term policy rate further until inflation is firmly positive and the risk of renewed deflation becomes negligible. The central bank's outlook of a 0.4% rise in the consumer price index in FY 2008 is not sufficient to justify interest rate hikes for the time being, particularly as inflation has consistently undershot past projections. Waiting until inflation is significantly above zero would support the expansion and reduce the risk that a negative shock could push Japan back into deflation. The central bank's Policy Board should thus review the understanding of price stability and increase the lower end of the range to give an adequate buffer against deflation, as the zero floor is too close to deflation for comfort. While the announcement of the Board members' understanding of price stability enhances transparency, the fact that the inflation range will be reviewed each year makes it less useful as a guide for market expectations over the medium term. The course of monetary policy should take into account progress in fiscal consolidation, which will influence the pace of economic growth and the evolution of inflation.

Japan has made progress in fiscal consolidation…

Japan has reduced its fiscal deficit from 8.2% of GDP in 2002 to around 4% in 2007 (on a general government basis excluding one-off factors), with the improvement divided almost equally between spending cuts and revenue increases. Government expenditure has fallen in nominal terms, primarily as a result of continued declines in public investment and the public-sector wage bill, although this has been partially offset by increased social security spending in the context of population ageing. On the revenue side, the government phased out the temporary income tax reduction and raised social security contributions, but a significant share of the increase in revenue was due to the economic expansion. Overall, about one quarter of the decline in the budget deficit since 2002 is explained by cyclical factors. On a primary budget basis, the deficit fell at an annual pace of around ½ per cent of GDP, adjusted for cyclical factors, between 2002 and 2007.

... but achieving a further cut in the budget deficit to meet the government's medium-term fiscal objectives is crucial ...

Despite the reduction in the budget deficit, government debt has continued to rise, reaching around 180% of GDP in 2007, the highest level ever recorded in the OECD area. Further progress in fiscal consolidation is urgent, as Japan is increasingly vulnerable to a rise in the long-term interest rate from its current low level of around 1½ per cent. The government's medium-term plan targets a small surplus in the primary budget of central and local governments combined by FY 2011 as a first step to reduce the government debt ratio in the 2010s. With the primary budget deficit on a general government basis estimated at 3% of GDP in 2007 (excluding one-off factors), achieving a surplus in 2011 would require an acceleration in the pace of consolidation to about ¾ per cent of GDP per year. Moreover, stabilising the government debt ratio may require a significant primary surplus of 1% to 2% of GDP (on a general government basis), while an even larger surplus is necessary to achieve the objective of reducing the debt ratio.

... with the priority on further reductions in government expenditure...

Further cuts in government outlays should be the priority to achieve the fiscal targets. In 2006, the government announced reductions by spending category through FY 2011. This important step should help maintain public confidence in the government's fiscal consolidation plan. However, the spending cuts are calculated relative to a baseline of 3% nominal output growth – higher than the 1.7% projected by the OECD for 2007-09 – which implicitly allows government expenditures to increase at an annual rate of between 1.2% and 1.7% over the period 2007-11. Thus, the medium-term spending plan is not sufficiently ambitious and may allow government outlays to rise as a share of GDP. A stricter spending plan is needed to make sure that the fall in government expenditures over the period 2002-07 is not reversed. Maintaining the sustainability of the social security system, which is excluded from the government's medium-term fiscal target, is important to ensure that a primary budget surplus for central and local governments combined is not achieved through a deterioration in the fiscal balance of the social security system.

... focusing on public investment, government employment...

Much of the spending restraint to date has been achieved by cutting public investment from 6% of GDP in 2002 to 4% in 2007, but even this lower level is still above the OECD average of 3%. This suggests that there may still be scope for further reductions, which should be accompanied by a better allocation of investment to enhance its productivity. Indeed, public investment has not been an efficient instrument to reduce regional disparities, which should be addressed by other policies. The government expects the cost of maintaining existing infrastructure to exceed new investment by 2011 and completely crowd out new investment by 2022. It is important to develop a plan to close underutilised infrastructure, based on strict cost-benefit analysis in the context of a declining population, to retain some room for productivity-enhancing public investment. Spending has also been reduced by a cut in the total compensation of central government workers (including employees of central government corporations) from 2% of GDP in FY 2001 to 1.7% in FY 2005. The government aims to reduce it further so as to halve its share of GDP by FY 2015. Spending reductions should be extended to local governments, all public enterprises and government-affiliated organisations, which account for more than 90% of public-sector employment. In any case, the scope for expenditure cuts in this area is limited by the fact that public-sector employment per population in Japan is already well below the level in other major OECD economies. In addition to public investment and government wages, it is thus important to identify other areas for spending reductions.

... and the social security system

Controlling social security spending in the context of rapid population ageing is essential to limit the growth of government expenditures. Despite the reform of the public pension system in 2004 and some changes planned in healthcare, the government projects that gross public social spending – pensions, healthcare, long-term nursing care and welfare – will rise at a 3% annual rate over the next decade, boosting it by almost 1% of GDP to 18.4% by FY 2015. Pension reform was intended to limit pension spending to around 9¼ per cent of GDP over the next decade and ensure the sustainability of the system for 100 years, but the recent confusion about the accuracy of pension records creates doubts about pension administration. Moreover, the 2004 projections were based on strong assumptions. Despite the fact that some of these assumptions were revised downward in 2007, they are based on past trends and could prove to be fairly optimistic. Any slippage from the spending target should be resolved by a hike in the pension eligibility age, rather than by a further rise in the contribution rate, which is already set to increase from 13.6% in FY 2004 to 18.3% by FY 2017, and by measures to boost the return on the pension fund's assets. As for public healthcare spending, the government aims to limit the rise from 5.4% of GDP in FY 2006 to 5.8% in FY 2015, a figure still below the current OECD average of 6%, despite population ageing. The increase in public healthcare spending is expected to be reduced by a number of reforms, including a reduction in medical fees and a new healthcare system in FY 2008 for those over age 75. However, the hike in the share of medical expenses to be paid by patients between 70 and 74 has been postponed for a year. In addition, healthcare spending is to be limited by preventing lifestyle-related diseases and reducing the length of hospital stays, although the impact of these reforms on healthcare spending remains uncertain. The key to achieving higher quality and greater efficiency in healthcare is accelerating needed regulatory reforms, in part to allow a greater role for the private sector.

Fiscal consolidation will require increased tax revenues, preferably as part of a comprehensive tax reform

Given the substantial primary budget surplus needed to stabilise the government debt ratio and the difficulty of significantly reducing spending, achieving the fiscal targets will require as much as 6% of GDP in additional revenue in coming years, according to a government estimate. Moreover, reducing the debt ratio would require even more revenue. The government should implement a comprehensive reform of the tax system to raise the necessary revenue. However, it is important to boost revenues in a way that limits any negative impact on Japan's growth potential in the medium term. Moreover, changes in the tax system should be phased in so as to help sustain the current economic expansion. At the same time, an overhaul of the tax system should address the upward trend in income inequality and improve the local tax system. Tax reform should thus aim at balancing the objectives of efficiency, equity and simplicity.

Revenue should be increased primarily through a hike in the consumption tax rate…

The negative impact of taxes on growth can be minimised by shifting the composition of taxes from direct to indirect taxes. Given the need for additional revenue in Japan, the amount of direct tax revenue should be maintained while increasing indirect tax revenue. This requires a hike in the consumption tax rate from its current level of 5%, the lowest in the OECD area. A one percentage-point hike in the consumption tax rate would boost government revenue by about ½ per cent of GDP. In seeking additional revenues in this area, Japan should maintain a single consumption tax rate applied to a broad tax base and retain flexibility in allocating the additional revenues.

… while broadening the corporate income tax base and cutting the rate to promote growth…

This should be accompanied by broadening the corporate tax base by cutting tax expenditures and reducing generous deductions, thereby lowering the proportion of firms that do not pay tax. Indeed, only one-third of firms – and one-half of large firms – pay corporate taxes. Broadening the tax base would enhance potential growth by improving the allocation of resources and investment. The additional revenue generated by base-broadening would allow some reduction in the corporate tax rate, currently the highest among OECD countries at 40%, to a level closer to the OECD average of 29%, which would also promote growth. The negative effect on tax revenue from such a rate cut would be limited by positive supply effects, notably increased investment and a larger corporate sector.

… reforming the personal income tax system, in part to reverse the deterioration in income inequality…

There is also considerable scope for boosting revenue by broadening the personal income tax base, given that less than half of wage income is taxed. This partly reflects the large deduction for wage earnings, which exempts more than a quarter of employees' earnings from the tax base, in part to improve horizontal equity between employees and the self-employed. A reduction in the exemption for wage income must be accompanied by measures to increase the proportion of self-employed income that is taxed. Higher personal income tax revenue resulting from base broadening would help to offset any decline in corporate taxes, thus maintaining the overall level of direct taxes. A greater role for the personal income tax, which has a positive impact on income distribution, may also be beneficial from an equity perspective. The additional revenue from base broadening could be used to finance an Earned Income Tax Credit, as well as perhaps reducing personal income tax rates so as to increase work incentives. An Earned Income Tax Credit provides support to low-income households while strengthening work incentives, although there could be difficulties in administration and possible fraud. Such an approach is likely to be effective in Japan, given its relatively wide earnings distribution, low taxes on labour and low benefits for the non-employed. In addition, equity concerns should be met by strengthening the inheritance tax, which is applied to only 4% of persons at the time of death. Finally, elements of the personal income tax system that discourage work – such as the exemptions and deductions for secondary earners – should be reformed, while improving the taxation of financial income to reduce distortions in the allocation of capital, thereby promoting growth.

... and improving the local income tax system

Tax reform should also focus on improving the local tax system, which is exceptionally complicated, with 23 taxes, while allowing only limited autonomy to local governments. Barriers to the effective use of existing powers to set local tax rates should be removed. The priority should be to phase out the local tax on corporations, while increasing revenue through the existing local taxes on personal income, consumption and property. Such taxes are more stable and have less adverse effects on the potential growth rate than taxes on corporations. Raising the overall consumption tax rate would boost the local consumption tax rate if it remains at a quarter of the national rate, thus providing additional revenue to local authorities. In addition, the effective rate of tax on property should be increased by bringing property evaluations closer into line with market prices. Greater revenue from these taxes would more than offset the abolition of local taxes on corporations, which are excessively volatile and discourage employment and investment. Moreover, eliminating the local corporate tax would bring the overall statutory rate more into line with the OECD average and thus have a positive impact on growth.

The key to boosting Japan's growth potential is to enhance productivity growth in the service sector by...

While a well-designed tax reform could have a positive effect on Japan's growth potential, the key priority for long-term growth is to improve the labour productivity performance. The potential growth rate in Japan is estimated at 1.4% over the period 2004 to 2013, the lowest rate in the OECD area, reflecting a large negative contribution from a declining working-age population. As the drag on economic growth from population ageing increases in the years to come, sustaining an improvement in living standards will depend on accelerating labour productivity growth. Given that labour productivity per hour worked in Japan is 30% below the US level, there appears to be a large potential for faster productivity growth. To accomplish this, it is essential to reverse the decline in productivity growth in the service sector, from 3.5% a year in the period 1976 to 1989 to only 0.9% between 1999 and 2004, in contrast to the high and sustained growth of productivity in the manufacturing sector.

… strengthening competition through regulatory reform…

The slowdown in productivity growth in services, in contrast to manufacturing, highlights the importance of strengthening competition. Indeed, the OECD indicator of the stringency of product market regulations in the non-manufacturing sector ranks Japan in the middle of OECD countries and well below the top performers. It is important, therefore, to strengthen competition by accelerating regulatory reform, as well as by upgrading competition policy and increasing international openness. The 2007 Regulatory Reform Programme, which includes a number of services, such as education, distribution and energy, should focus on lifting key regulations on entry and operations. It should also accomplish its goal of improving administrative tools, such as the "No-Action Letter" scheme, which allows a firm to seek advance clarification about the application of regulations to its business plan. Finally, it is important to strengthen the links between regulatory reform and the Special Zones for Structural Reform initiative introduced in 2003, which appears to be losing momentum. The initiative should be made more effective by removing barriers to the implementation of reform measures in the zones and ensuring that the initiative focuses on its key objective of nationwide regulatory reform rather than on regional development.

… upgrading competition policy, increasing international openness…

Enforcement of competition law by the Japan Fair Trade Commission has been strengthened by the 2005 revision of the Anti-Monopoly Act (AMA). Nonetheless, the legal framework and enforcement should be further reinforced. *First*, administrative penalties and fines, which are relatively low compared with other countries and compared with the potential gains from violating the AMA, should be increased to strengthen the deterrent effect. *Second*, explicit exemptions from the AMA in a wide range of areas, such as insurance, the liquor business, hair cutting, agricultural co-operatives and air and maritime transport, should be reduced. Exemption is appropriate only when necessary to correct clear market failures. *Third*, the special treatment of small and medium-sized enterprises, which play a dominant role in the service sector, should be scaled back. *Fourth*, the Japan Fair Trade Commission should ensure that the large number of trade associations do not limit competition. Foreign competition is also important to boost productivity, in part as foreign affiliates have higher productivity than domestic firms. However, the share of foreign affiliates in total service turnover in Japan, as well as the proportion of services in the total turnover of foreign affiliates in Japan, are the lowest in the OECD area. It is thus important to remove barriers to inward foreign direct investment, as well as product market regulations that discourage foreign investors, in order to strengthen competition. In addition, Japan is relatively closed to international trade in services. Indeed, the import penetration rate for services in Japan is the lowest among OECD countries, indicating the need to reduce trade barriers.

... and carrying out the privatisation of Japan Post

The privatisation of Japan Post, which began in October 2007 with its division into four companies, should be fully carried out in line with the announced schedule. This important initiative is likely to shift the flow of funds away from the public sector and towards the private sector, thus promoting the dynamism of the Japanese economy. Moreover, in December 2007, Japan announced a plan to strengthen the competitiveness of its financial and capital markets, including measures to enhance the transparency of regulations.

It is also necessary to address regulatory problems in key service industries

Competition in key service industries should be strengthened through wide-ranging reforms, while strictly enforcing competition law:

- *Retail sector*: The transparency and predictability of the Large-scale Retail Store Location Law, which aims at "maintaining the living environment", and the City Planning Law, which is intended to revitalise urban areas, should be improved to ensure that they do not act as entry barriers to large stores.

- *Energy sector*: A single independent sectoral regulator should be established for both the electricity and gas sectors to ensure competition and the share of consumers allowed to choose their suppliers should be expanded. In electricity, although Japan has introduced accounting separation of vertically-integrated incumbents, competition should be further strengthened through formal separation, reducing barriers to new entrants and expanding the interconnection capacity.

- *Transport industry*: Competitive pressures should be enhanced in ports by relaxing entry barriers and reforming the "Prior Consultation Process". In the air transport industry, the current slot allocation scheme based on IATA guidelines should be improved by introducing market mechanisms. Moreover, airlines should be able to sell tickets directly to consumers at competitive prices. Airports should be privatised and their capacity expanded in order to increase efficiency and reduce high charges.

- *Business services*: Pervasive regulation, including by professional associations, should be relaxed, while encouraging international competition through increased recognition of foreign certificates.

- *Public services*: Reforms in areas such as education and healthcare should be advanced, in part through the special zone initiative and expanded use of market testing to outsource government activities to the private sector.

*Reforms are needed in the labour market
to reverse increasing dualism…*

Product market reforms should be accompanied by reforms in the labour market to increase efficiency and equity. Japan has experienced a sharp rise in labour market dualism, with the share of non-regular workers rising from 20% in 1994 to 34% in 2007. Firms are achieving employment flexibility through increased hiring of non-regular workers, who have temporary contracts, boosting their share of employment. In addition, non-regular workers are relatively inexpensive; the average hourly wage of part-time employees, who account for three-quarters of non-regular workers, is only 40% of that of regular workers, and they are exempt from some social insurance systems. The increasing dualism is creating a large segment of the population, concentrated among young people, with only short-term employment experience and limited opportunities to enhance their human capital, given that they do not benefit fully from firm-based training, which plays an important role in Japan. There are also serious equity problems, given that the difference in productivity between regular and non-regular workers is much smaller than the wage gap. The equity concern is magnified by the lack of movement between the two segments of the workforce, trapping a significant portion of the labour force in a low-wage category from which it is difficult to escape. Reversing the trend towards increased dualism requires a comprehensive approach. This should include enhancing the flexibility of regular employment, increasing the coverage of temporary workers by social security insurance schemes and upgrading training programmes to enhance the employment prospects of non-regular workers.

*… while promoting higher labour force
participation of women*

With women accounting for more than two-thirds of non-regular workers, reversing the trend towards labour market dualism as suggested above may help to boost female participation rates by providing more attractive job opportunities and encouraging flexibility in working arrangements. A higher participation rate of women would help buffer the impact of the decline in the working-age population, which is projected to fall by 9% in the decade beginning in 2007. The priority is to remove aspects of the tax and social security systems that discourage employment of secondary earners. In addition, private-sector practices, such as company allowances for spouses, the importance of tenure in setting wages and the use of age limits on potential new workers, may also discourage female participation in the labour force. The government should also reduce or eliminate aspects of the tax and social security systems that discourage women from working full-time. Indeed, the proportion of women employed part-time, at 41%, is one of the highest in the OECD area. Improved access to childcare would be effective in boosting both female labour force participation and the fertility rate. Finally, efforts to promote better work-life balance, in part through stricter enforcement of the Labour Standard Law, may encourage greater female labour force participation.

ISBN 978-92-64-04306-0
OECD Economic Surveys: Japan
© OECD 2008

Chapter 1

Key challenges to sustaining the expansion in Japan

The economic expansion, the longest in Japan's post-war history, remains on track, though at a slower pace. The upturn is driven by business investment and exports, while other components of demand remain sluggish. Although growth is projected to continue at a 1½ to 2% rate through 2009, Japan must address a number of problems to sustain the expansion over the medium term. This chapter identifies five key challenges: i) ensuring a definitive end to deflation under the new monetary policy framework; ii) achieving progress in fiscal consolidation in the context of high public debt and rapid population ageing; iii) implementing a comprehensive tax reform to increase government revenue, while promoting economic growth, addressing rising income inequality and improving the local government tax system; iv) enhancing productivity growth in the service sector; and v) reforming the labour market to reverse rising dualism and boosting labour force participation to offset demographic trends.

The current expansion, which began in early 2002, reversed a decade of economic stagnation in Japan. Output growth had averaged less than 1% a year during the decade from 1992 to 2002, the lowest in the OECD area, as Japan worked through the aftermath of the collapse of the asset price bubble (Table 1.1). Consequently, Japan's ranking in terms of per capita income fell from fifth highest in the OECD in 1992 to nineteenth in 2002. During the current expansion, GDP per capita has increased at a 2.1% rate, matching the OECD average over the period 2002-07. The improved performance of Japan during the last five years has been driven by the acceleration of productivity growth, which nearly doubled from the 1% rate recorded during the 1992 to 2002 period, promoted by progress in structural reform (see Annex 1.A1). Nevertheless, the labour productivity gap relative to the United States was large at 30% in 2006 (Figure 1.1).

This expansion has been led by business investment, which has accounted for almost 40% of the rise in output since 2002, thanks to growth at an annual rate of more

Table 1.1. **Japan's rebound from a decade of economic stagnation**

A. International comparison (annual average percentage change)

	1992-2002		2002-2007	
	Japan	OECD average	Japan[1]	OECD average[2]
Real GDP	0.9	2.6	2.1	2.7
Real GDP per capita	0.6	2.0	2.1	2.0
Labour productivity	1.0	1.6	1.9	1.5

B. Components of Japanese growth (annual average percentage change)

	1992-2002	2002-2007[1]	Change
Private consumption	1.3	1.4	0.1
Government consumption	2.9	1.2	−1.7
Fixed investment	−1.2	1.0	2.2
Public[3]	−0.6	−8.1	−7.5
Residential	−2.2	−1.9	0.3
Business	−1.2	5.1	6.3
Final domestic demand	0.9	1.3	0.4
Stockbuilding[4]	−0.1	0.1	0.2
Total domestic demand	0.8	1.4	0.6
Exports	3.6	9.7	6.1
Imports	3.9	4.7	0.8
Net exports[4]	0.1	0.7	0.6
GDP	0.9	2.1	1.3

1. The second preliminary estimate of GDP in the fourth quarter of 2007, which was made on 12 March 2008 – after the publication of Economic Outlook No. 82 – was included in the data for 2007.
2. OECD estimate for the OECD average in 2007.
3. Including public corporations.
4. Contribution to GDP growth.
Source: OECD, OECD Economic Outlook, No. 82 (December 2007), OECD, Paris.

Figure 1.1. **Explaining differences in income**
2006

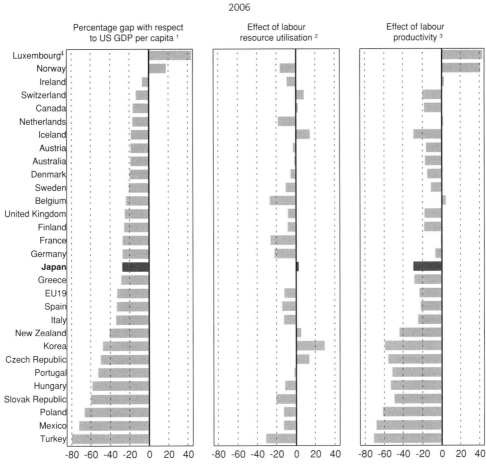

StatLink ⟲ http://dx.doi.org/10.1787/276811101571

1. Based on 2006 purchasing power parity exchange rates.
2. Labour resource utilisation is measured as the total number of hours worked divided by the population.
3. Labour productivity is measured as GDP per hour worked.
4. In the case of Luxembourg, the population is augmented by the number of cross-border workers.

Source: OECD, *Going for Growth 2008*, OECD, Paris.

than 5% (Table 1.1, Panel B). A number of factors have sustained business investment. *First*, the restructuring of the corporate sector reduced excessively high levels of debt, production capacity and employment, which, in turn, had depressed capital expenditures during the decade 1992 to 2002. Successful restructuring released pent-up demand for capital goods. *Second*, the improved financial soundness of the banking sector has supported business investment. A sharp increase in non-performing loans had undermined the capital base of the banking sector, contributing to a steady decline in bank lending beginning in the mid-1990s. With the progress in reducing non-performing loans since 2002, bank lending started to increase again in 2005.[1] *Third*, the acceleration in export growth from less than 4% in the decade beginning in 1992 to nearly 10% during the past five years has boosted corporate profitability and created demand for additional capacity, thus encouraging greater business investment. Exports have been sustained by Japan's increasing integration with Asian economies, which have accounted for more than half of Japan's export growth during this expansion. In addition, the significant decline in the yen between 2005 and mid-2007 has supported export growth. In sum, the external sector has accounted for about one-third of increased output during this expansion.

The corporate-led expansion has sustained growth at 2.1% over the past five years, a pace substantially above Japan's potential growth rate of about 1½ per cent, despite a weak contribution from the household sector and a small drag from fiscal policy. Private consumption has increased at a 1.4% annual pace, about the same as during the decade 1992 to 2002 (Table 1.1), as the benefits of the long expansion led by business investment and exports have not spread fully to the household sector. Indeed, sluggish wage growth has reduced labour income as a share of GDP to its lowest level since 1990. On the fiscal side, the government faced a deficit of 8% of GDP in 2002, reflecting weak economic growth and a sharp increase in public spending, which had accounted for half of the increase in GDP during the decade 1992 to 2002. To reduce the deficit, the growth of government consumption was halved during the period 2002 to 2007, while public investment declined at an 8% annual rate.

The economic expansion is projected to remain on track through 2009. After discussing the short-term outlook, this chapter analyses a number of imbalances in the economy that pose risks to a continued expansion. The chapter then outlines the key economic challenges facing Japan.

Recent economic trends in Japan and the short-term economic outlook

After expanding at a 4% annual rate between the third quarter of 2006 and the first quarter of 2007, the economy slowed, with in the third quarter of 2007 slightly below that in the first quarter. This long-lasting expansion has already overcome soft patches in 2003 and 2004, when output stagnated or actually declined,[2] and it is projected to rebound again with output growth of between 1½ and 2% during 2008 and 2009 (Table 1.2). Business investment is likely to continue to lead the expansion, given the overall high level of confidence, capacity utilisation and profits. The pre-tax profits of listed companies are expected to rise by nearly 6% in FY 2007, setting a record high for pre-tax profits for the fifth consecutive year. The large gap between the rate of profitability and borrowing costs should support continued capital spending (Figure 1.2). The gap reached 4 percentage points for large manufacturers in mid-2007 and 2 points for large non-manufacturing firms (Panels A and B). In addition, improved growth expectations have been driving demand for new capacity (Panel C). At the beginning of this expansion in 2002, manufacturers expected demand to increase at only a 1% annual rate over the following five years, while non-manufacturing firms were even more pessimistic. By 2006, growth expectations in both sectors had risen by almost 1 percentage point. These factors should sustain business investment, though at a pace well below the nearly 7% annual rate recorded between 2004 and 2006.

Export growth has been strong, increasing at an 11.6% rate in value terms in 2007 despite weak demand from the United States (Figure 1.3). Buoyant export growth with little increase in sales to the United States reflects the downward trend in the US share of Japanese exports, from 30% in 2000 to 20% in 2007, while the share of Asian countries rose from 41% to 48% over that period thanks to China (Panel B). Export growth has also been supported by the depreciation of the yen, which fell by 18% in effective terms between the end of 2004 and the second quarter of 2007 (Panel C), partly as a result of the yen carry trade (Box 1.1). However, the downward trend in the yen was reversed during the second half of 2007. Export growth is projected to continue to support economic activity in

Table 1.2. **Short-term economic projections**[1]

	2006	2007	2008	2009	2007		2008		2009	
					1st half	2nd half	1st half	2nd half	1st half	2nd half
Demand and output (volumes)										
Consumption										
Private	2.0	1.4	1.1	1.3	2.4	0.6	1.0	1.1	1.3	1.4
Government	−0.4	0.8	1.9	1.4	0.4	1.5	2.3	1.3	1.4	1.5
Gross fixed investment	1.3	−0.3	−0.3	1.8	0.3	−4.4	0.3	1.8	1.7	2.2
Public[2]	−8.1	−2.2	−4.9	−4.4	8.3	−8.2	−3.7	−2.6	−5.1	−4.9
Residential	0.9	−9.5	−7.6	4.9	−4.9	−27.1	−4.6	1.7	6.0	6.0
Business	4.3	2.4	2.4	2.8	−0.4	2.3	2.4	2.9	2.5	3.1
Final domestic demand	1.4	0.9	0.9	1.4	1.5	−0.4	1.1	1.3	1.4	1.6
Stockbuilding[3]	0.2	0.1	0	0	0.1	−0.1	0.0	0.0	0.0	0.0
Total domestic demand	1.6	1.0	0.9	1.4	1.6	−0.5	1.1	1.3	1.4	1.6
Exports of goods and services	9.7	8.8	7.8	7.2	9.3	10.5	7.4	7.6	7.2	6.8
Imports of goods and services	4.2	1.7	4.5	5.5	2.7	0.8	4.8	5.6	5.4	5.5
Net exports[3]	0.8	1.2	0.7	0.4	1.0	1.5	0.5	0.4	0.4	0.3
GDP	2.4	2.1	1.6	1.8	2.7	1.1	1.6	1.7	1.8	1.9
Inflation and capacity utilisation										
GDP deflator	−1.0	−0.8	−0.3	0.3	−0.6	−1.3	−0.3	0.2	0.3	0.5
Private consumption deflator	−0.3	−0.5	0.1	0.3	−0.7	−0.1	0.1	0.2	0.3	0.5
CPI[4]	0.2	0.1	0.3	0.4	−0.5	0.8	0.2	0.3	0.4	0.5
Core CPI[4]	−0.4	−0.2	−0.1	0.3	−0.2	−0.1	0.0	0.1	0.3	0.5
Unemployment rate	4.1	3.9	3.7	3.6	3.9	3.8	3.8	3.7	3.6	3.5
Output gap	0.0	0.2	0.2	0.5	0.7	0.1	0.2	0.3	0.5	0.6
Memorandum items:										
Net government lending[5]	−4.9	−4.0	−3.8	−3.4						
Net primary balance[5]	−4.1	−3.2	−2.9	−2.3						
Gross debt[6]	179.2	180.3	181.6	183.3						
Net debt[6]	85.6	88.1	90.8	92.4						
Current account[6]	3.9	4.8	4.8	5.2						

1. Assuming an exchange rate of 109.4 yen to the dollar – the level on 12 November 2007 – and a $90 price for Brent oil in 2008 and 2009. All growth rates are annual rates relative to the preceding period. Data announced on 12 March 2008 – after the finalisation of *Economic Outlook*, No. 82 – are included in the historical data for 2006 and 2007. The numbers for 2008 and 2009 are identical to those in *Economic Outlook*, No. 82.
2. Including public corporations.
3. Contribution to GDP growth.
4. Compared to the same semester of the previous year. The core CPI is the OECD definition, which excludes both food and energy.
5. Per cent of GDP. Excluding one-off factors.
6. Per cent of GDP.
Source: OECD, *OECD Economic Outlook*, No. 82 (December 2007), OECD, Paris.

2008-09, although its momentum is likely to slow as the impact of past exchange rate depreciation fades (Table 1.2).

In contrast, private consumption has been somewhat sluggish in 2007, constrained by increased taxes[3] and a renewed decline in wages. After turning positive in 2005-06, wages dropped by 0.7% in 2007 (Figure 1.4) despite a fall in the unemployment rate to 3.9% in 2007 – the lowest level since 1998 – and a job-offer-to-applicant ratio above unity. The decline in wages in the context of a tighter labour market reflects several structural factors. First, the increasing proportion of lower-paid part-time workers has reduced the overall average wage level. Second, the large-scale retirement of baby boomers is resulting in the replacement of high-paid workers by younger workers at lower wages. However, these

Figure 1.2. **Factors supporting business investment**

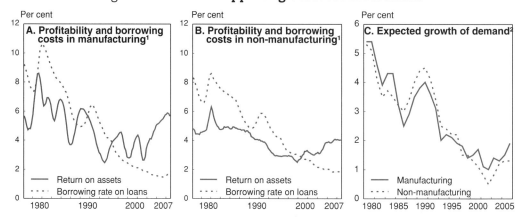

StatLink ⸺ http://dx.doi.org/10.1787/276873677036

1. Return on assets corresponds to operating profits divided by assets. Figures are a moving average of four quarters. The figures are for large firms.
2. Over the next five years.

Source: Cabinet Office, *Annual Survey of Corporate Behaviour* and Ministry of Finance, *Financial Statements Statistics of Corporations by Industry.*

structural factors depressing wages are expected to fade, leading to wage increases during 2008-09. Indeed, the proportion of non-regular workers (which consist primarily of part-time workers) is unlikely to continue its steady upward trend now that it has risen to one-third of the labour force. In addition, the number of baby boomers reaching retirement age will peak in early 2008. Rising wages are projected to help sustain private consumption at a rate of around 1¼ per cent during 2008-09.

A sharp drop in construction activity, though, is likely to be a drag on business investment and private consumption in the short term. A revision of the Building Standards Law in June 2007, aimed at improving the inspection process after a scandal in 2005, is causing severe bottlenecks in the approval process. Consequently, housing starts fell by 37% (year-on-year) in the third quarter of 2007 and this was immediately reflected in

Figure 1.3. **Exports and exchange rate**

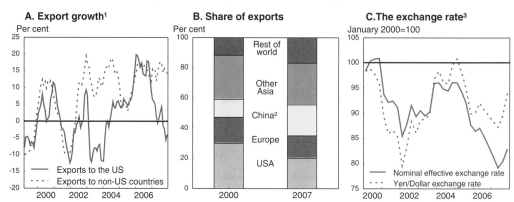

StatLink ⸺ http://dx.doi.org/10.1787/277027437244

1. Year-on-year growth rates of a moving average of export values over three quarters.
2. Includes Hong Kong, China.
3. A decline indicates a depreciation of the yen. The effective exchange rate is calculated *vis-à-vis* 41 trading partners.

Source: Ministry of Finance, *Trade Statistics* and OECD, *OECD Economic Outlook*, No. 82 Database, OECD, Paris.

Box 1.1. **The yen carry trade and its economic impact**

A carry trade is generally defined as a trade in which an investor borrows funds in one currency (the funding currency) at a low interest rate and invests in higher-yielding assets in another currency (the target currency) to take advantage of interest rate differentials. There are two potential sources of instability in a carry trade; a leveraged investment and an exposure to foreign exchange risk, as it is unhedged.[1] The Japanese yen has been one of the most favoured funding currencies in the context of persistently low interest rates close to zero in Japan. The yen carry trade has been used by large international financial institutions, such as hedge funds and investment banks. A second aspect has been carry trades by Japanese domestic investors, including both financial institutions and individuals. For example, life insurers purchase foreign bonds to support yen-denominated liabilities, while individual investors have been shifting a share of their wealth away from bank deposits or other low-yielding yen investments towards foreign bonds and equities. Given the lack of data on the outstanding size of yen carry trade positions, it is difficult to quantify the amount of carry trade. Nevertheless, it appears to have been an important factor explaining the doubling of Japanese holdings of foreign equities and bonds from 150 trillion yen in 2000 (30% of GDP) to 297 trillion yen (58% of GDP) by mid-2007. In addition, the net outward yen-denominated assets held by Japanese financial institutions sharply increased from $100 billion at the end of 2003 to $255 billion in mid-2007.

The impact of the carry trade on financial markets, notably for foreign exchange, appears to have been significant. The build-up of short open positions in yen – an un-hedged selling position in yen – tends to weaken the yen, while strengthening the target currency. The impact can be seen in the trends in the yen/dollar exchange rate, given that the dollar has been one of the major target currencies of the yen carry trade, especially since 2004. Indeed, the US short-term policy rate rose from 1% at the beginning of 2004 to 5¼ per cent by the second half of 2006, significantly expanding the interest rate differential with Japan. The dollar appreciated 8% relative to the yen over that period, compared to its 4% fall in effective terms. Another example is the 40% rise in the Korean won against the yen between the end of 2003 and mid-2007, as the increase in the Korean policy rate from 3¼ to 5% over this period widened the interest rate gap between the two countries. Over the same period, the balance of yen-denominated loans held by the Korean banks increased by around 40% in response to strong demand from private-sector investors wanting to take advantage of the large interest rate differentials. In sum, the yen carry trade has put downward pressure on the Japanese currency, thus contributing to the easing of monetary conditions in Japan and helping to sustain the current expansion.

The increased liquidity resulting from the yen carry trade also affects asset prices, notably bonds and equities in target countries, while tending to reduce the risk premium in global financial markets. However, there is a risk that a sudden unwinding of the yen carry trade – which implies the selling of the target currency accompanied by the purchase of the funding currency – might adversely affect financial stability and ultimately damage the real economy. The risk stems from the possibility of a rapid unwinding of leveraged and un-hedged positions accumulated over time. Such an unwinding could result from a significant rise of the yen that more than offset the gains from the interest rate differential or from a narrowing of the interest rate differential. If a significant rise in the yen triggered the process, the unwinding of the yen carry trade would reinforce the upward pressure on the yen, leading to a vicious circle and a significant spike in volatility in foreign exchange markets.[2] Such a development would negatively affect Japanese exports and could strengthen deflationary pressure. Moreover, the unwinding of the yen carry trade could spark a sell-off in financial markets of target countries, resulting in a sharp fall in those markets.

Box 1.1. **The yen carry trade and its economic impact** *(cont.)*

Despite these risks, there is an incentive for the yen carry trade to continue as long as there is a substantial gap in interest rates between Japan and other countries, other things being equal. However, it is neither desirable nor possible to curb such capital flows in globally-integrated financial markets. Given the potential risks for financial markets and consequently for economic activity, the authorities should closely monitor financial markets to limit the risks associated with the yen carry trade.

1. Holding an unhedged position allows the investor to fully realise the gain from the interest rate differential. Such an approach has been encouraged by the relatively low volatility of exchange rates in recent years.
2. For example, the sudden reversal of speculative "short positions in yen" in 1998 led to a sharp rise in the yen from 137 yen per dollar in September to 115 yen per dollar in October.

Figure 1.4. **Wage growth has turned negative**

Year-on-year percentage change

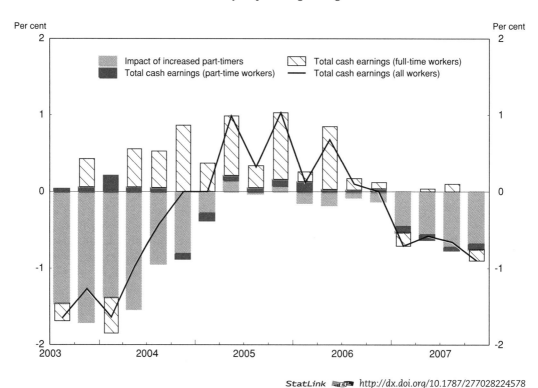

StatLink 🔗 http://dx.doi.org/10.1787/277028224578

Source: Ministry of Health, Labour and Welfare, *Monthly Labour Survey.*

a 27% decline (seasonally-adjusted annual rate) in residential construction in the second half of 2007 (Table 1.2). This regulatory change also reduced corporate construction starts by 41% in the third quarter, thus dampening business investment, which nevertheless recorded a strong rise. The projection assumes that, with the correction of the regulatory problem, residential construction will begin expanding at a 6% annual pace from 2009.[4]

Despite the continued economic expansion and the decline of the yen, prices are still falling. After turning positive during 2006, both the headline and the official Japanese measure of core consumer prices (excluding fresh food only) decreased during the first three quarters of 2007 on a year-on-year basis (Figure 1.5), before jumping up by 0.5%

Figure 1.5. **Japan remains in mild deflation**
Year-on-year percentage change

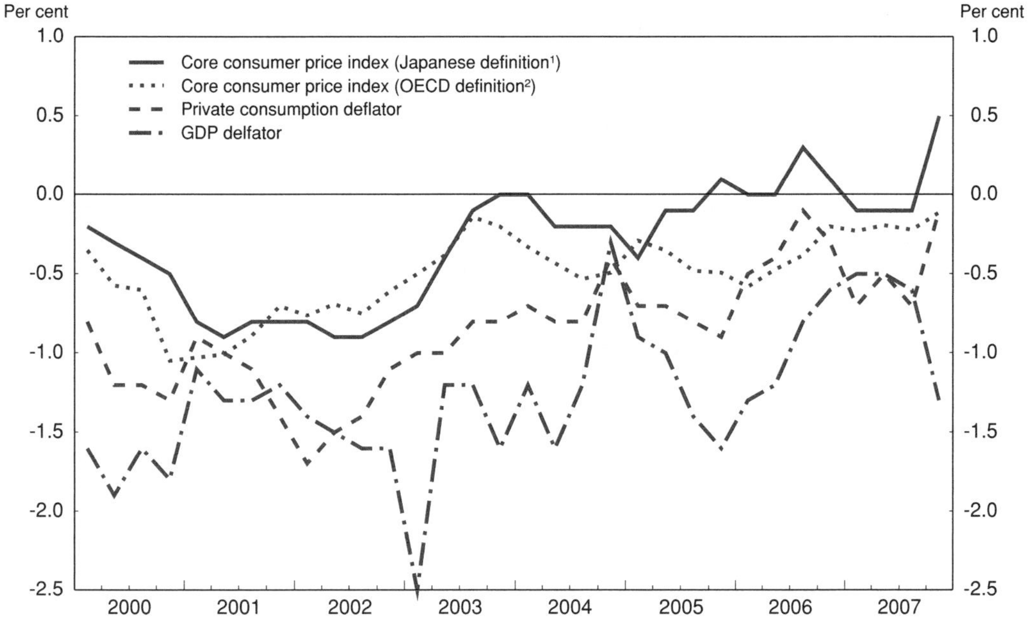

StatLink ⬛⬛ http://dx.doi.org/10.1787/277058488018

1. Japanese definition of core CPI excludes fresh food only.
2. OECD definition of core CPI excludes food and energy products.

Source: OECD, *OECD Economic Outlook*, No. 82 Database, OECD, Paris; Ministry of Internal Affairs and Communications; and Cabinet Office.

in the fourth quarter, primarily due to higher oil prices.[5] The OECD definition of core consumer prices, which excludes both food and energy, continued to decline in each quarter of 2007 as it has in every quarter since 1998. Price deflators for GDP and private consumption are falling at a faster rate. One factor putting downward pressure on prices has been the decline in unit labour costs at a 2% annual rate since 2002. With the expected return to positive wage growth, unit labour costs are projected to stabilise by 2009, reducing downward pressure on prices. The continued expansion should push inflation into positive territory, although it is likely to remain at between 0 and 0.5% until late in 2009.

In sum, after somewhat weak growth between mid-2007 and mid-2008, reflecting the sharp decline in construction activity and falling wages in 2007, the expansion is projected to pick up, keeping annual growth rates at between 1½ and 2% through 2009. However, the risks to the expansion appear to be larger than before. On the external side, the increased turbulence in world financial markets since mid-2007 may result in a decline in overseas demand and slower export growth. A sudden and marked appreciation of the yen as the current account surplus rises to over 5% of GDP in 2009 could have a similar impact. Maintaining buoyant export growth is important to revitalise domestic demand. However, a delay in the expected rebound in wage growth in 2008 would weaken private consumption. There is also uncertainty about how quickly the regulatory problem in the Building Standards Law will be fixed, allowing housing and corporate construction starts to stabilise. In addition to these risks, the increasing polarisation of the expansion by sector, size of firm and region poses a threat to the continued expansion.

The polarisation of this economic expansion poses risks

The narrow base of this expansion and the key role of exports help to explain the significant divergence in performance between sectors and regions. The unbalanced nature of growth is reflected in the widening gap between the manufacturing sector, which has benefited from buoyant exports, and the non-manufacturing sector, which depends more on domestic demand. Indeed, the rate of return on assets in manufacturing, which was 2.6% at the beginning of the expansion in 2002 – slightly below that in non-manufacturing – reached almost 6% in 2007, the highest since the 1980s (Figure 1.2, Panels A and B). In contrast, the rate for non-manufacturing increased only modestly. The difference is even more marked in terms of profits per employee, which were around 0.3 million yen in both sectors in 2002 (Figure 1.6, Panel A). By 2006, profits per employee in manufacturing were double those in the non-

Figure 1.6. **An unbalanced economic expansion in Japan**

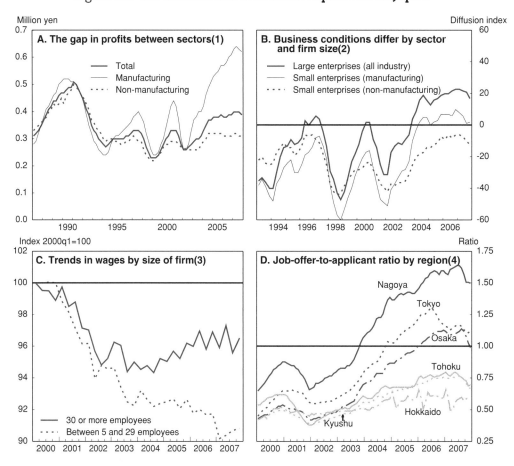

StatLink 🔗 http://dx.doi.org/10.1787/277063343015

1. Per capita profits are defined as business profits/the number of employees. The figures are a four-quarter moving average.
2. Diffusion index of "favourable" minus "unfavourable" business conditions in the Tankan Survey. There is a discontinuity between the third and fourth quarters of 2003 due to data revisions. Large enterprises are defined as those with more than one billion yen of capital, while small enterprises have between 20 and 100 million yen.
3. Seasonally-adjusted series. Quarterly data are a simple average of months. The data series for firms with less than 30 employees is calculated by the OECD.
4. Tokyo is actually the Minami-Kanto region, Osaka is the Kinki region and Nagoya is the Tokai region.

Source: Ministry of Finance, *Financial Statements Statistics of Corporations by Industry*; Bank of Japan, *Tankan Survey*; and Ministry of Health, Labour and Welfare, *Monthly Labour Survey* and *Report on Employment Service*.

manufacturing sector. Firms in non-manufacturing have been more affected by rising input prices, notably for energy and raw materials, given that they have more difficulty in passing those price increases on to domestic consumers due to weak domestic demand and deregulation. Low productivity growth in the service sector has also squeezed profitability.[6]

Given that 90% of small and medium-sized enterprises (SMEs) are in non-manufacturing, the dichotomy between different sectors has also created a significant gap between large and small firms. Indeed, the Bank of Japan's indicator of business conditions shows a large and growing disparity by size of firm (Figure 1.6, Panel B). Business sentiment in small manufacturing firms has fallen close to zero, while remaining in negative territory for those in non-manufacturing. The growing variance in performance by firm size is also reflected in a divergence in wage growth (Panel C). At firms with less than 30 employees, wages have fallen 9% since 2000, compared to only 3% at those with 30 or more employees. This has widened the already significant wage gap between small and large firms.

The dualistic expansion has also increased the disparity between regions in Japan. In its January 2008 *Regional Economic Report*, the Bank of Japan stated that the economy as a whole was on a "moderate expansion trend" although there are regional differences. Consequently, the Bank downgraded its overall assessment for four of Japan's nine regions, while leaving the other five unchanged.[7] Growing regional disparity is particularly evident in the labour market. For example, in Hokkaido, the northern island with little manufacturing activity, the job-offer-to-applicant ratio was only 0.6 in December 2007, only slightly higher than at the beginning of the recovery in 2002 (Figure 1.6, Panel D). In contrast, the ratio jumped from 0.7 to 1.5 over the same period in the region of Nagoya, which includes many large manufacturers. Regional disparity is also reflected in land prices, which rose in the three major urban areas in 2007, while falling in the rest of the country (Figure 2.4).

Another important dualism in the economy is found in the labour market. As noted above, the proportion of non-regular workers rose to one-third of employees in 2007. The sharp increase in the share of non-regular workers, who earn significantly less than regular workers, is a key factor reducing average wages, while contributing to the rising trend in income inequality. In addition, the lack of training for non-regular workers, many of whom are under the age of 30, has negative implications for Japan's growth potential over the medium term.

Key challenges facing the Japanese economy

In addition to overcoming these imbalances, sustaining the upturn over the medium term requires meeting a number of difficult challenges, which are discussed in this *Economic Survey*:

- Achieving a definitive end to almost a decade of deflation under the new monetary policy framework introduced in March 2006 (Chapter 2).
- Ensuring fiscal sustainability in the context of exceptionally rapid population ageing (Chapter 3).
- Implementing a comprehensive tax reform to achieve the medium-term fiscal consolidation targets, while supporting economic growth, addressing the deterioration in income equality and improving the local government tax system (Chapter 4).
- Enhancing productivity growth in the service sector (Chapter 5).
- Reforming the labour market to reverse the trend towards dualism and to encourage labour force participation (Chapter 6).

Underlying each of these challenges is the rapid ageing of Japan's population. Population projections through the year 2050 are presented in Box 1.2.

Box 1.2. **Population projections for Japan**

Rapid demographic change has already made Japan's population one of the oldest in the OECD area. Since its peak from 1991 to 1993, the working-age population (15 to 64) has fallen by 3.7%, and the annual pace of decline accelerated to 0.5% in 2005. This boosted the share of the elderly (over age 65) to 20.2% of the total population in 2005. The increase in the share of elderly from 7% to 20% was exceptionally rapid in Japan, taking only 35 years (1970 to 2005). In comparison, this transition is projected to take 86 years in the United States and 156 years in France.

Japan's total population peaked in 2004 at 127.8 million and is projected to decline at an accelerating pace through the middle of this century, according to the government's official projection (Table 1.3). Indeed, by 2050, Japan's total population is expected to be less than 100 million, boosting the median age from 43 years at present to 57 years. Population decline is driven by an accelerating drop in the working-age population, which is projected to fall to less than 50 million in 2050. Consequently, the number of elderly is projected to rise from 28% of the working-age population (aged 20 to 64) in 2000 to 72% in 2050, making it the second highest in the OECD area (Figure 1.7).

Table 1.3. **Population indicators and projections for Japan**

	Total population		Working-age population[2]		Fertility rate	Life expectancy		Median age	Share of elderly[4]
						Male	Female		
	(millions)	(growth in %)[1]	(millions)	(growth in %)[1]	(TFR)[3]	(years)	(years)	(years)	(%)
1990	123.6	0.5	85.9	0.9	1.54	75.9	81.9	37.7	12.0
2000	126.9	0.3	86.2	0.0	1.36	77.7	84.6	41.5	17.3
2010	127.2	0.0	81.3	−0.6	1.22	79.5	86.4	45.1	23.1
2020	122.7	−0.4	73.6	−1.0	1.23	80.9	87.7	49.0	29.2
2030	115.2	−0.6	67.4	−0.9	1.24	81.9	88.7	53.0	31.8
2040	105.7	−0.9	57.3	−1.6	1.25	82.7	89.4	55.4	36.5
2050	95.2	−1.0	49.3	−1.5	1.26	83.4	90.1	57.0	39.6

1.   The average annual growth rate in per cent for the decade.
2.   Population between the ages of 15 and 64.
3.   Total Fertility Rate (TFR) is the average number of children that a woman expects to bear during her lifetime.
4.   The number of persons over the age of 65 as a percentage of the total population.

Source: Ministry of Internal Affairs and Communications, *Population Census*, and National Institute of Population and Social Security Research, *Population Projection (2006 December version)*.

The government's population projection is based on a fertility rate that remains steady around its 2006 level of 1.26, while life expectancy continues to increase. Any increase in fertility, as well as greater immigration, could moderate the pace of population ageing. Nevertheless, it is clear that demographic changes will have a marked impact on all aspects of the Japanese economy. Rapid population ageing thus underpins the key challenges addressed in this Survey: ensuring fiscal sustainability (Chapter 3), reforming the tax system (Chapter 4), accelerating productivity growth (Chapter 5) and improving the labour market (Chapter 6).

Box 1.2. **Population projections for Japan** *(cont.)*

Figure 1.7. **Population ageing in OECD countries**
Population aged 65 and over, relative to the population aged 20-64

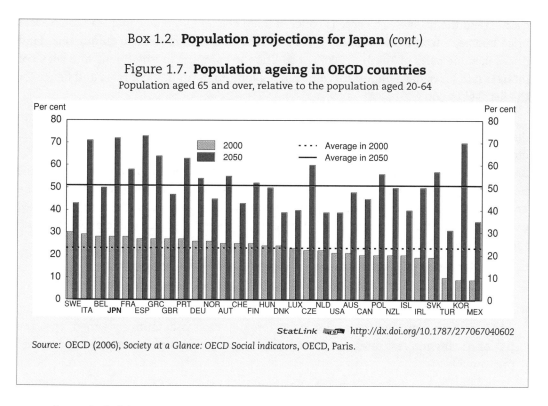

StatLink http://dx.doi.org/10.1787/277067040602

Source: OECD (2006), *Society at a Glance: OECD Social indicators*, OECD, Paris.

Ensuring a definitive end to deflation under the new monetary policy framework

As noted above, Japan remains in a state of mild deflation, with the core consumer price index falling in 2007 for the ninth consecutive year (Figure 1.5). The current rate of deflation does not constrain real interest rates at inappropriately high levels – as during the early 2000s – and there is little risk of a deflationary spiral. Nevertheless, deflation is still a concern, both directly, as it may act as a drag on the economy,[8] and because it leaves monetary policy with insufficient margin to respond to shocks that could once again drive the level of real interest rates above that required by economic conditions.

In March 2006, the Bank of Japan ended the quantitative easing policy introduced in 2001 to fight deflation and announced a new framework for monetary policy.[9] As part of this framework, it stated that inflation in the 0 to 2% range is the Policy Board's understanding of price stability. In July 2006, the central bank raised the overnight rate (the policy interest rate which had been fixed at zero since 2001) by 0.25%, followed by a similar hike in February 2007. Despite the interest rate hikes, the real short-term interest rate remains below 1%, raising the question about the appropriate degree of monetary stimulus in the sixth year of an economic expansion. The monetary authorities have made clear their intention to "normalise" interest rates, which it believes "are very low relative to economic activity and price conditions".[10] However, it is difficult to forecast the path of inflation, as there has been little correlation between the output gap and the rate of inflation in recent years.

The decision to raise interest rates by 50 basis points while consumer prices were still falling reflects, in part, the central bank's longer-term perspective that considers risk factors that may significantly impact economic activity and prices. One concern is that an excessively long period of low interest rates relative to economic and price conditions would result in an "inefficient allocation of resources as firms and financial institutions over-extend themselves".[11] There is concern that such an outcome could lead to an asset price bubble, a worry that was reinforced by double-digit increases in commercial land prices in some parts of Tokyo in 2007. In addition to asset prices, the timing and speed of interest rate hikes have important implications for long-term interest rates and hence for the fiscal situation.

Although financial markets expected further increases in the overnight interest rate during 2007, the Bank of Japan has left the rate at 0.5% in the context of slowing economic growth. Moreover, turbulence in international financial markets since the summer of 2007 has raised concern about the risk of slower growth in the world economy and a possible negative impact on Japanese exports. In sum, there is considerable uncertainty about the appropriate path of monetary policy in the context of slower output growth, increased economic uncertainty, persistent deflation despite a sustained economic expansion and the long-term risks of leaving interest rates too low for too long.

Chapter 2 examines monetary policy, focusing on the following issues:

● How can monetary policy help bring a definitive end to a decade of deflation?

● How should the Bank of Japan balance the risk of an early monetary policy tightening, which could undermine the expansion before deflation is definitively ended, with the risk of leaving interest rates too low for too long, creating distortions such as an asset price bubble?

● How could the new policy framework be improved to promote effective monetary policy?

Achieving progress in fiscal consolidation

Government debt has risen to 180% of GDP, the highest ever recorded in the OECD area, making fiscal consolidation an urgent task (Figure 1.8). The run-up in debt has raised concern about the vulnerability of the government's financial position to a rise in the long-term interest rate from its current low level of around 1½ per cent. Japan has made progress in fiscal consolidation, reducing its budget deficit from 8.2% of GDP in 2002 to an estimated 4% (excluding one-off factors) in 2007. About a quarter of the reduction over that period was a result of the economic expansion. The remainder was accomplished through cuts in government spending, primarily in public investment, and measures to boost revenue, including annual hikes in the pension contribution rate and the ending of the temporary personal income tax cut. In addition, corporate tax revenue has been exceptionally buoyant.

The government has set a target of a primary budget surplus for central and local governments combined by FY 2011 as a first step to reducing the government debt ratio in the 2010s. According to OECD estimates, the primary budget deficit (for the general government excluding one-off factors) has fallen by about ½ per cent of GDP a year since 2002 on a cyclically-adjusted basis, reducing it to 3% of GDP in 2007. Achieving a primary budget balance in 2011 would thus require accelerating the pace of fiscal consolidation to around ¾ per cent of GDP a year. However, stabilising the government debt ratio by 2011 would likely require a surplus as large as 1% to 2% of GDP. Moreover, achieving the longer-term objective of reducing the government debt ratio would require a still larger surplus.

Japan cut government expenditures from nearly 39% of GDP in 2002 to around 36.5% in 2007. The biggest reduction was in public investment, which fell by about 2% of GDP over that period. However, achieving the medium-term fiscal targets entirely through additional

Figure 1.8. **The fiscal situation in Japan**
For general government, as per cent of GDP[1]

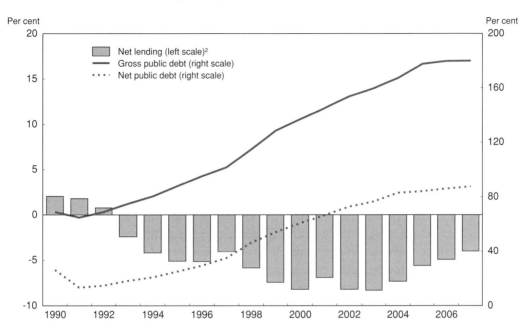

StatLink ᵃ🔗 http://dx.doi.org/10.1787/277134173324

1. OECD estimates for 2006 and 2007.
2. Excludes one-off factors related to the transfer of pension funds, the privatisation of highway corporations and transfers from the Fiscal Loan Funds Special Account.

Source: OECD, *OECD Economic Outlook*, No. 82 Database, OECD, Paris.

spending cuts would be very difficult. *First*, population ageing will put continued upward pressure on outlays for pensions, healthcare and long-term nursing care. *Second*, it will be difficult to achieve further large spending cuts in public investment, as it has already fallen to a level close to the OECD average as a share of GDP. Moreover, the cost of maintaining existing infrastructure, which already accounts for a third of total public investment, limits the scope for future spending reductions. In addition, growing public concern about the regional inequalities is creating pressure to maintain or even increase public investment. *Third*, realising the government's aim of reducing its wage bill as a share of GDP by half over the next decade is a difficult challenge, given that public employment is already quite low compared to other major OECD countries.

The fall in the budget deficit, excluding one-off factors, is projected to slow to about ¼ per cent of GDP in both 2008 and 2009 under current policies, highlighting the need for additional fiscal consolidation measures. The *Integrated Expenditure and Revenue Reform*, announced in July 2006, set out the amount of deficit reduction needed to meet the FY 2011 target, as well as spending cuts in broad areas (social security, personnel expenses, public investment and other). However, the expenditure reductions are not binding on the annual budgeting process. Moreover, details on how the target for public healthcare spending is to be achieved are not spelled out.

The fiscal policy challenges are analysed in Chapter 3, emphasising the following issues:

● What size of primary budget surplus should Japan target to stabilise and then reduce the government debt ratio?

- To what extent can the fiscal goals be accomplished through spending cuts and in what areas can reductions be achieved?

- How can the government strengthen the medium-term plan to maintain confidence in its fiscal consolidation programme and avoid a rise in the risk premium as public debt continues to rise?

Implementing a comprehensive tax reform

Given the pressures for increased expenditure, spending cuts alone cannot achieve the government's fiscal targets, making it necessary to boost tax revenue. There appears to be significant scope to raise revenue as the share of taxes in GDP in Japan is one of the lowest in the OECD area (Figure 1.9). However, there is evidence that higher taxes can reduce the level of GDP per capita, although the extent of the reduction depends on the way in which the tax increase is designed and implemented. With population ageing putting downward pressure on Japan's potential growth (see below), it is important to limit the negative impact of higher taxes on growth. Japan thus faces a number of difficult trade-offs between raising additional revenue and promoting growth. In particular, personal income tax revenue is relatively low in Japan, reflecting the small tax base and the fact that more than half of taxpayers are in the lowest tax bracket of 5%. There is thus significant scope for boosting revenue from personal income taxes, although this may slow growth by weakening work incentives. As for the corporate income tax, the rate is the highest in the OECD area, suggesting that cutting the rate may have a positive impact on growth, although at the risk of reducing tax revenue.

Figure 1.9. **Tax revenue in OECD countries**
Per cent of GDP in 2005

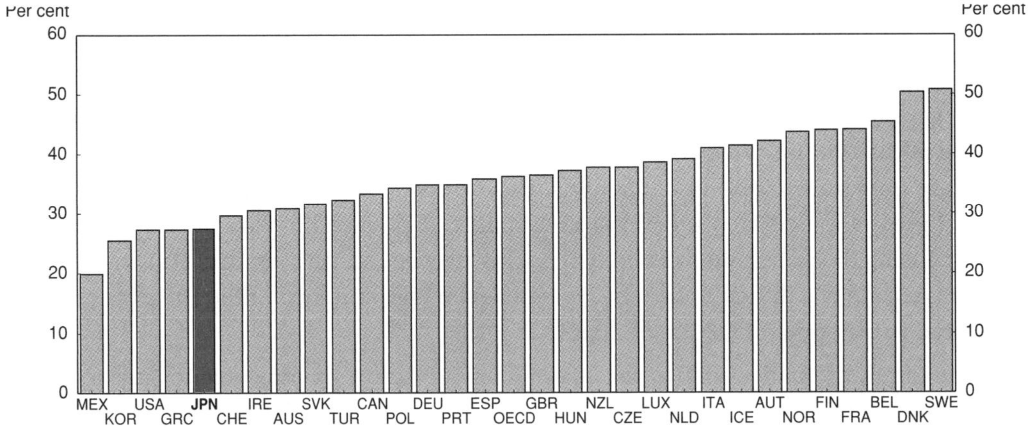

StatLink http://dx.doi.org/10.1787/277164218143

Source: OECD (2007), Revenue Statistics 1965-2006, OECD, Paris (http://dx.doi.org/10.1787/366725334503).

In addition to the trade-off between boosting tax revenue and promoting economic growth, the impact of the tax system on income inequality and relative poverty is another important consideration. Income inequality among the working-age population has risen significantly in recent years, making it the fifth highest in the OECD area in 2000. The relatively high level of inequality reflects the small impact of Japan's tax system on distribution, in part due to large tax exemptions for personal income and weak progressivity in tax rates. However, strengthening the redistributive effect of the tax system by making tax rates more progressive and expanding the role of the personal income tax would tend to have a negative impact on Japan's potential growth rate, as noted above. On the other hand, relying on the consumption tax to generate additional revenue would not contribute to reducing income inequality, although its effect on economic growth would be less negative.

Tax reform should also include measures to improve the local tax system, which is exceptionally complicated, with 23 major taxes. Moreover, the autonomy of local governments in determining tax rates and bases is limited in practice. Fiscal relations between the central and local governments need to be improved in order to maximise the benefits of decentralisation.

Chapter 4 analyses the tax system and proposes the key elements of a comprehensive reform, focusing on a number of questions:

- How can tax reform raise sufficient revenue, while minimising the negative impact on economic growth? Should efforts to raise additional revenue focus on hiking the consumption tax rate or broadening the base of direct taxes?

- Should any broadening of the personal and corporate income tax bases be offset by a revenue-neutral reduction in tax rates in order to promote economic growth?

- Do concerns about income distribution justify strengthening the redistributive impact of the personal income tax even though this may reduce hours worked, with potentially negative effects on economic growth?

- How can the local tax system be improved and simplified, while increasing the autonomy of local governments?

Enhancing the productivity of the service sector

Japan's potential growth rate has fallen from 4% in the 1980s to around 1½ per cent since 2004 and it is projected to remain at that level, the lowest in the OECD area, over the period 2009-13 (Table 1.4). Potential growth has been sustained by an increase in potential labour productivity growth from 1% in the second half of the 1990s to a projected 2.2% over the period 2009-13, above the rate expected for the United States and the euro area. However, a large and growing negative contribution from declining employment, despite a further expected rise in the labour force participation rate, is projected to reduce Japan's potential growth rate to 1.5%, compared to the OECD average of 2.2%. The key factor is the accelerating fall in the working-age population, which lowers the potential growth rate by nearly one percentage point per year during the period 2009 to 2013 (see Box 1.2). Labour utilisation, which was a factor narrowing the per capita income gap with the United States in 2006 (Figure 1.1), will widen the gap instead. Consequently, narrowing, or even maintaining, the size of the income gap with the United States will require faster productivity growth in Japan.

The large labour productivity gap with the United States – 30% in 2006 – suggests considerable scope for boosting productivity in Japan. Achieving faster productivity growth depends primarily on the service sector, given its dominant share of employment and output. However, productivity growth in services slowed from 3.5% in the 1976-89 period to only 0.9% between 1999 and 2004, with a particularly sharp decline in ICT services. In contrast, in manufacturing, which is more exposed to competition, productivity growth has remained steady at around 4% since the 1970s. Accelerating productivity growth,

Table 1.4. **Potential economic growth in OECD countries**

Annual averages, percentage points for the total economy

	Potential GDP growth		Potential labour productivity growth (output per employee)		Potential employment growth		Components of potential employment growth[1]					
							Trend participation rate		Working-age population		Structural unemployment[2]	
	2004-08	2009-13	2004-08	2009-13	2004-08	2009-13	2004-08	2009-13	2004-08	2009-13	2004-08	2009-13
Australia	3.2	2.7	1.7	2.0	1.5	0.7	0.1	0.0	1.2	0.7	0.1	0.0
Austria	2.2	1.9	1.7	1.8	0.5	0.1	0.1	0.1	0.4	0.1	0.0	0.0
Belgium	2.1	1.8	1.2	1.6	0.8	0.2	0.3	0.1	0.6	0.1	0.0	0.0
Canada	3.0	2.4	1.4	1.7	1.6	0.7	0.3	0.1	1.3	0.6	0.1	0.0
Denmark	1.7	1.4	1.6	1.7	0.1	−0.2	−0.2	−0.1	0.2	−0.2	0.1	0.0
Finland	3.0	2.1	2.4	2.3	0.6	−0.2	0.3	0.1	0.2	−0.4	0.1	0.0
France	1.8	1.9	1.3	1.6	0.6	0.4	−0.1	−0.2	0.6	0.5	0.0	0.0
Germany	1.5	1.7	1.3	1.6	0.2	0.1	0.4	0.2	−0.3	−0.1	0.1	0.0
Greece	4.1	3.5	3.2	3.2	0.9	0.3	0.7	0.3	0.1	−0.2	0.1	0.1
Iceland	4.4	2.4	2.5	1.7	1.9	0.7	0.0	0.0	1.9	0.7	0.0	0.0
Ireland	5.4	4.6	1.9	2.1	3.4	2.5	1.0	0.8	2.3	1.6	0.2	0.0
Italy	1.3	1.3	0.8	1.5	0.5	−0.2	0.5	0.1	−0.1	−0.3	0.2	0.0
Japan	**1.5**	**1.5**	**2.0**	**2.2**	**−0.4**	**−0.7**	**0.2**	**0.2**	**−0.7**	**−0.9**	**0.0**	**0.0**
Korea	4.5	5.0	3.6	4.5	0.7	0.6	0.2	0.1	0.5	0.3	0.1	0.1
Netherlands	1.8	1.7	1.2	1.3	0.6	0.3	0.5	0.3	0.1	0.0	0.0	0.0
New Zealand	2.9	2.3	1.1	1.6	1.8	0.6	0.3	0.0	1.3	0.6	0.2	0.0
Norway[3]	3.3	2.6	2.2	2.3	1.1	0.4	0.0	0.0	1.1	0.3	0.0	0.0
Spain	3.2	2.3	0.3	1.2	2.9	1.1	0.9	0.2	1.6	0.9	0.5	0.1
Sweden	3.1	2.6	2.3	2.4	0.8	0.1	0.2	0.0	0.7	0.1	0.0	0.0
Switzerland	1.7	1.8	0.8	1.0	0.9	0.7	0.1	0.1	0.8	0.6	0.0	0.0
United Kingdom	2.7	2.4	1.8	2.1	0.8	0.3	0.1	0.1	0.7	0.2	0.0	0.0
United States	2.7	2.7	2.0	2.1	0.7	0.6	−0.5	−0.5	1.2	1.1	0.0	0.0
Euro area	2.0	1.9	1.1	1.6	0.9	0.2	0.5	0.1	0.3	0.2	0.1	0.0
Total OECD	2.3	2.2	1.6	1.9	0.7	0.3	−0.1	−0.3	0.7	0.6	0.1	0.0

1. Percentage-point contributions to potential employment growth.
2. Estimates of the structural rate of unemployment are based on the concepts and methods described in "Revised OECD Measures of Structural Unemployment", *OECD Economic Outlook*, No. 68 (2000), OECD, Paris.
3. Excluding the oil sector.
Source: OECD, *OECD Economic Outlook*, No. 81 (June 2007), OECD, Paris.

therefore, depends on reversing the slowdown in the service sector. Productivity growth, in turn, is determined by a number of factors, including the regulatory framework and the strength of competition, which is influenced by international trade and inflows of foreign direct investment.

In addition to the overall deceleration in productivity growth in the service sector, there is concern about the weak performance of key service industries. In particular, the retail sector appears to be relatively inefficient, while prices are high by international comparison for transport industries, notably air transport and harbours, and for network industries, such as electricity. The rapidly growing area of business services appears hampered by pervasive regulations aimed at ensuring adequate quality. Finally, public services, such as health and education, have remained largely closed to market forces.

Chapter 5 discusses how productivity growth in the service sector can be accelerated, focusing on the following issues:

● What are the key factors limiting productivity growth in the service sector?

● How can government initiatives to develop the service sector be improved?

- What measures are needed to strengthen competition? How can competition policy be improved and regulatory reform accelerated?

- What are the major obstacles to productivity growth in key service industries, such as the retail sector, transport, network industries, business services and public services?

Reversing the trend towards dualism in the labour market while increasing labour force participation

Nominal wages resumed falling in 2007 despite the tightening of the labour market noted above. Although wages of regular and non-regular workers, such as part-timers and those with temporary contracts, have been fairly constant (Figure 1.4), the continuing shift to lower-paid non-regular workers is pushing down the overall average wage (Figure 1.10). Firms have an incentive to hire non-regular workers in order to reduce costs. For example, part-time workers (the key component of non-regular workers) are paid only 40% as much on an hourly basis as full-time workers. The total savings to firms is even larger since employees working less than 30 hours a week are exempt from all social insurance charges except employment insurance. In addition, firms use non-regular workers, which include dispatched workers and persons on temporary contracts, to provide greater flexibility than is possible in the case of regular workers.

Figure 1.10. **The share of non-regular workers is rising**

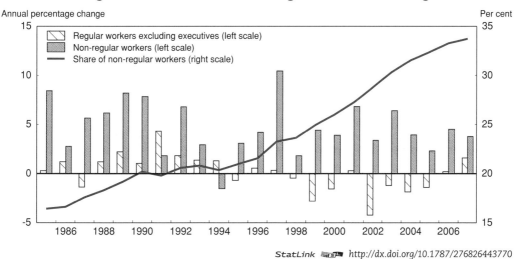

StatLink ⇒ http://dx.doi.org/10.1787/276826443770

Source: Ministry of Internal Affairs and Communications.

While the expanded availability of non-regular employment provides job opportunities to some people who would otherwise be unable to find work, the increasing dualism of the labour market poses a number of efficiency and equity concerns. Non-regular workers, who have less education on average than regular workers,[12] tend to be excluded from on-the-job training. Given the important role of firm-based training in Japan, such workers are at risk of being left behind with a low level of human capital. Not surprisingly, the proportion of non-regular workers is the highest in the service sector – at 41% of employment – where productivity growth has decelerated sharply. In addition, there are serious equity problems. Although there is little evidence, productivity differences between regular and non-regular workers are likely to be much smaller than the 60% wage gap. The equity concern is magnified by the fact that there is little movement of workers between regular and non-regular jobs, even though around three-quarters of non-regular workers between the ages of 20 and 35 prefer regular employee status.[13] Consequently, a significant portion of the labour force is trapped in a low-wage category from which it is difficult to escape. In sum, a third of the labour force is subject to low wages and reduced social protection, while bearing the brunt of adjustments in employment.

Increased dualism is also a cause of growing inequality. Since the mid-1980s, the Gini coefficient, a broad measure of income inequality, has risen by more than 11% according to Japan's *Survey on the Redistribution of Income*. In addition, an OECD study that provides an international comparison of income distribution using national data sources found that the Gini coefficient for the working-age population in Japan, which was below the OECD average in the mid-1980s, was the fifth highest in 2000.[14]

Japan is one of only four OECD countries in which the working-age population is already declining. The population in the 15 to 64 age group began to fall in 1996 and the pace of decline has accelerated to an annual rate of close to 1% (see Box 1.2). Although this is partially offset by the upward trend in participation rates, the size of the labour force is shrinking. In addition, the number of hours worked, which remains higher than in most other major countries, may fall further. The accelerating decline in labour inputs will put a growing burden on workers as the population ages. The scope for boosting labour force participation of older workers (ages 55 to 64) is limited, given that it is already the highest in the OECD. On the other hand, there is scope to increase the female participation rate, which is low compared to some other major economies. Moreover, 41% of women who do work are employed part-time, one of the highest in the OECD area. The fact that women account for two-thirds of non-regular employment may discourage their participation in the labour force.

In sum, the key challenges to improving the labour market, which are discussed in Chapter 6, are:

● How can the trend of increasing dualism in the labour market be reversed despite the preference of firms to hire non-regular workers?

● How can the human capital of non-regular workers be increased in an economy that emphasises on-the-job training?

● How can the participation rate be increased, particularly for women and older persons, thereby limiting the pace of the decline in the labour force?

Conclusion

Buoyant business investment supported by progress in corporate restructuring and strong export demand, primarily from Asia, has driven Japan's economic expansion and brought an end to a decade of economic stagnation. Sustaining the upturn is essential to stop deflation and achieve the government's fiscal targets. Achieving these goals requires appropriate monetary and fiscal policies, as well as an overhaul of the tax system that raises the necessary revenue without derailing the expansion. With the working-age population declining by almost 1% a year, further improvements in living standards depend increasingly on productivity, particularly in the service sector, which has experienced a sharp slowdown. Labour market reform is needed to cope with the declining population and to reverse the rising dualism between regular and non-regular workers, which is increasing income inequality. The following chapters analyse the challenges outlined in this chapter and develop specific policy recommendations to meet them.

Notes

1. This is important particularly for small and medium-sized enterprises, which account for almost half of bank loans. Larger companies, in contrast, rely more on internal financing and capital markets.

2. Indeed, output fell at a 0.6% annual rate from the third quarter of 2002 to the first quarter of 2003 and was basically unchanged during the final three quarters of 2004.

3. Higher tax payments resulted from the phasing out in FY 2006-07 of the temporary income tax reduction introduced in 1999 and a temporary impact from the shift of part of the income tax to the local inhabitant tax in the second quarter of 2007.

4. Under this assumption, half of the decline recorded in the level of housing investment in the third quarter of 2007, on a national accounts basis, would be recovered by the end of 2009.

5. Indeed, energy prices rose 8.3% in December (year-on-year), accounting for 0.64 percentage point of the 0.7% rise in overall inflation.

6. There is also a marked difference between manufacturing and non-manufacturing sectors in their expectations of future growth (Figure 1.2, Panel C), thus dampening capital investment in the latter.

7. In its quarterly reports between April 2005 and July 2007, only one region had been downgraded, in contrast to three in the October 2007 report alone. In January 2008, Hokkaido, Tohoku, Hokuriku and Kanto Koshinetsu were downgraded. The assessment of Hokkaido was changed from "flat" to "sluggish".

8. See IMF (2003), "Deflation: Determinants, Risks, and Policy Options – Findings of an Interdepartmental Task Force" for a discussion of the costs of deflation. Many economists view inflation at a small positive rate as beneficial for economic growth, as such a rate facilitates adjustments in relative prices and wages. For a discussion of these issues, see Anne-Marie Brook, Ozer Karagedikli and Dean Scrimgeour, "An optimal inflation target for New Zealand: lessons from the literature", *Reserve Bank of New Zealand Bulletin*, Volume 65, No. 3, September 2002, pp. 5-16.

9. This change followed the announcement that the Japanese measure of the core CPI, which excludes only fresh foods, had risen by 0.5% (year-on-year) in January 2006, its third consecutive monthly increase. However, following the revision of the consumer price index in August 2006, the core CPI actually declined by 0.1% in January 2006.

10. See the Bank of Japan's October 2007 *Outlook for Economic Activity and Prices*, page 2.

11. See the Bank of Japan's October 2007 *Outlook for Economic Activity and Prices*, page 6.

12. Only 12% of non-regular workers have a university education compared to 31% of regular workers.

13. This is based on the "Survey of actual conditions on the attributes of young people" in 2003 by the Cabinet Office. See Chapter 6 for details.

14. See Förster and Mira d'Ercole (2005), "Income Distribution and Poverty in OECD Countries in the Second Half of the 1990s", OECD Social, Employment and Migration Working Paper No. 22, OECD, Paris.

ANNEX 1.A1

Taking stock of structural reforms

This annex reviews actions taken on the structural policy recommendations in the 2006 *OECD Economic Survey of Japan*. Recommendations made in this *Survey* are shown in the boxes at the end of each chapter.

Recommendations in the 2006 *Survey*	Actions taken or proposed by the authorities
A. Maintaining the financial soundness of the banking system	
Continue strong prudential supervision over the banks by requiring them to keep non-performing loans (NPLs) at low levels and further strengthen their capital.	The ratio of NPLs to total credit for the major banks declined from 2.9% in March 2005 to 1.5% in March 2007.
Encourage the regional banks to further reduce their NPL ratios, which remain higher than in the major banks, and to strengthen their capital base.	The ratio of NPLs to total credit for regional banks declined from 5.5% in March 2005 to 4.0% in March 2007.
Avoid moral hazard in government supervision of regional banks, which would create additional non-performing loans.	No action taken.
Follow through on the privatisation of Japan Post in order to shift the flow of funds away from the public sector, while ensuring a level playing field with private-sector financial institutions.	The privatisation of Japan Post has advanced according to its initial plan, as it was split into four companies in October 2007.
Scale back the role of public financial institutions, preferably by closing them, and subject them to clear budget constraints to reduce the amount of government funding.	The Japan Finance Corp. for Municipal Enterprises will be closed. The Shoko Chukin Bank and the Development Bank of Japan are to be privatised. Five other public financial institutions are to be combined into the "Japan Finance Corporation" in 2008 and their activities will be scaled back.
Ensure that the new institution to be created by the merger of five public financial institutions operates efficiently to limit the need for government subsidies.	The *Law on Administrative Reform Promotion* states that there will be no financial subsidies to the Japan Finance Corporation to compensate its losses.
B. The public expenditure and tax systems	
The public expenditure system	
Develop a comprehensive plan to close inefficient public infrastructure to avoid a significant rise in renewal and maintenance costs.	No action taken.
Raise public-sector efficiency, in part by reforming the employment system, rather than by implementing across the board cuts in employment.	The government revised the evaluation system for central government workers. A dual career path system and a reform of the personnel exchange system with private firms will be proposed in 2008.
Promote the effective use of market testing to transfer some government tasks to the private sector.	After starting with pilot projects in three areas in 2005, market testing was expanded to seven sectors in 2007.
Introduce more market mechanisms into healthcare and nursing care in order to limit spending increases.	No action taken.
Policies to improve the efficiency of the tax system	
Broaden the personal income tax base in order to eliminate distortions.	No action taken.
Introduce a taxpayer identification number system to improve compliance with the tax system.	No action taken.

Recommendations in the 2006 *Survey*	Actions taken or proposed by the authorities
Consolidate corporate tax credits to broaden the tax base, ensuring that remaining tax credits are well targeted.	The number of tax expenditures was reduced from 64 in FY 2006 to 61 in FY 2007, although the amount remained unchanged at about 7% of corporate tax revenue.
Pursue the plan to sell government assets with an aim of increasing efficiency, while using the receipts to reduce gross government debt.	The FY 2007 central government budget contains 240 million yen (0.1% of GDP) of revenue from the sale of assets, a 26% increase from the previous budget.

C. Address inequality and relative poverty

Reverse the trend towards increasing labour market dualism through a comprehensive approach

Reduce employment protection for regular workers to reduce the incentive for hiring non-regular workers to enhance employment flexibility.	No action taken regarding regular workers. The *Part-time Work Law* was revised, in principle, to strengthen protection for part-time workers. Some employers have already implemented required changes.
Expand the coverage of non-regular workers by social insurance systems based in workplaces, in part by improving compliance with current insurance systems.	The revision of the *Employees' Pension Insurance Law*, which has been submitted to the Diet, will slightly boost the number of non-regular workers covered by the employees' pension system.
Increase training to enhance the employability of non-regular workers.	Several reforms have been implemented under the *Challenge Again Action Plan*.

Using social spending and tax reform to address inequality and relative poverty

Shift the allocation of social spending to increase the share received by low-income households.	No action taken.
Target social spending on vulnerable groups, such as single parents, while taking care to limit the creation of poverty traps and work disincentives.	Several reforms aiming at those groups were implemented under the *Challenge Again Action Plan*.
Take account of income distribution in tax reform.	No action taken.

D. Encourage innovation

Reform framework conditions to support innovative activities

Promote the development of venture capital markets, while moving away from public debt guarantees and finance.	Disclosure by firms has been improved to encourage investment by individual investors in venture businesses.
Scale back the size of public financial institutions, thereby enhancing the availability of funds for venture business and new start-ups.	See the actions listed in Section A.
Enhance the mobility of labour, including researchers, by increasing the portability of pensions and reforming retirement allowances at public research institutes.	The MEXT launched a project to promote the diversification of the career path for researchers in FY 2006 and FY 2007.
Expand the use of open competition in hiring, performance-based pay and fixed-term contracts in order to enhance labour mobility and reduce "in-breeding" in public research institutes and universities.	Following the *3rd Basic Plan of Science and Technology* (March 2006), research institutes and universities are to increase the number of researchers with fixed-term contracts.
Reduce labour practices that limit the scope for organisational changes that would allow firms to benefit more fully from introducing new technology.	No action taken.
Improve the regulatory framework continuously to reflect technological progress, particularly in the areas of medical and social welfare services, while further strengthening competition policy.	The three-year *Regulatory Reform Plan* included 154 reforms in healthcare and 79 in social welfare. In FY 2006, 53 were implemented in healthcare, while 32 were implemented in social welfare. In competition policy, four reforms were implemented.
Upgrade the regulatory framework for network industries.	The guideline for fair trade in electricity was revised and the threshold for consumer choice in the gas sector was lowered from 0.5 to 0.1 million m^3 in 2007.
Boost productivity in the retail sector, in part by avoiding policies that favour small stores.	The CEFP's *Program for Enhancing Growth Potential* in 2007 included strategies for innovation in services. In addition, METI established the *Service Industry Productivity Council* to address low productivity in services.
Use the special zone initiative to quickly advance nationwide structural reforms and provide greater information on the nationwide implementation of reforms and their economic impact.	A total of 45 reforms implemented in special zones were expanded nationwide in FY 2006, followed by five reforms in FY 2007. A survey on the economic effects of the special zone policy was issued in September 2006.
Further improve the framework for evaluating patents to make the system more efficient.	An action plan to reform the patent evaluation system was updated in January 2007.

Recommendations in the 2006 *Survey*	Actions taken or proposed by the authorities
Promote creativity in education and the diffusion of knowledge	
Give more autonomy to local governments and individual schools in setting curriculum, hiring teachers and setting wages to increase competition between schools and reverse declining levels of performance.	Local schools are allowed to hire additional teachers paid by the municipalities. There is to be more flexibility in the choice of textbooks and a larger role for municipalities.
Reform the entrance exams for secondary schools and universities to test a broader range of knowledge.	No action taken.
Encourage competition among universities by allowing more flexibility in their management, enhancing transparency in evaluating performance and further reducing regulations, including those that prevent foreign universities from entering Japan.	A survey on reforms of education at universities was conducted to facilitate competition by providing greater information.
Enhance vocational training by establishing a well functioning system of recognition and certification of learning that is co-financed by public and private sources.	The *Challenge Again Action Plan* includes several programmes to enhance vocational training and proficiency examinations and certificates were strengthened.
Upgrade the policy framework to improve innovation-specific policies	
Strengthen links between public research institutes and the business sector.	The *3rd Basic Plan of Science and Technology* promotes co-operation between business and R&D organisations through conferences.
Avoid mixing national innovation policies with measures to promote balanced regional development.	Measures aimed at the revitalisation of regional economies through R&D investment were included in the *3rd Basic Plan* in March 2006 and the *Innovation 25* plan in June 2007.
Further increase the share of competitive grants in the allocation of public R&D funds.	The amount of competitive grants rose from 471 billion yen in FY 2006 to 477 billion yen in FY 2007, boosting its share in central government outlays on science and technology from 12.6% to 13.6%.
Attach greater importance to the non-manufacturing sector in the allocation of public R&D funds.	The CEFP's and METI's policies related to the service sector noted above focus on increasing innovation in service.
Maintain flexibility in allocating public R&D funds, thereby limiting the risks inherent in concentrating R&D efforts in the sectors identified as priority areas.	The allocation of funds is made based on reviews of past policies, opinions from experts and the mid-term plan.
Focus support for R&D on new start-ups.	No action taken.
Expand the CSTP's work to include framework measures to promote innovation, while strengthening the link with other councils, including the CEFP and the Council for the Promotion of Regulatory Reform.	No action taken.
E. Strengthen integration in the world economy	
Improve the climate for inflows of foreign direct investment	
Use the FDI doubling objective as a spur to create a more open and transparent climate for FDI.	A "Program for Acceleration of Foreign Direct Investment in Japan" was put forward in 2006 aiming at improving the investment environment.
Fully open the M&A market to foreign firms by allowing them to use their own shares to finance M&As and granting them the same tax deferrals that are available in the case of domestic M&As.	The necessary policy changes were enacted in the FY 2007 tax reform. Following this reform, one "triangular" merger by a foreign company has taken place.
Further lift specific restrictions on FDI, especially in the service sector and network industries.	No action taken.
Accelerate regulatory reform in product markets, such as removing entry barriers for both foreign and domestic firms, notably in medical care, education, transport, electricity and professional services.	Demand and supply adjustment in harbor transport was abolished in all ports in FY 2006 and the permission requirement for setting prices was replaced by prior notification for all ports by FY 2006. An Anti-Monopoly Act guideline for agricultural co-operatives was issued in FY 2007 to deter unfair trade practice and to promote new entry.
Relax employment protection for regular workers, which tends to also help encourage foreign investment.	No action taken.
Remove obstacles to international trade	
Pursue the liberalisation of trade barriers, giving priority to multilateral trade negotiations, complemented by regional trade agreements, to further reduce the level of trade restrictions, including tariff and non-tariff barriers.	In addition to its active participation in the Doha Round, Japan signed Economic Partnership Agreements (EPA) with the Philippines and Chile in FY 2006, and with Thailand, Brunei and Indonesia in FY 2007. Participation in conformity assessment bodies of other countries was permitted in the field of electrical products and telecom equipment, based on mutual recognition agreements. The list of qualified food additives was gradually increased.
Strengthen market forces in the agricultural sector, in part by reducing market price supports, thereby promoting trade liberalisation in a multilateral context and broadening the scope for EPAs.	In order to accelerate the structural reform of agriculture, the price support for sugar crops was replaced by a non-product specific direct payment system in 2007.

Recommendations in the 2006 *Survey*	Actions taken or proposed by the authorities
Allow greater flexibility in the inflow of human resources, including both specialists and non-specialists, which would also facilitate EPAs.	The recent Economic Partnership Agreements with the Philippines and Indonesia will allow entry and temporary stay for individuals who work as nurses and care workers in Japan once the agreements enter into force.
Pursue further regulatory reform in product markets in part to improve access for imports.	The Regulatory Reform Plan has addressed a number of product market regulations.
Encouraging the inflow of human resources to Japan	
Improve the immigration control system to allow more highly qualified persons to work in Japan.	Preferential measures in the special zone have been expanded nationwide to give foreign researchers and data processing engineers, who work in designated facilities, residence status and the maximum period of stay was extended from 3 to 5 years in November 2006. Specific dependent relatives of such foreigners can also enter Japan under certain conditions beginning in March 2007.
Expand the range of qualifications that permit foreign personnel to work in Japan and increase recognition of qualifications and diplomas acquired overseas.	No action taken.
Increase the number of occupational categories where foreigners are allowed to work to include non-specialised and non-technical professions.	No action taken.

ISBN 978-92-64-04306-0
OECD Economic Surveys: Japan
© OECD 2008

Chapter 2

Bringing an end to deflation under the new monetary policy framework

With the end of quantitative easing in 2006, the Bank of Japan introduced a new monetary policy framework that includes an understanding of price stability as 0 to 2% inflation and raised interest rates from zero to 0.5%, although most measures of inflation have remained negative. Given remaining deflationary pressures, slower economic growth in 2007 and increased uncertainty about the outlook for growth, the central bank should not raise the short-term policy rate further until inflation is firmly positive and the risk of renewed deflation becomes negligible. In addition, the lower end of the inflation range should be increased to provide an adequate buffer against deflation.

Monetary policy faces the challenge of bringing a definitive end to deflation by supporting the economic expansion. Deflation has become entrenched in Japan, as reflected in the fall in the core consumer price index (excluding food and energy) in the fourth quarter of 2007, the 37th consecutive quarterly decline (year-on-year). At the same time, the central bank is concerned about the risk that maintaining a low interest-rate environment for too long relative to economic and price conditions may lead to distortions, notably an asset price bubble. The appropriate path of monetary policy depends in part on the pace of fiscal consolidation. After discussing the challenges facing monetary policy, this chapter concludes with a set of recommendations, which are presented in Box 2.3.

Monetary policy since the end of quantitative easing

The end of the quantitative easing policy in March 2006 marked the beginning of a new monetary policy framework (Box 2.1). With the return to the orthodox approach of

---

Box 2.1. The new monetary policy framework

In March 2006, the Bank of Japan announced the end of the quantitative easing policy that it adopted in 2001 (Table 2.1). This unorthodox approach, which sharply increased the monetary base by targeting bank reserves, played a positive role in stabilising the banking sector and achieving a sustained expansion (see the 2006 OECD Economic Survey of Japan). In addition, it helped to keep the long-term interest rate at a low level, averaging only 1.3% between 2001 and 2006, despite large government budget deficits and rising debt.

With the end of quantitative easing, the Bank of Japan introduced a new framework for monetary policy. The main elements of the framework are:

1. A statement of what price stability means to members of the Policy Board.

2. A two-pronged approach in deciding the conduct of monetary policy. First, the Bank of Japan considers whether the economic outlook that it deems most likely one to two years in the future is consistent with a path of sustainable growth under price stability. Second, it examines, from a longer-term perspective, risk factors that may significantly impact economic activity and prices.

3. The publication of the Bank of Japan's views on the economy and monetary policy in the bi-annual Outlook for Economic Activity and Prices.

In presenting the new framework, the Policy Board stated that 0 to 2% is its "members' understanding of medium to long-term price stability". Each member specified a range and the overall median value was around 1%. This was the first time that the Bank of Japan has announced an inflation range. The central bank stressed that this is neither an inflation target nor an inflation objective because it is not binding. In addition, the range refers to the medium to long term. Nevertheless, the adoption of a numerical range for inflation is a positive step towards transparency, as it is a guide to monetary policy decisions. Indeed, as the October 2007 Outlook for Economic Activity and Prices stated, the Bank of Japan decides

---

Box 2.1. **The new monetary policy framework** (*cont.*)

Table 2.1. **A chronology of Japanese monetary policy issues**

1998	April	The revised Bank of Japan (BOJ) Law comes into effect, giving the central bank greater independence in currency and monetary policy management.
	September	The BOJ cuts the overnight call rate to 0.25%.
1999	February	The BOJ adopts a zero interest rate policy.
	September	The BOJ announces that it will maintain the zero interest rate policy until the end of deflation is in sight.
2000	August	The BOJ ends the zero interest rate policy by raising the overnight rate to 0.25%.
2001	February	The BOJ cuts the overnight rate to 0.15%.
	March	The BOJ cuts the overnight rate to 0% and launches the quantitative easing policy, setting the target for banks' current account balances at the central bank at around 5 trillion yen (1% of GDP).
	August	The quantitative easing target is raised to around 6 trillion yen.
	December	The quantitative easing target is raised to around 10 to 15 trillion yen (2-3% of GDP).
2002	October	The quantitative easing target is raised to around 15 to 20 trillion yen (3-4% of GDP).
2003	April	The quantitative easing target is increased twice – first to around 17 to 22 trillion yen and later in the month to around 22 to 27 trillion yen.
	May	The quantitative easing target is increased to around 27 to 30 trillion yen.
	October	The quantitative easing target is raised to around 27 to 32 trillion yen.
2004	January	The quantitative easing target reaches its peak of around 30 to 35 trillion yen (6-7% of GDP).
2006	March	The government announces that core CPI for January 2006 rose 0.5% – the third straight monthly increase and the strongest growth in nearly eight years.
	March	The BOJ ends the quantitative easing policy and introduces the new monetary policy framework, while leaving the overnight call rate at 0%.
	July	The BOJ raises the overnight call rate from 0% to 0.25%.
	August	The revision of the CPI lowers the inflation rate by about 0.5%. Consequently, the rate of inflation in January 2006 is lowered from 0.5% to 0%.
2007	February	The BOJ increases the overnight call rate to 0.5%.

the future conduct of monetary policy while "taking account of the understanding". However, there are several issues related to the new framework.

First, the inflation range represents the diversity of views within the Board and will be re-considered each year and possibly adjusted. Consequently, it may change as new members are appointed to the Board.* Such an approach gives the Bank of Japan considerable flexibility in setting monetary policy but also increases uncertainty among market participants about future policy directions.

Second, the inclusion of zero in the inflation zone is problematic. Of the approximately 25 central banks that target inflation, only one (Thailand) includes zero in its objective. The Bank of Japan justified its low range on the grounds that "Japan experienced a prolonged period of low rates of inflation since the 1990s". Indeed, the average annual growth rate of the consumer price index (CPI) since 1990 has been 0.4% in Japan compared to 2% in Germany and 2.7% in the United States. As economic decision-making in Japan has been based on low inflation expectations, the Bank argues that an inflation target significantly higher than recent experience could have a negative impact on the economy. However, the low inflation rate since 1990 includes a prolonged period of deflation following the collapse of the asset price bubble. Hence, the low rate of inflation in recent years is not a good rationale for a definition of price stability that includes zero. Instead, it suggests the need for a higher inflation zone, more in line with the 2.1% average inflation rate during the 1980s, as a commitment not to risk a recurrence of deflation. A definition of inflation that includes zero increases the risk that negative demand shocks would push the economy back into deflation.

* The members of the Policy Board have five-year terms and there is at least one change in the Board membership each year.

Figure 2.1. **Interest rate developments in Japan**

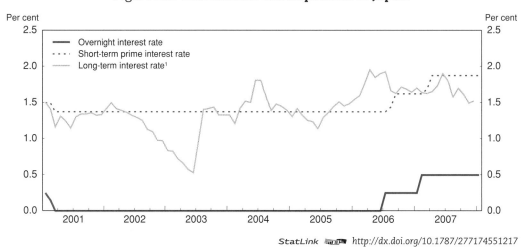

StatLink ⟶ http://dx.doi.org/10.1787/277174551217

1. Ten-year government bonds.

Source: OECD, *Analytical Database* and Bank of Japan.

targeting short-term interest rates, the Bank of Japan unwound the large build-up in reserves accumulated between 2001 and 2006, reducing it to a level in line with the reserve requirement for banks during a period of several months. Following the end of quantitative easing, the long-term interest rate increased to 2% – its highest level since 1999 – but it has since stabilised at around 1½ per cent (Figure 2.1). In July 2006, the Bank of Japan ended the zero interest rate policy, introduced along with the quantitative easing policy in 2001, by raising the overnight call rate to ¼ per cent, followed by a second hike to ½ per cent in February 2007 (Table 2.1). The rate has remained constant at that level in the context of a renewed decline in consumer prices beginning in the first half of 2007 and increased uncertainty about the world economy in the wake of financial turbulence since the summer of 2007.

The conduct of monetary policy has helped to reduce expectations of long-term inflation significantly, as shown by developments in the bond market.[1] The expected rate of inflation over ten years, which reached as high as 1% between 2004 and 2006, has fallen to 0.4%, matching the average rate of inflation since 1990. Moreover, most of the expected inflation can be explained by the anticipated rise in the consumption tax rate from the current 5%. A mechanical calculation suggests that a hike to 10%, as proposed by some economists,[2] could generate inflation of up to 0.3% a year over the next decade.

The direction of monetary policy

At the end of October 2007, the Bank of Japan presented its bi-annual *Outlook for Economic Activity and Prices*, which includes its perspective on the course of the economy and the direction of monetary policy. The main points in the *Outlook* include:

● "The level of short-term interest rates has been very low relative to economic activity and price conditions."

● "Unit labor costs, although currently still declining, are likely to stop falling along with gradual rises in wages."[3]

● "The year-on-year rate of change in the CPI (excluding fresh food) is likely to be around 0% in the short run, but is expected gradually to rise in the longer run" (Table 2.2).

Table 2.2. **The Bank of Japan's economic outlook**

Percentage change (median value shown in parentheses)[1]

		April 2007 *Outlook*	October 2007 *Outlook*
FY 2007	Real GDP	+2.0 to +2.1 (+2.1)	+1.7 to +1.8 (+1.8)
	Core CPI[2]	0.0 to +0.2 (+0.1)	0.0 to +0.1 (0.0)
FY 2008	Real GDP	+2.0 to +2.3 (+2.1)	+1.9 to +2.3 (+2.1)
	Core CPI[2]	+0.4 to +0.6 (+0.5)	+0.2 to +0.4 (+0.4)

1. From the Bank of Japan's semi-annual *Outlook for Economic Activity and Prices*.
2. Excludes fresh food only.
Source: Bank of Japan.

- "In sum, while confirming that the Japanese economy remains likely to follow a path of sustainable growth under price stability in light of the 'understanding' (of price stability) and assessing relevant risk factors, the Bank will adjust the level of interest rates gradually in accordance with improvements in the economic and price situation."

The monetary policy response of the Bank of Japan to its projected rise in inflation from 0% in FY 2007 to 0.4% in FY 2008 depends on its economic outlook and associated risks together with its understanding of price stability. The exceptionally low inflation range of 0 to 2% predisposes the central bank to react swiftly, as shown by the two hikes in the overnight rate while inflation and nominal wage growth were still negative. As noted above (Box 2.1), an inflation zone including zero is rare, as monetary authorities believe that it is necessary to have a cushion to ensure that demand shocks do not result in deflation. For example, the European Central Bank (ECB), which initially focused on a 0 to 2% inflation zone, added "close to 2%" to its definition in May 2003. This change "underlines the ECB's commitment to provide a sufficient safety margin against the risks of deflation" (ECB, 2003). A number of problems are associated with deflation:[4] i) the central bank loses the ability to achieve negative real interest rates, given the zero lower bound on nominal interest rates, preventing monetary policy from being sufficiently expansionary at certain times;[5] ii) expected price declines can result in the deferral of consumption and investment, thus dampening output growth; and iii) the negative redistributive effects of deflation in a debt-deflation scenario are contractionary. While inflation can also have a negative economic impact, there is some evidence that a small positive inflation rate has the beneficial effect of allowing relative prices to adjust smoothly (the so-called "grease effect").

The appropriate size of the safety margin against deflation in the inflation target should be larger the lower the flexibility of wages, the weaker the financial system, the lower the rate of potential growth and the smaller the scope for fiscal stimulus.[6] While Japan has a high degree of wage flexibility, its potential growth rate is low compared to other OECD countries (see Chapter 1), making it more vulnerable to recession and deflation after negative shocks. In addition, the room for manoeuvre in fiscal policy, which allows a country to offset negative demand shocks more easily, is extremely limited in Japan, given that its public debt to GDP ratio is the largest in the OECD area. In addition, the difficulty in accurately measuring inflation makes a zero lower limit problematic.[7] The CPI is thought to overstate inflation in a number of countries, in part due to the failure to adequately account for quality improvements in goods and services. Consequently, a rate close to zero may actually imply that the correctly-measured price level is declining (Box 2.2). Finally,

Box 2.2. **How large is the bias in Japan's consumer price index?**

Accurate measurement of the CPI is essential for appropriate monetary policy, especially in Japan, where the central bank's understanding of price stability is inflation in the range of 0 to 2%. An upward bias in the measurement of inflation can thus lead to a situation in which the actual price level is declining while the reported inflation rate still falls within the range identified as price stability.

The CPI in Japan in the mid-1990s was estimated to be biased upwards by 0.9%, according to research done at the Bank of Japan (Shiratsuka, 2005 and 2006). The bias was explained mainly by the failure to fully account for new products and for quality changes in existing products, as well as by the under-representation of new retail outlets in the survey of prices. In addition, the "upper-level substitution" effect – consumers replacing more expensive items in the CPI with cheaper ones – was found to add 0.1 percentage point of bias. In shifting the base year to 2000, the Ministry of Internal Affairs and Communications (MIC) introduced the hedonic method, which is now used for personal computers, printers and digital cameras to reflect quality changes in prices. In addition, MIC increased the number of data collection points by adding more discount stores and began to introduce new items without waiting for the change in the base year of the CPI, which occurs every five years.[1] As a result, the CPI bias has fallen significantly, according to Shiratsuka (2005 and 2006).

In introducing its new monetary policy framework in March 2006, the Bank of Japan stated that "Price stability is, conceptually, a state where the change in the price index without measurement bias is zero per cent. Currently, there seems to be no significant bias in the Japanese consumer price index" (Bank of Japan, 2006). However, the revision of the CPI in August 2006, which included shifting the base year from 2000 to 2005, lowered the rate of CPI inflation by 0.5%, pushing it back into negative territory. The impact of the revision was larger than the 0.3% fall in the index in 2001, when the base year was moved from 1995 to 2000. The decline in the CPI in August 2006 was mainly due to a change in weights, such as a tripling of the weight accorded to mobile telephone charges,[2] improvements in quality and the introduction of new products in the index. The August 2006 revision revealed that the reported rate of inflation when the central bank hiked the policy interest rate in July 2006 was overstated.

Additional debate about the accuracy of price statistics has been prompted by Broda and Weinstein (2007a), who compared the CPI in the United States to that in Japan. The study concluded that the upward bias in Japanese CPI inflation is 1.8% per year compared to 1% for the US CPI. According to this study, the bias in the Japanese index is explained by:

● Unaccounted improvements in the quality of certain products explain 1.0 percentage point of the bias. This includes 0.8 percentage point from quality adjustment, based on Broda and Weinstein (2007b), and 0.2 percentage point from the limited use of the hedonic method in Japan.

● The "upper-level substitution" effect explains 0.2 percentage point of the bias. This reflects the fact that the arithmetic averaging method used in Japan does not allow for substitutability between the 584 items in the Japanese CPI as relative prices change.

● The "lower-level substitution" effect – the fact that consumers shift away from a brand with a high price to a lower-priced brand of a particular item – accounts for 0.4 percentage point of bias. The United States corrects for this by randomly sampling prices – approximately ten price quotations per item in each geographic area. In contrast, the Japanese CPI includes the price of only one item.

● The outlet effect explains 0.2 percentage point of the bias. The effect is caused by the rapid growth of large-scale retail stores, expanding the floor space per retail establishment and reducing the unit price of goods.

Box 2.2. **How large is the bias in Japan's consumer price index?** *(cont.)*

However, these results have been criticised on a number of grounds. Research in MIC (Sato, 2007) argues that the hedonic method is not always superior in adjusting for quality than other methods, such as the overlap method. Concerning the bias due to the upper-level substitution effect, this study finds that the arithmetic averaging formula used in Japan gives nearly identical results to geometric averaging. Shiratsuka (2007) argued that the Broda and Weinstein study ignored structural difference between Japan and the United States. Specifically, the lower-level substitution effect is thought to be unimportant on the grounds that the Japanese CPI employs a "one specification for one item method" in surveying individual prices, which is less influenced by the difference in lower-level aggregation formulas.

While it is difficult to give definitive answers to these technical statistical issues, it appears clear that there are upward biases in the CPIs of both Japan and the United States. The extent of the bias depends on a number of issues: i) whether the limited use of hedonic methods in Japan to measure quality adjustment results in an overestimate of the CPI; ii) whether the arithmetic averaging method used in Japan allows the upper-level substitution effect to be captured in the CPI; and iii) whether the current method employed in Japan effectively limits the lower-level substitution bias. Perhaps the most important conclusion is that it is important to continue efforts to improve the quality of CPI statistics, which are crucial to guide monetary policy decisions.

1. For a discussion of recent developments in the calculation of Japan's CPI, see Shimizu (2005). The website of MIC (*www.stat.go.jp/english/data/cpi/1584.htm*) also provides detailed information on this issue.
2. The introduction of a new price plan for mobile telephones at the beginning of 2007 put additional downward pressure on the CPI.

there is evidence that a higher rate of inflation is justified in countries where adjustment in the real sector is limited, as is the case in Japan, by a high level of employment protection (see Chapter 6) and low labour mobility (Brook *et al.*, 2002). In sum, a number of factors suggest that Japan needs a relatively large buffer. The Bank of Japan's Policy Board should therefore review the understanding of price stability and increase the lower end of the range to provide an adequate buffer against deflation, as the zero floor is too close to deflation for comfort.[8] It may be beneficial to change the mechanism for setting the understanding of price stability. In some OECD countries, the inflation range is set by the government (the United Kingdom and Norway) or by consultation between the government and the central bank (Canada, Australia, New Zealand, Iceland, Hungary and Turkey), rather than independently by the monetary authority, as in the case of the euro area.

Even with the low inflation zone, the Bank of Japan should be cautious in raising interest rates given the uncertainty about the strength of the expansion (see Chapter 1). The central bank's October 2007 *Outlook* assumes "A virtuous circle of growth in production, income and spending that is expected to remain in place". However, the decline in nominal wages in 2007 puts such a virtuous circle at risk by limiting the impact of production gains on household income and spending.[9]

Even if the expansion continues as projected, it is very difficult to pinpoint the end of deflation, which has shown a high degree of inertia.[10] Indeed, the annual decline in the core CPI (excluding food and energy) has remained between 0.3% and 0.9% since 2000, despite significant fluctuations in the real economy. This suggests that when inflation is close to zero, it is relatively insensitive to changes in economic activity.[11] The difficulty of projecting the inflation rate is reflected in the Bank of Japan's bi-annual *Outlook for Economic Activity and Prices*. In the April 2006 *Outlook*, the median forecast of core CPI inflation by

Policy Board members was 0.8% for FY 2007 (Figure 2.2), suggesting a possible response by a forward-looking monetary authority. Moreover, this projection incorporated market expectations about the future course of the short-term policy rate, which at the time was expected to rise from 0% to 1.25% in 2007. However, the Bank of Japan's outlook for inflation turned out to be substantially too high, even without the assumed increase in the short-term policy rate. In the October 2007 *Outlook*, the forecast for core CPI in FY 2007 was revised down to 0%. Inflation undershot the Bank of Japan's projection even though the growth path of GDP was in line with its *Outlook*. Given such uncertainty, the Bank of Japan should not raise the short-term policy rate further until inflation is firmly positive and the risk of renewed deflation becomes negligible. This is consistent with its stated approach of adjusting "the level of interest rates gradually in accordance with improvements in the economic and price situation".

Figure 2.2. **Projections by the Bank of Japan's Policy Board members**
Percentage change projected for FY 2007

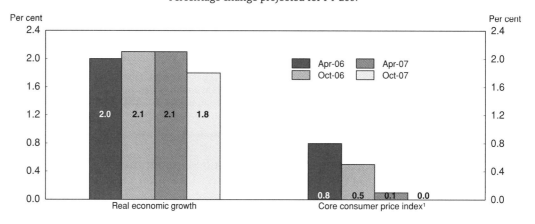

StatLink 🖳🛲 http://dx.doi.org/10.1787/277176801130

1. Excludes fresh food only.
Source: Bank of Japan.

Given the slowdown in growth, the uncertainty about the prospects for the expansion and the persistence of deflation, the Bank of Japan should avoid further interest rate hikes, which would risk undermining the expansion. The short-run impact of higher short-term interest rates is illustrated by the 50 basis-point rise in the overnight rate since July 2006, which was matched by an increase in the short-term prime rate from 1.4% to 1.9% (Figure 2.1).[12] Higher interest rates have a negative effect on the non-financial corporate sector, whose net financial liabilities amounted to nearly 50% of GDP in 2005. The depressing impact is strongest in the non-manufacturing sector and among small and medium-sized enterprises (SMEs), which have benefited only to a limited extent from the growth of this expansion (Figure 1.6). Indeed, despite the improving financial soundness of the banking sector, bank lending has slowed from a peak of 2.5% (year-on-year) in the second quarter of 2006 – just before the first interest rate hike in July 2006 – to 0.7% in the fourth quarter of 2007 (Figure 2.3). Moreover, bank lending to the corporate sector fell by 0.6% in the fourth quarter of 2007, while lending to SMEs, which accounts for almost half of total bank lending, declined by 1.0%. By sector, lending to non-manufacturing firms has fallen while that to manufacturing firms has remained steady, thus reinforcing the uneven nature of this expansion (see Chapter 1).

Figure 2.3. **Bank lending is decelerating**
Year-on-year percentage change

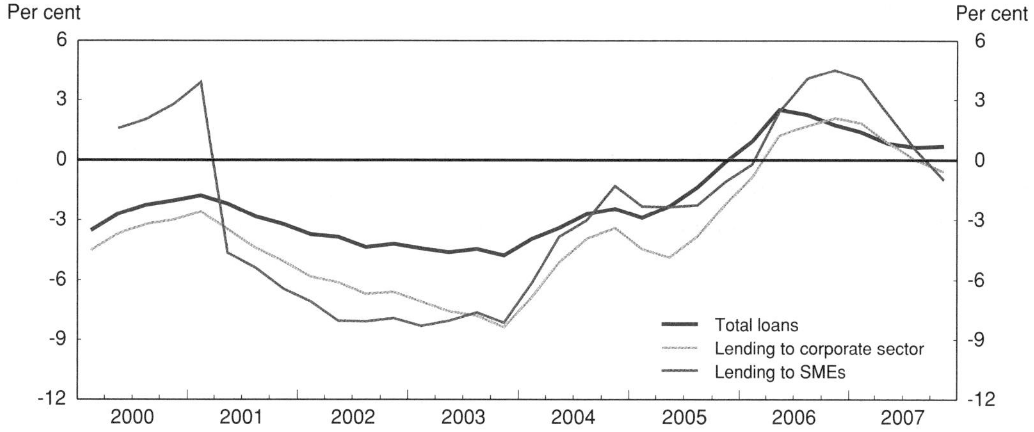

StatLink ⬛ᴵˢᴸ http://dx.doi.org/10.1787/277253135102

Source: Bank of Japan, *Loans and Discounts Outstanding by Sector.*

A negative impact from interest rates hikes is also suggested by the macroeconomic model of the Japanese government, which estimates that a 100 basis-point rise in the short-term interest rate would reduce the level of output by 0.4% in the first year and by 0.8% after three years due to declines in business and housing investment (Masubuchi *et al.*, 2007). Output would fall despite a projected rise in private consumption (by 0.2% after three years), which reflects the fact that the household sector is a net creditor and would thus benefit from a rise in interest income. However, it is not certain to what extent households would consume their additional income given that it is accompanied by an increase in government debt (see below). In addition, while higher interest rates would boost the income of the household sector as a whole, the gains would tend to be concentrated in high-income households. In 2007, the top income quintile accounted for 40% of the net financial assets held by worker households. The impact on private consumption is dampened by the fact that the marginal propensity to consume among the top income quintile, at 67% in 2006, was significantly lower than the bottom quintile, at 83%.

The Japanese government's macroeconomic model suggests another reason for being cautious in raising interest rates: a hike in short-term rates that is incorporated into long-term rates would have a negative impact on the fiscal situation, given that public debt is 180% of GDP. Indeed, the model estimates that a 100 basis-point increase in the short-term interest rate would increase the government budget deficit by 0.4% of GDP.

Monetary policy in the light of longer-term risks

The Bank of Japan's October 2007 *Outlook* also highlights the risk that an extended period of low interest rates may lead to distortions, as firms and financial institutions overinvest in certain areas.[13] However, the long period of low interest rates in Japan is justified by economic conditions. Indeed, the Taylor-rule interest rate estimated by the OECD was negative between 1998 and 2006.[14] Even at the end of 2007, the Taylor rule suggests an interest rate of 0.4%, slightly below the 0.5% overnight rate set by the Bank of Japan.

A major concern of the Bank of Japan seems to be the possible influence of low interest rates on asset prices, notably real estate, given the difficult adjustment following the collapse of the land price bubble in the early 1990s (Figure 2.4). This risk, though, seems to be overstated at present. After fifteen consecutive years of decline, the nationwide average land price rose by 0.4% in 2007, reflecting increases for both residential (0.1%) and commercial land (2.3%) in 2007. Moreover, there is a marked contrast between the three major metropolitan areas (Tokyo, Osaka and Nagoya), where prices have risen, and the rest of the country, where prices are still falling for both residential and commercial land, reflecting in part the uneven nature of the current expansion (Panel A).

Figure 2.4. **Land prices in Japan**

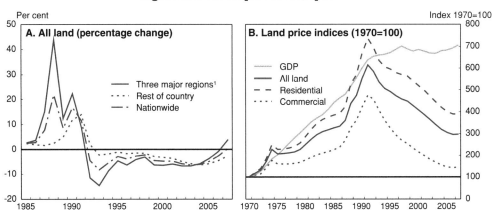

StatLink ᗡᗡᔧ http://dx.doi.org/10.1787/277310344620

1. Includes Tokyo (Tokyo, Kanagawa, Saitama and Ibaraki prefectures), Osaka (Osaka, Hyogo, Kyoto and Nara prefectures) and Nagoya (Aichi and Mie prefectures).

Source: Ministry of Land, Infrastructure and Transport.

The largest rise in land prices in 2007 occurred in Tokyo – 9.4% for commercial land – and this has created some concern about the development of a new bubble. However, even after this increase, the price of commercial land in Tokyo is still 78% below its 1991 peak. Taking a long-run perspective, there appears to be considerable scope for a further increase in land prices. While nominal GDP has expanded seven-fold since 1970, land prices have only increased by a factor of three (Figure 2.4, Panel B). The gap is especially large for commercial land prices, which have risen only 44% since 1970. Nevertheless, the outlook for land prices is modest, suggesting little urgency to "normalise" the policy rate, which has been below 1% since 1995. According to a quarterly survey by the Bank of Japan, the share of respondents that expect land prices to rise in the future declined from 46% in December 2006 to 33% in December 2007, while the share that expect land prices to fall increased from 17% to 21% over the same period.[15] Moreover, the amount of outstanding loans to firms in the real estate sector has remained steady at around 65 to 70 trillion yen since 2004, well below the peak of nearly 100 trillion yen in the mid-1990s.[16] In sum, the stabilisation of land prices is a positive signal of economic recovery and there are few warning signals that suggest the creation of a price bubble. In general, monetary policy should not target asset prices over and above their impact on output and consumer price inflation.

Conclusion

The priority for the monetary authorities should be to bring a definitive end to deflation in the context of slowing growth during 2007 and the continued decline in the CPI. Given the weakness of the non-manufacturing sector and the fall in bank lending following the hikes in interest rates in 2006 and 2007, the Bank of Japan should be cautious in further tightening monetary policy. Waiting until inflation moves significantly above zero before raising interest rates further would help sustain the expansion. Although there is a small risk that maintaining low rates for an extended period of time would allow inflation to exceed the 0 to 2% range defined as price stability by the central bank, raising interest rates too fast and too early would put the economic expansion at risk. The cost of ending the upturn before deflation is vanquished is clearly greater than temporarily overshooting the desired level of inflation. In addition, hikes in short-term interest rates may be accompanied by a run-up in long-term bond yields, which have remained exceptionally low. A significant rise in long-term rates prior to a complete end to deflation, including a rise in the GDP deflator, would be problematic for a number of reasons. *First*, higher long-term borrowing costs would impose a headwind on economic activity. *Second*, it would aggravate the fiscal situation, given the high level of public debt. Finally, improving the monetary policy framework would encourage appropriate policy decisions. In particular, the understanding of price stability of the Bank of Japan's Policy Board should be revised to raise the lower bound above zero in order to provide an adequate buffer against renewed deflation. The plan to review the inflation zone annually makes it less appropriate as a guide to expectations over the medium and long term. Instead, a fixed definition of price stability would provide more transparency for monetary policy.

Box 2.3. **Summary of recommendations for monetary policy**

- Be cautious in raising short-term interest rates, given the remaining deflationary pressures, such as falling wages and unit labour costs.

- Take into account the progress in fiscal consolidation in setting monetary policy.

- Revise the understanding of price stability to exclude zero to ensure an appropriate buffer to avoid a recurrence of deflation.

- Once the understanding of price stability is at an appropriate level, avoid frequent changes in the range so as to provide a useful guide to inflation expectations over the medium and long term.

Notes

1. The expected rate of inflation is calculated as the spread between the yields on ten-year government bonds and indexed bonds.

2. Indeed, a hike in the consumption tax to between 11% and 17% may be necessary, according to a 17 October 2007 briefing by the Cabinet Office's Council on Economic and Fiscal Policy (2007), which is discussed in Chapter 3.

3. However, this was less optimistic than the April 2007 *Outlook for Economic Activity and Prices*, which stated that unit labour costs "are likely to stop falling and start showing modest increases".

4. See Brook *et al.* (2002) for a discussion of the risks associated with deflation.

5. This was a serious problem for Japan during the downturn of 2001. While real GDP was falling at a 2.9% annual pace between the first and fourth quarters of 2001, the real short-term interest rate averaged nearly 2% even though the nominal short-term policy interest rate was set at zero. Real interest rates in the United States were negative about one-third of the time between 1945 and 1990.

6. This is explained in an article by Toshiro Muto (2006), Deputy Governor of the Bank of Japan.

7. The ECB recognised the risk of measurement bias in the CPI in its May 2003 decision on its inflation zone (ECB, 2003).

8. The Bank of Japan in fact recognised this argument in presenting its new policy framework in March 2006: "If there is a risk of falling into a vicious cycle of declining prices and deteriorating economic activity, depending on the weight attached to the risk, the accommodation of slight inflation may be deemed consistent with an understanding of price stability in the conduct of monetary policy." Moreover, a recent study at the Bank of Japan concluded "that the steady-state inflation rate that minimises the social loss is generally between 0.5% and 2%" (Fuchi, Oda and Ugai, "The Costs and Benefits of Inflation: Evaluation for Japan's Economy", Bank of Japan Working Paper No. 07-E-10, May 2007, Bank of Japan).

9. In the press conference following the release of the October 2007 *Outlook for Economic Activity and Prices*, the governor of the Bank of Japan stated that the "immediate downside risks are big".

10. The Bank of Japan's *Outlook for Economic Activity and Prices* in October 2007 reflects this uncertainty: "It is also possible that prices will continue not to rise despite the improvement in economic conditions."

11. In other words, the Philips curve, which shows the trade-off between inflation and output gaps, is relatively flat at rates of inflation close to zero. According to one study, the Philips curve for Japan becomes flat when the inflation rate falls below ½ per cent, at a quarter-on-quarter non-annualised rate (Mourougane and Ibaragi, 2004).

12. Bank of Japan data shows that banks have been able to pass on the increase in the overnight rate in lending rates. The rate on new short-term loans rose 49 basis points between the second quarter of 2006 and the third quarter of 2007, matching the 50 basis-point increase in the overnight rate by the Bank of Japan. The rate on the stock of existing short-term loans rose by 41 basis points over the same period. The re-pricing of existing long-term loans has increased more slowly, rising by 24 basis points.

13. On page 6 of the *Outlook*, it states, "If, for instance, the expectation takes hold that interest rates will remain low for a long time regardless of developments in economic activity and prices, there is a medium- to long-term risk of larger swings and of inefficient allocation of resources as firms and financial institutions over-extend themselves". In the press conference following the release of the October *Outlook*, the governor of the Bank of Japan went on to say "we must not underestimate the risks of extending low interest rates too long, including the risks of skewed asset allocation and big fluctuations in the economy".

14. The Taylor rule rate is a function of an equilibrium real interest rate (short term), the implicit inflation target, the average output gap and the gap between actual inflation and the implicit inflation target. Equal weight is given to the inflation gap and the output gap. In the case of Japan, the price stability target is inflation of 1.0% (the midpoint of the 0 to 2% understanding of price stability) and an equilibrium real interest rate of 1.2%.

15. This is from the *Opinion Survey on the General Public's Views and Behaviour*. Consequently, the diffusion index (the proportion of respondents who expect land prices to rise minus those who expect them to fall) declined from 29 in December 2006 to 12 in December 2007.

16. Moreover, another factor suggesting that a real estate price bubble is not imminent is the financial situation of real estate firms, which have recorded a drop in their ratio of interest-bearing liabilities to assets from more than 80% in 1990 to less than 60% (Bank of Japan, 2007a).

Bibliography

Bank of Japan (2006), *The Bank's Thinking on Price Stability*, 10 March 2006, *www/boj.or.jp/en/type/release/ zuiji_new/data/mpo0603a1.mpf*.

Bank of Japan (2007a), *Financial System Report*, March, Tokyo.

Bank of Japan (2007b), *Outlook for Economic Activity and Prices,* October, Tokyo.

Broda, Christian and David Weinstein (2007a), "Defining Price Stability in Japan: A View from America", *Monetary and Economic Studies*, Vol. 25, No. S-1, Bank of Japan.

Broda, Christian and David Weinstein (2007b), "Price Indexes and Deviations from the Law of One Price", University of Chicago Graduate School of Business, mimeo.

Brook, Anne-Marie, Ozer Karagedikli and Dean Scrimgeour (2002), "An optimal inflation target for New Zealand: lessons from the literature", *Reserve Bank of New Zealand Bulletin*, Volume 65, No. 3, September.

Council on Economic and Fiscal Policy (2007), *On the Promotion of the Integrated Reform of Social Security and Taxation – For the Safe and Sustainable Social Security System and Taxation in the 21st Century*, a paper submitted by expert members, 17 October 2007, Tokyo (in Japanese).

European Central Bank (2003), "The ECB's monetary policy strategy", Press Release, 8 May 2003, *www.ecb.int/press/pr/date/2003/html/pr030508_2.en.html#*.

Fuchi, Hitoshi, Nobuyuki Oda and Hiroshi Ugai (2007), "The Costs and Benefits of Inflation: Evaluation for Japan's Economy", Bank of Japan Working Paper No. 07-E-10, May, Bank of Japan.

IMF (2003), "Deflation: Determinants, Risks, and Policy Options – Findings of an Interdepartmental Task Force", Washington.

Ito, Takatoshi and Tomoko Hayashi (2006), *Inflation Targeting and Monetary Policy*, Toyo Keizai Shinposha, Tokyo (in Japanese).

Masubuchi, Katsuhiko *et al.* (2007), "The ESRI Short-Run Macroeconometric Model of the Japanese Economy (2006 version) – Basic Structure, Multipliers, and Economic Policy Analyses", ESRI Discussion Paper Series No. 173, Economic and Social Research Institute, Cabinet Office, Tokyo.

Mourougane, Annabelle and Hideyuki Ibaragi (2004), "Is there a change in the trade-off between output and inflation at low or stable inflation rates? Some evidence in the case of Japan", OECD Economics Department Working Paper No. 379, OECD, Paris.

Muto, Toshiro (2006), "Price Stability and Central Banks' Responsibility", *Bank of Japan Quarterly Bulletin*, February 2006.

OECD (2006), *OECD Economic Survey of Japan*, OECD, Paris.

Sato, Masaaki (2007), "Comments on Dr. Weinstein's Paper," Ministry of Internal Affairs and Communications, mimeo.

Shimizu, Makoto (2005), "Recent Methodological Developments in the CPI in Japan," a paper presented at the OECD conference on "Inflation Measures: Too High – Too Low – Internationally Comparable?" Paris, 21-22 June 2005.

Shiratsuka, Shigenori (1999), "Measurement Errors in the Japanese Consumer Price Index", *Monetary and Economic Studies*, Vol. 17, No. 3, December, Bank of Japan.

Shiratsuka, Shigenori (2005), "Measurement Error of Japan's Consumer Price Index: What do We Know of the Upper-Level Bias?", *Bank of Japan Review*, November, Tokyo (in Japanese).

Shiratsuka, Shigenori (2006), "Measurement Errors in the Japanese CPI", *IFC Bulletin*, No. 24, Irving Fisher Committee on Central Bank Statistics, Washington, D.C.

Shiratsuka, Shigenori (2007), "Comments on Dr. Weinstein's Paper,"*Monetary and Economic Studies*, Vol. 25, No. S-1, Bank of Japan.

ISBN 978-92-64-04306-0
OECD Economic Surveys: Japan
© OECD 2008

Chapter 3

Achieving progress on fiscal consolidation by controlling government expenditures

With gross debt of 180% of GDP, further measures to reduce the large budget deficit are increasingly urgent. An improvement in the budget balance of between 4% and 5% of GDP (on a primary budget basis) is needed just to stabilise the government debt to GDP ratio, a first step towards the government's goal of lowering the ratio in the 2010s. The first priority is to further cut government spending, which has fallen by 2½ percentage points as a share of GDP during the past five years, focusing on public investment and the government wage bill. Expenditure reductions should be accompanied by reforms to improve efficiency in the public sector. In addition, policies to limit the increase in social spending, in the context of rapid population ageing, are essential for fiscal consolidation. However, expenditure cuts alone are insufficient to achieve Japan's fiscal objectives, making it necessary to raise additional revenue.

Japan has substantially reduced its fiscal deficit since the beginning of the economic expansion in 2002, despite the weak growth of nominal GDP in the context of persistent deflation. Spending cuts and revenue increases have each lowered the budget deficit by about 2% of GDP over the past five years. Nevertheless, much remains to be done to achieve fiscal sustainability in Japan. Indeed, the central government budget relies on borrowing to finance one-third of its spending, further pushing up public debt as a share of GDP, which is already the highest ever recorded among OECD countries. The government is committed to curbing the growth of expenditure to meet its target of a primary budget surplus for central and local governments combined by FY 2011. However, achieving large spending cuts in the major spending categories of social security, public investment and the government wage bill is becoming increasingly difficult. This chapter reviews the progress in fiscal consolidation, examines the government's medium-term fiscal objectives and discusses major spending issues. Policy recommendations are presented in Box 3.2.

How much progress has Japan made in addressing its fiscal problem?

The budget deficit declined from 8.2% of GDP in 2002 to 4% in 2007, excluding one-off factors (Table 3.1). Increased revenue accounted for 1.8% of the improvement (Panel B), driven primarily by buoyant corporate tax revenue, which in turn reflected record high corporate profits and shrinking loss carryovers as the economic expansion continues. In addition, the phasing out of the temporary personal income tax cut introduced in 1999 boosted revenues. Spending cuts, amounting to 2.4% of GDP, were concentrated in public investment, accompanied by a significant fall in the government wage bill. However, these reductions were partly offset by a rise in social welfare-related outlays amounting to 1% of GDP in the context of population ageing. Overall, fiscal policy measures accounted for about three-quarters of the decline in the deficit since 2002, with the remainder explained by cyclical factors.[1]

Despite rising debt, the government's net interest payments declined by about ½ per cent of GDP between 2002 and 2007, reflecting falling interest rates.[2] Indeed, the effective interest rate paid on government net debt dropped from an average of 5.5% in the 1990s to less than 2% during the current expansion. The effective interest rate has been kept low by a number of exceptional factors, including the Bank of Japan's quantitative easing policy between 2001 and 2006, the persistence of deflationary expectations and the risk aversion of investors and banks (2006 OECD Economic Survey of Japan).

Although the deficit is on a steady downward trend, government debt continues to increase. On a gross basis, it has been rising at an annual rate of 7% since 1991, boosting its share of GDP from 65% to around 180% in 2007, the highest in the OECD area (Figure 3.1). Similarly, on a net basis, government debt rose at a 13% rate over that period.[3] The decomposition of changes in the net debt to GDP ratio (Figure 3.2) shows that the dominant cause of rising debt is the primary budget deficit. In addition to 15 consecutive years of

Table 3.1. **The evolution of the fiscal situation in Japan between 2002 and 2007**

A. Fiscal situation (per cent of GDP)

Calendar years	2002	2003	2004	2005	2006[1]	2007[1]	Change 2002-07[2]
A. Total							
Net lending	−8.0	−7.9	−6.2	−6.4	−2.9	−3.4	4.6
Primary balance	−6.6	−6.6	−5.0	−5.6	−2.1	−2.5	4.1
Cyclically-adjusted net lending	−7.0	−6.9	−5.6	−6.0	−2.8	−3.5	3.6
Cyclically-adjusted primary balance	−5.7	−5.6	−4.4	−5.2	−2.0	−2.6	3.1
B. Excluding one-off factors							
Net lending	−8.2	−8.3	−7.3	−5.6	−4.9	−4.0	4.1
Primary balance	−6.8	−6.9	−6.2	−4.8	−4.1	−3.2	3.6
Cyclically-adjusted net lending	−7.2	−7.2	−6.7	−5.2	−4.8	−4.1	3.1
Cyclically-adjusted primary balance	−5.8	−5.9	−5.6	−4.4	−4.0	−3.2	2.6
One-off factors[3]	0.1	0.4	1.2	−0.8	2.0	0.6	
C. Spending and revenue levels							
General government expenditure	38.8	38.4	37.0	38.2	36.6	36.5	−2.4
General government revenue	30.6	30.2	29.7	32.5	31.7	32.4	1.8

B. Contribution to fiscal change by item (calendar years)

	Per cent of GDP		Change 2002-07[2]
	2002	2007[1]	
Revenue items			
Direct taxes on households	5.2	5.6	0.4
Direct taxes on business	2.9	4.0	1.2
Social security contributions received by government	10.5	10.9	0.4
Indirect taxes	8.4	8.4	−0.1
Interest receipts	1.6	1.7	0.0
Others	2.0	1.9	−0.2
Total revenues	30.6	32.4	1.8
Expenditure items			
Government wage expenditure	6.7	6.1	−0.7
Government consumption on social benefits[4]	3.7	4.2	0.5
Other government consumption	7.5	7.6	0.1
Social security benefits paid by government	11.1	11.6	0.6
Government fixed capital formation	4.8	3.2	−1.6
Interest payments	3.0	2.5	−0.5
Other expenditures[5]	2.0	1.2	−0.7
Total expenditure	38.8	36.5	−2.4
Budget balance	−8.2	−4.0	4.1
Primary budget balance[6]	−6.8	−3.2	3.6

1. OECD estimates.
2. Difference in percentage points.
3. Major one-off factors include the transfer of the basic part of corporate pension funds to the government, the transfer of debt from the highway corporations to the newly established Expressway Holding and Debt Repayment Agency, and the transfer of the reserve fund from the Fiscal Loan Fund Special Account to the central government.
4. Mainly healthcare and long-term nursing care.
5. Includes subsidies, other current payments, capital transfer payments and consumption of fixed capital.
6. Excludes net interest payments.
Source: Cabinet Office and OECD, OECD Economic Outlook, No. 82 Database, OECD, Paris.

Figure 3.1. **OECD countries with a large public debt ratio**
As a share of GDP[1]

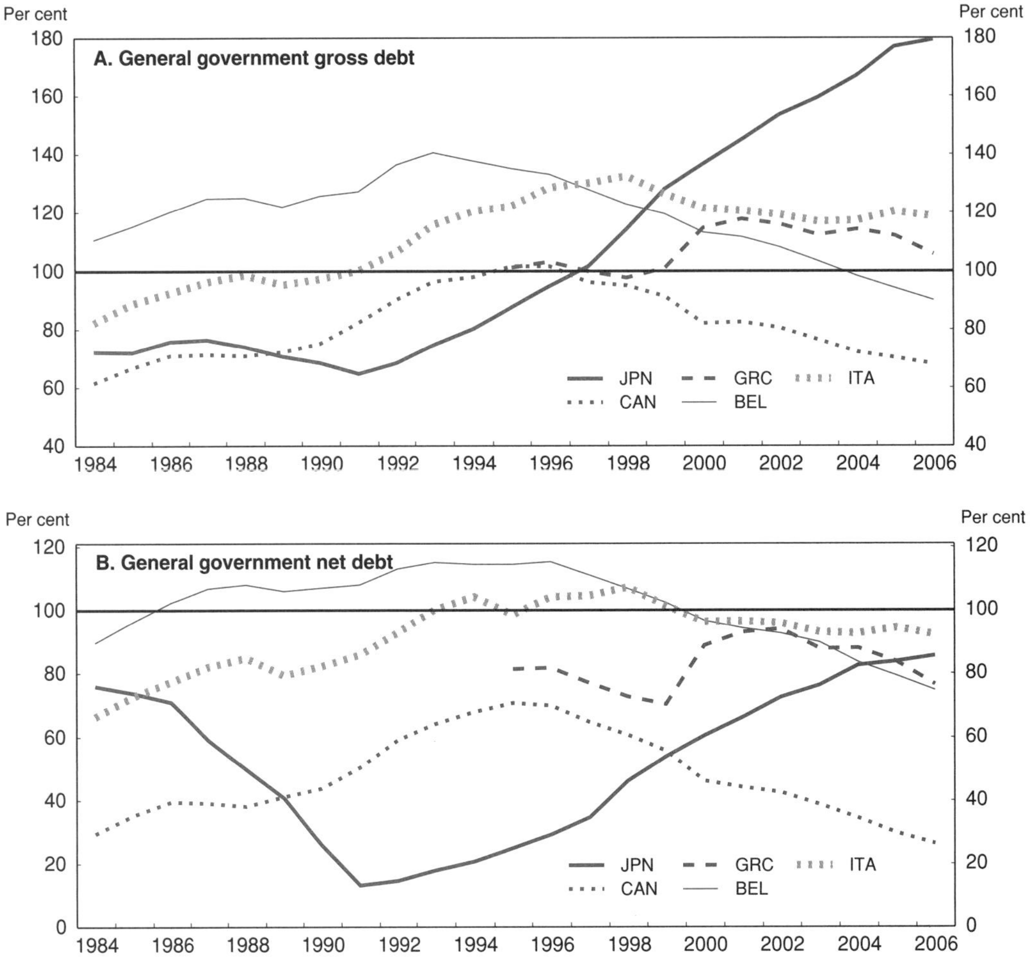

StatLink ⟨⟨⟨⟨ http://dx.doi.org/10.1787/277327363337

1. The five countries in this figure had the highest gross debt ratios in the OECD area in 2000.

Source: OECD, OECD Economic Outlook, No. 82 (December 2007), OECD, Paris.

deficits, the slow growth of nominal GDP made it difficult to stabilise the upward trend in the government debt ratio, which requires that nominal GDP grow at least as fast as the stock of government debt. However, nominal GDP growth has been sluggish, at an annual rate of less than 1% since 1991 in the context of deflation. A positive factor for stabilising debt was the decline in interest payments, as noted above, thanks to lower interest rates. The challenge for Japan is to resolve the budget deficit problem before the period of low interest rate comes to an end and rising interest payments on the accumulated debt result in a further deterioration in the fiscal situation.

The government's medium-term fiscal plan

The government's *Direction and Strategy*, announced in January 2007, established three fiscal objectives:[4] i) curb the expansion in the size of the government; ii) achieve a surplus in the primary balance of the combined central and local government budgets by FY 2011;[5]

Figure 3.2. **Decomposition of debt dynamics**

Change in government's net debt as a per cent of GDP[1]

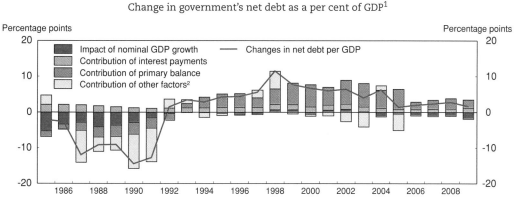

StatLink ᴍ᷐ᴤ᷐ http://dx.doi.org/10.1787/277421518443

1. The formula is as follows: $(B_0/Y_0) - (B_{-1}/Y_{-1}) = (B_{-1}/Y_0) * (i-g) + PB_0/Y_0 + e$, where B, Y, I, g, PB and e represent net debt, nominal GDP, the effective interest rate, the GDP growth rate, primary balance and other factors, respectively.

2. Other factors, which are calculated as a residual, include changes in asset prices. In addition, net income from asset sales, dividends from equity held by the government, and acquisition of asset and liabilities from non-government institutions that are not recorded in flow data are included.

Source: OECD, *OECD Economic Outlook*, No. 82 Database, OECD, Paris.

and *iii)* stabilise the government debt to GDP ratio and decrease it in the mid-2010s. The plans calls for fiscal consolidation of around ½ per cent of GDP a year, the rate achieved between FY 2001 and FY 2006, in order to achieve the FY 2011 target. The *Reference Projection* provides a quantitative picture of how the policy goals in the *Direction and Strategy* can be achieved (Table 3.2). According to the latest version (January 2008), the combined central and local government primary budget deficit is estimated to have fallen from the 2.9% of GDP recorded in FY 2005 to 0.7% in FY 2007.[6] It is projected to fall further to 0.1% in FY 2011 without any tax increases, according to the "growth scenario" shown in Table 3.2, which assumes that the expenditure reductions included in the 2006 fiscal consolidation plan are implemented.

In addition, there is a plan for fiscal consolidation of the social security fund, which accounts for about 40% of total expenditure in the general government budget. *First,* the government will increase its contribution to the basic pension from one-third at present to one-half by FY 2009, at a cost of around 2.3 trillion yen (0.4% of GDP). *Second,* the rise in the pension contribution rate from 14.6% in FY 2007 to 16.1% in FY 2011 will generate an additional ½ per cent of GDP in revenue for the social security system. The additional revenue is projected to help improve the balance of the social security fund by ½ per cent of GDP, from a deficit of ¼ per cent of GDP in FY 2007 to a surplus of a similar magnitude in FY 2011 (Figure 3.3).[7] Although the government's medium-term plan does not explicitly include the social security fund, it should be considered simultaneously with central and local government balances, given that the general government balance determines the evolution of government debt. It is important, therefore, to carefully monitor developments in the social security fund, which depends on demographic trends and other unpredictable factors, to ensure that the *Direction and Strategy's* target for a primary budget surplus for central and local governments combined is not achieved through a deterioration in the social security fund. Finally, the contribution rates for pensions, healthcare and nursing care should be taken into account in the government medium-term plan in determining the appropriate overall burden on households.

Table 3.2. **Evolution of the medium-term plan of the government**[1]

Fiscal year	Year of plan	2005	2006	2007	2008	2009	2010	2011
A. Macroeconomic indicators (per cent change from proceeding year)								
Real GDP	2006	2.7	1.9	1.8	1.8	1.7	1.7	1.7
	2007	2.4	1.9	2.0	2.1	2.2	2.4	2.5
	2008	2.4	2.3	1.3	2.0	2.3	2.5	2.6
Nominal GDP	2006	1.6	2.0	2.5	2.9	3.1	3.1	3.2
	2007	1.0	1.5	2.2	2.8	3.3	3.7	3.9
	2008	1.1	1.6	0.8	2.1	2.5	2.9	3.3
GDP deflator	2006	−1.1	0.1	0.7	1.1	1.3	1.4	1.5
	2007	−1.3	−0.4	0.2	0.7	1.1	1.3	1.3
	2008	−1.3	−0.7	−0.5	0.1	0.2	0.4	0.7
CPI	2006	0.1	0.5	1.1	1.6	1.9	2.1	2.2
	2007	−0.1	0.3	0.5	1.2	1.7	1.9	1.9
	2008	−0.1	0.2	0.2	0.3	0.6	1.0	1.4
Nominal long-term interest rate (per cent)	2006	1.4	1.7	2.4	2.9	3.3	3.7	3.9
	2007	1.4	1.8	2.1	2.6	3.3	3.7	4.0
	2008	1.4	1.7	1.6	1.7	2.1	2.4	2.9
B. Fiscal Indicators (per cent of GDP)								
General government fiscal balance	2006	−5.4	−5.0	−4.0	−3.7	−3.4	−2.9	−2.8
	2007	−5.8	−3.6	−3.0	−2.8	−2.4	−2.0	−1.8
	2008	−4.3	−3.3	−2.8	−3.0	−2.7	−2.4	−2.2
of which: Central government	2006	−5.0	−4.5	−3.4	−3.2	−3.3	−3.2	−3.4
	2007	−5.9	−3.5	−2.7	−2.6	−3.0	−3.0	−3.0
	2008	−4.1	−3.4	−2.8	−2.9	−3.0	−3.0	−2.9
Local government	2006	−0.4	−0.2	−0.4	−0.3	−0.2	−0.1	0.1
	2007	−0.2	0.1	0.3	0.4	0.5	0.6	0.7
	2008	−0.4	0.2	0.2	0.5	0.3	0.4	0.5
Social security fund[2]	2006	0.0	−0.2	−0.2	−0.2	0.1	0.4	0.4
	2007	0.3	−0.2	−0.6	−0.6	0.1	0.4	0.5
	2008	0.3	−0.1	−0.2	−0.6	0.0	0.2	0.2
Primary balance of general government[2]	2006	−4.7	−4.2	−3.1	−2.6	−1.8	−0.9	−0.5
	2007	−5.1	−2.8	−2.1	−1.9	−1.3	−0.6	−0.2
	2008	−3.6	−2.7	−1.9	−2.1	−1.6	−1.2	−0.9
of which: Central and local government	2006	−3.3	−2.8	−2.0	−1.5	−1.0	−0.4	0.0
	2007	−2.9	−1.7	−0.6	−0.4	−0.5	−0.1	0.2
	2008	−2.9	−1.7	−0.7	−0.5	−0.6	−0.4	−0.1
Social security fund[2]	2006	−1.4	−1.4	−1.1	−1.1	−0.8	−0.5	−0.5
	2007	−2.2	−1.1	−1.5	−1.5	−0.8	−0.5	−0.4
	2008	−0.7	−1.0	−1.2	−1.6	−1.0	−0.8	−0.8
General government expenditure	2006	36.1	35.6	34.9	34.8	34.6	34.4	34.4
	2007	n.a	n.a	n.a	n.a	n.a	n.a	n.a
	2008	n.a	n.a	n.a	n.a	n.a	n.a	n.a

1. The *Reference Projection* is revised in January of each year. The figures for 2006 are from the "Base Case" in which the budget surplus is achieved in FY 2011. The figures for 2007 and 2008 are from the "growth scenario" (1-A), in which: i) output growth is sustained by supply-side reforms to improve potential growth and a favourable global environment; and ii) the spending reductions scheduled in the fiscal consolidation programme announced in July 2006 are implemented. The *Reference Projection* also includes a "risk scenario", shown in Annex 3.A1, in which growth is lower in the absence of reforms and a favourable growth environment.
2. The figures are calculated by the OECD based on the figures in the *Reference Projection* and the *OECD Economic Outlook*, No. 82 Database.
Source: Cabinet Office (2006, 2007c and 2008) and OECD calculations.

In sum, the government's medium-term plans would result in fiscal consolidation of around 1% of GDP by FY 2011, in terms of the primary general government balance, a pace that is only half as fast as the ½ per cent of GDP per year achieved during this expansion

Figure 3.3. **Projection of the social security fund balance**

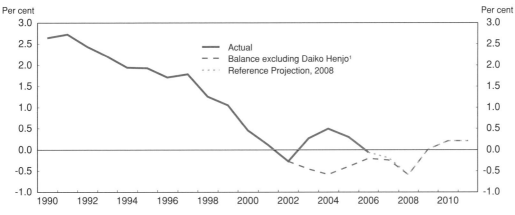

StatLink ⤢ http://dx.doi.org/10.1787/277425617131

1. Excludes Daiko Henjo from the actual balance (2002-2006) and from the Reference Projection for 2007. Daiko Henjo is the transfer of the basic part of the corporate pension funds to the government.

Source: Cabinet Office (2008) and OECD calculations.

(on a cyclically-adjusted basis).[8] Moreover, the overall general government primary balance may remain in deficit in FY 2011 (Table 3.2). It is appropriate, therefore, to accelerate the pace of fiscal consolidation. Excluding one-off factors, the OECD estimates the general government primary deficit at 3.2% of GDP in calendar year 2007 (Table 3.1), suggesting that the pace of consolidation would have to accelerate to around ¾ per cent of GDP a year to achieve a primary budget balance in calendar year 2011.

There is also a question of whether the 2008 *Reference Projection* is overly optimistic. In the "growth scenario", it projects that real GDP growth will accelerate from an average of 2% over the period 2002 to 2006 to 2.6% in FY 2011 (Table 3.2), thanks to positive supply-side factors, such as greater use of information technology, the implementation of free trade agreements and regulatory reform. However, this projection is higher than most other short-term projections, including those by the OECD, which expects that output will expand at an annual rate of less than 2% between 2007 and 2009 (Table 1.2). Moreover, the rate projected in the *Reference Projection* is well above Japan's potential growth rate, for the period 2007 to 2011, which is estimated by the OECD at 1½ per cent (Table 1.4), a rate close to the current estimate by the government of Japan. Policies to boost potential growth are certainly necessary and desirable. But given uncertainty about the impact and timing of policy changes on potential growth, it is risky to assume a substantial and prompt rise in potential growth as a basis for the medium-term fiscal plan. This risk is acknowledged in the "risk scenario" of the 2008 *Reference Projection,* which projects that real GDP growth will decelerate to 1.1% in the absence of the reforms noted above (see Annex 3.A1). In sum, basing the fiscal consolidation plan on the assumption that economic growth does not accelerate would be more reasonable.

In addition to overly optimistic economic assumptions, the FY 2011 objective of the *Direction and Strategy* is not likely to be sufficient to achieve the long-term goal of stabilising, and then reducing, the public debt ratio.[9] The size of the general government primary budget surplus necessary to stabilise the debt ratio depends on the level of the interest rate relative to the growth rate; the larger the gap between the interest rate and the nominal growth rate, the larger the necessary primary budget surplus. In the 2006 *Reference Projection,* the interest rate (3.9%) was substantially larger than the nominal growth rate

(3.2%), suggesting that a primary budget surplus of 1% of GDP would be required.[10] This was revised in the 2007 *Reference Projection*, which projected an interest rate and nominal growth rate of around 4% in FY 2011. Finally, in the 2008 *Reference Projection*, the nominal growth rate is above the interest rate. Looking at recent trends, the net effective interest rate on government debt since 1995 has averaged 2.6%, well above the 0.3% average nominal growth rate.[11] Such a gap would require a primary budget surplus of around 2% of GDP. In sum, achieving the government's objective of stabilising the public debt ratio would require a general government surplus of between 1% and 2% of GDP – an improvement of 4% to 5% of GDP from the deficit in FY 2007. Reducing the public debt ratio would require an even larger improvement in the primary budget balance. This conclusion is consistent with long-term projections by the Japanese government and the members of the Council on Economic and Fiscal Policy (CEFP) (Box 3.1).

Box 3.1. **Long-term fiscal projections by the Japanese government and the CEFP**

A projection by the CEFP examines the fiscal policy changes necessary to stabilise the public debt ratio through 2025 (Table 3.3). It concludes that an improvement in the primary budget balance of central and local governments of between 1.5% and 4.9% of GDP is necessary. The size of the needed improvement depends on the level of healthcare and long-term nursing care spending and on the macroeconomic assumptions. However, the lower end of this range assumes that real growth will accelerate to a pace of 2.4% between 2007 and 2011. Assuming growth of 1.6% – more in line with potential growth as estimated by the OECD – implies that the necessary improvement in the primary budget balance would be between 3.9% and 4.9% of GDP, in line with the OECD estimate above. Even this large increase in the primary budget surplus would not be adequate to reduce the public debt ratio, as planned by the government during the 2010s.

Table 3.3. **Long-term fiscal projections through 2025**
Primary budget surplus needed to stabilise the debt to GDP ratio (as a per cent of GDP)[1]

Expenditure cut between FY 2006-11	Social security policy[2]		Growth assumption[3]	Change in primary balance	Required change in tax burden[4]
	Burdens	Benefits			
−1.9%	Increase	Constant	Low	4.9%	5.9%
			High	2.7%	3.1%
	Constant	Decrease	Low	4.3%	5.1%
			High	1.8%	1.9%
−2.4%	Increase	Constant	Low	4.6%	5.5%
			High	2.4%	2.8%
	Constant	Decrease	Low	3.9%	4.6%
			High	1.5%	1.6%

1. Figures are derived endogenously based on the assumption that the debt service ratios in FY 2011 and FY 2020 do not exceed the level in FY 2025.
2. Social security policy includes healthcare and nursing care services.
3. In the high-growth scenario, real GDP growth is 2.4% between FY 2007-11 and 1.7% thereafter. In the low-growth scenario, real growth is 1.6% and 0.9%, respectively. The gap between the interest rate and the nominal growth rate ranges from 1.3 to 1.6 percentage points. The high-growth scenario assumes an increase in labour supply and regulatory reforms to boost productivity.
4. The required change in tax revenue is not equal to the change in the primary balance due to macroeconomic changes. The increase in tax revenue consists of greater consumption and income tax revenues.
Source: Council on Economic and Fiscal Policy (2007c).

Box 3.1. **Long-term fiscal projections by the Japanese government and the CEFP** (cont.)

Another long-term projection, by the Financial System Council of the Ministry of Finance in 2007, analysed fiscal sustainability through the year 2050 (Table 3.4). With no fiscal reforms, the primary budget deficit of central and local governments would rise to 4.5% of GDP by mid-century due to increasing social welfare expenditures.[1] As a result, the debt to GDP ratio, currently estimated at 144% by the government,[2] would reach nearly 400%. A primary budget surplus of 4.2% from FY 2007 onwards (compared to the deficit of 0.7% projected that year in the *Reference Projection* shown in Table 3.2) would be necessary to stabilise the debt ratio at its current level through 2050. Cutting the debt ratio in 2050 to 60%, the guideline set by the Maastricht Treaty, would require a surplus of 5.5% of GDP in the primary balance (shown under Estimate 1 of the baseline scenario in Table 3.4). Delaying fiscal consolidation imposes a high cost, according to this simulation. If the targeted budget surplus were only achieved in FY 2012, the size of the improvement in the primary balance to keep the debt ratio unchanged at around 140% would be about 4.8% of GDP – 0.6 percentage point larger. This projection also examines the effect of the government's fiscal consolidation plan. Even with the budget cuts incorporated in the *Reference Projection*, a primary budget surplus of 2.9% of GDP in FY 2007 would be necessary to stabilise the government debt ratio through 2050.[3]

Table 3.4. **Long-term fiscal projections through 2050**

Primary budget surplus (as per cent of GDP) needed in FY 2007 to stabilise the debt to GDP ratio by 2050

Debt ratio[1] target in 2050	Fiscal indicator	Baseline scenario[2]		MTO scenario[3]	
		Estimate 1[4]	Estimate 2[5]	Estimate 1[4]	Estimate 2[5]
140%	Primary balance	4.2%	2.9%	2.9%	1.6%
	Cost of delaying[6]	0.6%	0.4%	0.5%	0.2%
100%	Primary balance	4.8%	3.7%	3.5%	2.4%
	Cost of delaying[6]	0.6%	0.5%	0.6%	0.4%
60%	Primary balance	5.5%	4.5%	4.1%	3.2%
	Cost of delaying[6]	0.7%	0.6%	0.7%	0.5%

1. The coverage of debt is limited to central and local government bonds and the borrowing by the special account for local tax grants, and is thus below the OECD estimate based on a general government basis, which was 180% of GDP in 2007.
2. Baseline scenario assumes that current policies will continue up to FY 2050.
3. The MTO (Mid-Term Objective) scenario reflects the current reform plan included in the *Reference Projection* of the 2007 *Direction and Strategy*.
4. Estimate 1 uses the macroeconomic assumption in the *Structural Reform and Medium-Term Economic and Fiscal Perspectives – FY 2005 Revision* for the period 2007-11. The nominal growth rate is assumed to be 1.6% between 2012 and 2032 – a gap of 1.4 percentage point with the long-term interest rate. Nominal growth is assumed to be 1% between 2033 and 2050, a 2 percentage-point gap with the long-term interest rate.
5. Estimate 2 increases the nominal growth rate by 1 percentage point from Estimate 1 between 2012-2050.
6. The cost of delaying shows the additional primary budget surplus required if fiscal consolidation is delayed five years, *i.e.* from FY 2007 to FY 2012.
Source: Ministry of Finance, Financial System Council (2007).

1. While these simulations are useful to consider the necessary amount of fiscal consolidation to stabilise the debt to GDP ratio in the future, they are sensitive to the underlying assumptions. One of the risks is a further rise in the borrowing rate of the government. Although the Financial System Council assumes a gap of 2 percentage points between the long-term interest rate and the nominal GDP growth rate, a high level of debt and population ageing may lift the risk premium. The higher cost of borrowing increases the amount of fiscal consolidation needed to stabilise the debt ratio.
2. The government definition of debt is limited to central and local government bonds and the borrowings of the special account for local tax grants. It is thus less than the general government debt figure of 180% estimated by the OECD, which includes short-term borrowing and other financial liabilities.
3. These estimates are sensitive to the rate of output growth. In Estimate 2, nominal growth is boosted by 1 percentage point from the rate assumed in Estimate 1 (the growth assumption used by the Ministry of Health, Labour and Welfare in social security projections). This reduces the needed improvement in the primary budget balance by between 1% and 1.3% of GDP in the baseline scenario.

Continuing the downward trend in government spending

Expenditure cuts are the top priority for fiscal consolidation. Reducing spending would limit the amount of the additional tax burden necessary to achieve the fiscal objectives of the government, thus limiting the negative impact of taxes on growth. Moreover, empirical research indicates that deficit reductions achieved through spending cuts tend to be longer lasting than those resulting from tax increases. Furthermore, cross-country evidence suggests that expenditure reductions that focus on government wages and transfer spending have positive confidence effects that offset, at least in part, the contractionary impact of fiscal consolidation on economic activity (OECD, 2006a). This is particularly the case when government debt is high, as in Japan.

On the expenditure side, Japan has had some success: total government spending fell at an annual rate of 0.3% in nominal terms between 2002 and 2007, reducing it from 38.8% of GDP to 36.5%. In contrast, the spending target for FY 2007-11 in the 2007 and 2008 *Reference Projections* is less ambitious, as it allows government outlays to increase at an annual rate of between 1.2% and 1.7%.[12] Nevertheless, the high nominal growth rate of output assumed in the *Reference Projection* – 2.7% over the period FY 2007-11 – enables Japan to get close to the FY 2011 target of a primary budget surplus through expenditure cuts (as a share of GDP) alone. However, as noted above, this growth assumption appears overly optimistic. In contrast, the OECD projects that nominal output growth will pick up from an average of 0.9% between 2002 and 2007 to 1.7% between 2007 and 2009. If this pace of growth were extended to 2011, and expenditures expand at the 1.2% to 1.7% rate assumed in the *Reference Projection*, the decline in government expenditures over the period 2007-2011 would be 0.7% of GDP at most. Such a decline is well below the necessary improvement in the primary budget balance of 4% to 5% of GDP. This section focuses on the scope for spending cuts in some key areas, including pensions, healthcare, long-term nursing care, public investment and the government wage bill.

Social spending

Gross public social spending in Japan was 17.7% of GDP in 2006, well below the OECD average of 20.6%, according to the OECD Social Expenditure database. Indeed, Japan ranked eighteenth out of 24 OECD countries, despite its relatively aged population. Japan's Ministry of Health, Labour and Welfare reported the same level of social spending in FY 2006 (Table 3.5) as the OECD, although its more narrow measure excludes labour market and housing policies included in the OECD definition. Pensions, healthcare and long-term nursing care account for more than 90% of social expenditure in Japan. The government projects that social spending will grow at a 3% annual rate through FY 2015, boosting its share of GDP by less than 1 percentage point to 18.4%. With rapid population ageing, maintaining social expenditure well below the current OECD average is an ambitious target. Given that social spending accounts for 40% of total government outlays, containing expenditure increases in this area is a key to achieving fiscal consolidation in the medium term.

The 2004 reform of the public pension system was intended to ensure its sustainability for the next 100 years by introducing three measures (Table 3.6). *First*, the pension contribution rate is being gradually increased from 13.6% in FY 2004 to 18.3% by FY 2017. *Second*, pension spending will be limited through a system of "macroeconomic indexation", which adjusts pension benefits based on changes in the number of

Table 3.5. **Projection of social spending to FY 2015**

| | FY 2006 | | | | FY 2011 | | | | FY 2015 | | | |
| | Before reform | | After reform[1] | | Before reform | | After reform[1] | | Before reform | | After reform[1] | |
	Trillion yen	Share of GDP[2]	Trillion yen	Share of GDP[2]	Trillion yen	Share of GDP[2]	Trillion yen	Share of GDP[2]	Trillion yen	Share of GDP[2]	Trillion yen	Share of GDP[2]
Total outlays	**91.0**	**17.7**	**89.8**	**17.5**	**110.0**	**18.4**	**105.0**	**17.6**	**126.0**	**19.9**	**116.0**	**18.4**
Pensions	47.3	9.2	47.4	9.2	56.0	9.4	54.0	9.1	64.0	10.1	59.0	9.3
Healthcare	28.5	5.5	27.5	5.4	34.0	5.8	32.0	5.4	40.0	6.3	37.0	5.8
Welfare	15.2	3.0	14.9	2.9	20.0	3.3	18.0	3.1	23.0	3.6	21.0	3.2
of which:												
Elderly nursing care	6.9	1.3	6.6	1.3	10.0	1.7	9.0	1.4	12.0	2.0	10.0	1.6

1. Includes the impact of the 2004 pension reform, 2005 elderly nursing care reform and 2006 healthcare reform.
2. GDP growth rate until FY 2011 is based on the 2006 *Reference Projection* (Table 3.2). The Ministry of Health, Labour and Welfare assumes an annual growth rate of 1.6% after FY 2011.
Source: Ministry of Health, Labour and Welfare (2006).

contributors and life expectancy. Macroeconomic indexation will be introduced once the consumer price index rises 1.7% above its 2005 level,[13] a condition that has not yet been met. *Third*, as noted above, the government contribution rate to the basic pension is to be increased from one-third to one-half by FY 2009. These reforms are projected to limit pension outlays to around 9% of GDP through FY 2015. However, it became known in 2007 that individual pension contributions have not been registered accurately. This problem has increased uncertainty about benefit entitlements, creating doubts about pension administration, as well as deep anxiety among current and potential pension recipients. Consequently, the reliability of projections for the pension system is difficult to assess. The government stated that the cost of correcting this mistake will be financed by a reduction of management costs, which suggests scope to streamline the pension management system.

Table 3.6. **Long-run projections for the public pension system**[1]
Trillion yen

Year	Revenue (A)	Outlays (B)	Balance (A-B)	Fund (C)	Ratio of the Fund to outlays (C/B)
2005	32.3	36.1	−3.8	174.7	4.9
2006	34.1	37.4	−3.3	171.4	4.7
2007	35.8	38.6	−2.8	168.7	4.4
2008	37.8	39.9	−2.1	166.5	4.2
2009	41.5	41.5	0.0	166.5	4.0
2010	43.2	42.6	0.6	167.0	3.9
2015	50.5	47.3	3.2	176.3	3.7
2020	56.5	49.7	6.8	204.2	4.0
2025	61.8	52.5	9.3	246.3	4.5
2030	67.4	57.5	9.9	295.8	5.0
2040	77.4	73.5	3.9	368.8	5.0
2050	86.6	87.8	−1.2	377.0	4.3
2060	95.3	97.7	−2.4	356.3	3.7
2070	103.1	107.3	−4.2	324.1	3.1
2080	111.9	117.8	−5.9	273.1	2.4
2090	123.1	130.0	−6.9	207.4	1.6
2 100	136.7	143.9	−7.2	136.7	1.0

1. The National Pension Scheme and Employees' Pension System.
Source: Ministry of Health, Labour and Welfare (2005).

The 2004 pension reform also requires that the average replacement rate remain above 50%, although the rates for relatively high-income persons are already below that lower bound. In the initial projection, the replacement rate was expected to fall to 50.2% in 2023, which would force an end to the system of macroeconomic indexation given the requirement that the replacement rate remain above 50%.[14] In 2007, the government recalculated the future replacement rates based on new population estimates and economic assumptions. In this new projection, the replacement rate falls from 59.7% in FY 2006 to 51.6% in 2026. The 1.4 percentage-point rise in the replacement rate compared with the previous projection is mainly explained by a positive impact from economic factors based on the optimistic growth scenario included in the 2007 *Reference Projection*. The economic effect partially offsets the negative impact from demographic factors – 4.5 percentage points – based on the medium-case scenario for population changes, which has tended to be overly optimistic in the past. If the economic factors and demographic trends do not turn out as assumed in the projection, it will be difficult to maintain the replacement rate above the lower bound of 50%. One option is to change the law to allow the average replacement rate to fall below 50%. However, the scope for decline is limited as it may discourage contributions to the public pension scheme in favour of relying on social assistance, although the latter is subject to an asset test. A second option – a further hike in the contribution rate – should be avoided as it would have an adverse impact on the labour market. The best option would be to further raise the pension eligibility age in line with the increase in life expectancy.[15] This should be accompanied by reforms to increase the rate of return on accumulated assets in the social security funds.

Public healthcare expenditure in Japan, at 5.5% of GDP, was the ninth lowest among OECD countries in 2005. However, rapid ageing inevitably increases healthcare outlays; per capita spending for people aged from 65 to 74 was 3.2 times higher than for people under 65 in Japan. For those over age 75, the ratio is 5.1 times higher. Indeed, the changing age composition of the population alone would boost per capita healthcare expenditures by 1.3% per year until FY 2015. The government plans to reduce public healthcare spending from the 6.3% of GDP originally projected in FY 2015 to 5.8% through a number of reforms. *First*, the rate of co-payment by persons between the age of 70 and 74 with high incomes was increased from 20% to 30% and medical fees were cut by 3.2% in FY 2006. *Second*, a new medical insurance scheme for those over the age of 75 will be introduced in FY 2008. However, the hike in the standard co-payment rate for the 70 to 74 age group from 10% to 20% has been postponed for a year, although no new reforms to achieve the targeted cost reduction in FY 2008 have been proposed. *Third*, a large saving in the medium term is expected through a reduction in the average length of hospital stays, which is three to five times longer in Japan than in other OECD countries (OECD, 2007a). *Fourth*, healthcare costs are to be reduced through the prevention of lifestyle-related diseases. The government will further promote individual medical exams,[16] with the aim of reducing the number of persons with "metabolic syndromes"[17] by a quarter by FY 2015. However, the extent of savings that can be achieved by encouraging healthier lifestyles is uncertain. Moreover, the medical criteria underpinning this programme remain controversial even among healthcare professionals.

The government should pursue additional reforms to limit the increase in healthcare expenditure. *First*, it is important to make greater use of market mechanisms by allowing private-sector companies to manage hospitals, which is currently allowed only in one special zone (see Chapter 5). This would be encouraged by changing the regulation that prevents public insurance from being partially applied in cases where non-covered and covered medical treatments are provided together. *Second*, incentive structures should be improved to encourage greater use of generic medicines, which is low in Japan.[18] *Third*, further increasing the use of information technology in the medical billing systems would boost efficiency and the scope for third-party oversight. The share of electronic forms has jumped from less than 2% of medical bills in 2003 to 24% in mid-2007, although there remains substantial scope for greater use of information technology. In an attempt to limit the increase in healthcare spending, the government is planning to establish regionally-based insurers, which may help to reduce management costs through economies of scale. However, this reform will not provide incentives to insurers to monitor hospitals, individual clinics and doctors on behalf of their members, as there is little competition among insurers.

Reforms are also needed to contain spending on long-term nursing care, which is also rising rapidly due to population ageing. At present, private-sector firms certified by the government are allowed to provide some services at prices set by the government. Weak competition results in a lack of innovation, a limited variety of services and pricing and dissatisfaction among consumers. Relaxing price controls would improve efficiency and quality. In addition, in the long-term care insurance scheme, the "care managers", who decide the services for individuals qualifying for care, are expected to choose the optimal care package and service provider. However, most care managers are employed by service providers, and thus have no incentive to curb costs for users. Although the law states the fiduciary obligation of care managers, the legal deterrent is too weak to resolve the principle-agent problem. Instead, economic incentives are needed to guarantee that the elderly receive the appropriate nursing care at the lowest cost. In sum, it is necessary to reform the current system and reduce aggregate costs through greater use of market forces.

Public investment

Public investment, including that by public enterprises, has fallen from a peak of 8.4% of GDP in 1996 to 4.4% in 2006, in line with the government's medium-term plan. However, Japan is still the fourth highest in the OECD area in this regard and above the OECD average of 3.1% of GDP. While the medium-term plan calls for continuing reductions in public investment, further declines would raise concerns about regional income disparities and the need to maintain existing public infrastructure.

Traditionally, public investment has been used to promote regional equality. Indeed, the level of public investment by prefecture is negatively correlated with income levels (Figure 3.4). Not surprisingly, the size of the construction sector tends to be larger in low-income areas. However, between FY 1998 and FY 2004, the share of public investment fell in all prefectures and the negative correlation between per capita income and public investment weakened. Nevertheless, the regional variation in the unemployment rate declined between FY 1998 and FY 2004, suggesting that the sharp decline in public investment over that period had little impact. The regional variation in unemployment did widen between FY 2004 and FY 2006, but this is largely explained by the unbalanced nature of economic growth since 2004, with strong exports and sluggish domestic demand (see Chapter 1).[19] Consequently, areas where manufacturing is important have benefited the most from this expansion (Figure 1.6).

Public investment has not been an efficient tool for reducing regional inequality in Japan. In fact, the large disparity in levels between regions is explained primarily by differences in labour inputs and productivity, which is in turn determined by the industrial

Figure 3.4. **Public investment and level of income by prefecture**

As per cent of gross domestic expenditure

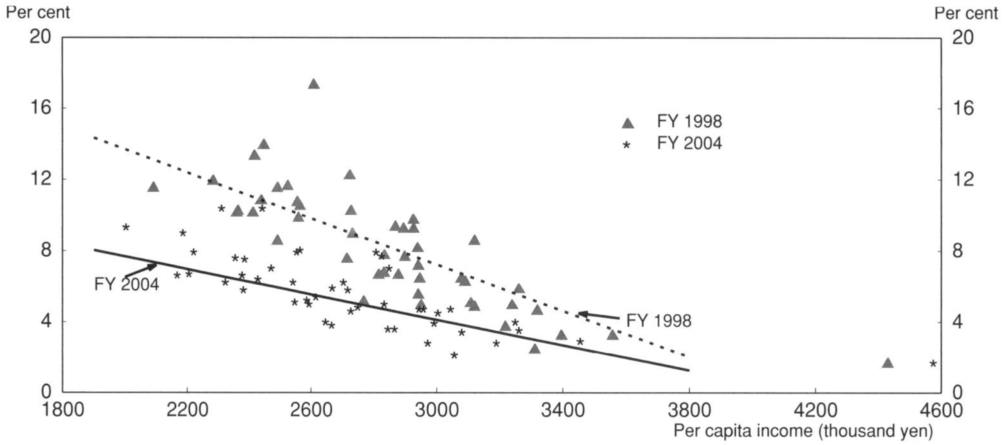

StatLink ᐊᑕᢖᗺ http://dx.doi.org/10.1787/277432711578

Source: Cabinet Office, *National Accounts by Prefecture*.

structure (Cabinet Office, 2004). Labour productivity growth in manufacturing has risen at an annual rate of around 4% since the 1970s, while that in the service sector slowed from 3.5% in the period 1976-89 to less than 1% between 1999 and 2004 (see Chapter 5). Consequently, regions focused on manufacturing have tended to experience faster per capita income growth. Policies to boost productivity growth in services are thus essential to narrow regional income gaps. While public investment can create some additional demand and improve local infrastructure so as to attract private investment, past experience suggests that the marginal gains are small relative to the cost. Indeed, the marginal productivity of public capital in the Tohoku region is only 5% of that in the southern Kanto region, which includes Tokyo (2006 *OECD Economic Survey of Japan*). As public infrastructure is an important intermediate input for the corporate sector, its allocation should be driven more by economic criteria. In addition, it has an important impact on social welfare, making it unfair to provide insufficient infrastructure in the major urban centres. Instead, regional inequality should be addressed through other measures, including well-targeted social welfare programmes, tax transfers among prefectures and policies to boost productivity growth in the service sector.

The rising share of public investment needed to maintain and renew existing infrastructure is another constraint on further reducing spending. According to the Ministry of Land, Infrastructure and Transport (2005), expenditure on maintenance and renewal will exceed the amount of new investment by 2011 and will totally crowd out new investment by 2022, if the current pace of spending cuts is maintained. However, this assumes that the existing stock of infrastructure is maintained, which is not an economically efficient choice in the context of a falling population, internal migration and a changing age composition. Indeed, the government projects that Japan's working-age population will fall by 16% by 2025, with the extent of the decline in Japan's 47 prefectures ranging from 4% to 32%. Meanwhile, the population over 65 years old will rise by 41% nationwide, with the rate of increase by prefecture varying between 12% and 73%. Such significant changes in total population and in its composition at the prefectural level over the next 18 years imply that the type and quantity of public infrastructure will need to adjust rapidly. Maintaining the existing stock of infrastructure in areas with large

Figure 3.5. **Renewal and maintenance costs of public infrastructure**[1]

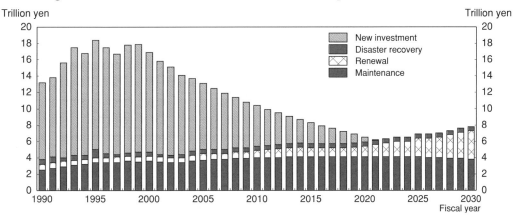

StatLink ⟨≋⟩ http://dx.doi.org/10.1787/277441866718

1. Social infrastructure built and managed by the Ministry of Land, Infrastructure and Transport only. Central government investment is assumed to fall by 3% and local government by 5% a year after FY 2005.

Source: Ministry of Land, Infrastructure and Transport (2005), *White Paper on Land, Infrastructure and Transport in Japan, 2005.*

population declines would limit the scope for new infrastructure needed for an ageing population. In sum, the government must decide to maintain infrastructure required to satisfy demographic and economic trends, while eliminating unnecessary infrastructure.

Further cuts in public investment should be accompanied by measures to increase its efficiency to ensure the adequate provision of public goods and services. Reforms to improve bidding, contracting and selection systems for public investment, in addition to strengthening the enforcement of competition policy,[20] have reduced the unit cost of public construction from 227.9 thousand yen (per square metre) in FY 1999 to 197.1 thousand yen in FY 2005 (Table 3.7).[21] However, it was still 18% higher than in the private sector in FY 2005, implying scope to further reduce construction costs. The gap is largest in the construction of factories, hospitals and offices. Although public construction accounts for only about 10% of total public

Table 3.7. **Comparison of the unit cost of public and private construction**

Thousand yen per square metre[1]

	FY 1999			FY 2005			Change in ratio
	Public (A)	Private (B)	Ratio (A/B)	Public (A)	Private (B)	Ratio (A/B)	
Residences	177.2	165.6	1.07	167.3	161.3	1.04	−0.03
Offices	255.3	197.3	1.29	265.1	175.1	1.51	0.22
Shops	194.6	110.8	1.76	153.5	102.5	1.50	−0.26
Factories and workplaces	242.2	103.0	2.35	188.1	109.3	1.72	−0.63
Warehouses	121.1	79.2	1.53	111.5	72.3	1.54	0.01
Schools	219.2	210.4	1.04	168.3	197.2	0.85	−0.19
Hospitals	346.0	207.1	1.67	338.9	209.4	1.62	−0.05
Other	252.7	167.6	1.51	213.7	143.0	1.49	−0.01
Average[2]	227.9	157.4	1.45	197.1	148.3	1.33	−0.12
Average[3]	227.9	175.4	1.30	197.1	167.1	1.18	−0.12

1. Original data is from Table 17 in the *Yearbook of Building Construction Started and New Dwellings Started*, Ministry of Land, Infrastructure, and Transport.
2. Public and private construction are each weighted by their individual composition.
3. Public and private construction are both weighted by the composition of public construction for comparison purposes.
Source: Council on Economic and Fiscal Policy (2007a) and OECD calculations.

investment, reducing costs should be a priority as it allows cuts in public expenditure without reducing the quantity or quality of public investment.

Reducing the size of the government and increasing its efficiency

The current administration aims to create a "small and efficient government", as stated in the *Basic Policies 2007*, by reducing the government wage bill by more than 2.6 trillion yen (0.5% of GDP) over a decade. The reduction will be achieved by simultaneously cutting employment and reforming the wage system. This will help achieve the government's target of halving the total compensation of central government workers (including employees of central government corporations) as a share of GDP in ten years.[22] There is public support for reducing government compensation before cutting other public expenditures or raising taxes, reflecting the fact that public wages have not experienced the marked decline recorded in the private sector (Figure 3.6). Indeed, wages of government

Figure 3.6. Comparison of wages and employment in the private and public sectors
1990 = 100

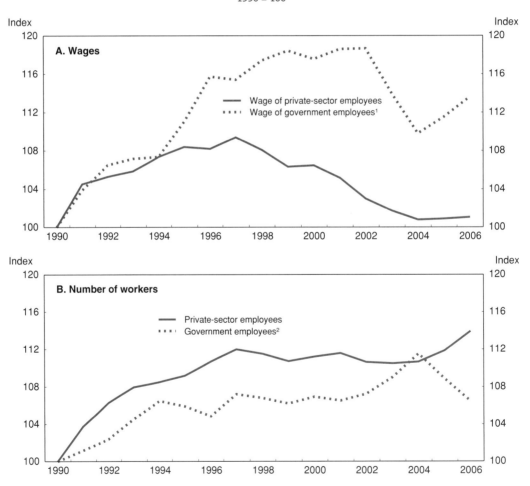

StatLink ⬛⬛ http://dx.doi.org/10.1787/277457868117

1. Wages are calculated as total labour compensation (SNA basis), divided by the number of employees, as defined below.
2. Government employees include workers engaged in public administration at the central and local levels, as defined in the Labour Force Survey.

Source: OECD, *OECD Economic Outlook,* No. 82 Database, OECD, Paris.

employees are 14% higher than in 1990 compared to only a 1% rise in the private sector. However, the impact of higher wage growth on total compensation was partially offset by a sharp decline in government employment beginning in 2004 (Panel B).

The scope for cutting the central government wage bill is limited by the fact that employment is already small. In 2006, there were only 2.6 central government workers per 1 000 population in Japan, compared to 4 in the United States and 33 in the United Kingdom (Figure 3.7). Given that central government workers account for only about 8% of public-sector employees in Japan, efforts to reduce the government wage bill should include local governments, public enterprises and other government-related organisations in accordance with the Law for the Promotion of Administrative Reform and other related reform plans. However, overall government employment is also low in Japan. Nevertheless, privatisation and the market-testing initiative, which was fully implemented in 2006, should be used to cut public employment by outsourcing government activities to private-sector firms (see Chapter 5). Reductions in the government wage bill should be accomplished by policies that enhance productivity and efficiency in the public sector, in particular by increasing labour mobility. In this regard, the priority should be to further reform aspects of the rigid and closed government wage and employment system, such as the steep seniority-based wage curve and the retirement pay structure that discourages job changes. The introduction of more flexible career paths and wage structures, combined with active personnel exchanges with the private sector, would enhance productivity and thereby reduce the government wage bill.

Figure 3.7. **An international comparison of public-sector employment**

Employees per 1 000 population

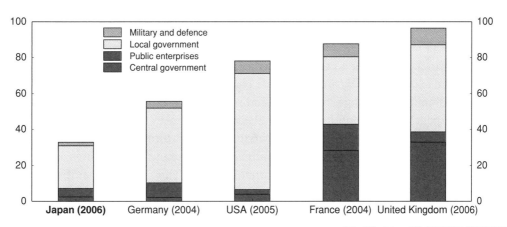

StatLink ⫟⫟⫟ http://dx.doi.org/10.1787/277467625288

Source: Ministry of Internal Affairs and Communications, Office for National Statistics (United Kingdom) and OECD.

Moreover, there is scope to reduce the wages of local government workers as part of the objective to cut the government wage bill. *First*, the estimates of the average wage of workers in local governments range from roughly equal to about 12% higher than those in the central government despite the lower living costs in regional areas. Unless there is clear evidence of higher productivity at the local level, there is room to reduce wages of local government workers relative to the central government. *Second*, the variation in public-sector wages across regions does not appear to accurately reflect differences in the cost of living (Figure 3.8). In particular, the gap between public and private-sector employees in low-income areas is large compared to high-income areas.[23] This suggests some scope for reduction in the local government wage bill, which in addition might boost productivity by making the private sector more attractive to talented individuals.

Figure 3.8. **Wage gap between private and public employees by prefecture**[1]

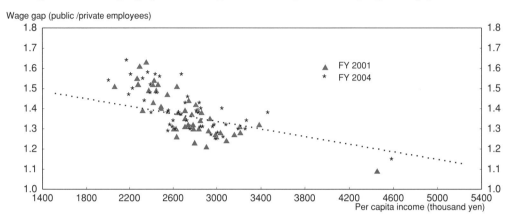

StatLink 📈 http://dx.doi.org/10.1787/277470163001

1. The private wage is the average scheduled cash earnings of private enterprises with ten or more employees. The public wage is the average monthly basic salary of employees engaged in general administration. As the type of job is not controlled, the level of the gap varies due to differences in the attributes of the jobs. The trend line is a regression that includes other variables such as the age and tenure of employees.

Source: Ministry of Health, Labour and Welfare, Ministry of Internal Affairs and Communications, Cabinet Office, and OECD calculations.

Conclusion: additional revenues are needed to achieve Japan's medium-term fiscal objectives

Japan still has some scope to reduce government outlays. In particular, cutting public investment to a level closer to the OECD average and lowering the government wage bill could reduce expenditures by around 1½ per cent of GDP. However, it will be more difficult to achieve significant savings in social spending, given its relatively low level at present and the impact of rapid ageing. Nevertheless, measures to slow the growth of social expenditure are crucial to the success of Japan's medium-term fiscal plan as it accounts for 40% of total spending. In sum, further reducing government expenditures as a share of GDP is still the top priority for fiscal consolidation. The cuts by specific spending programmes that were incorporated in the 2007 *Direction and Strategy* are an important addition to the medium-term plan, although the size of the reductions should be made more ambitious.

In any case, expenditure cuts alone are inadequate, given the size of Japan's fiscal deficits. Projections by the government show that an improvement in the primary budget surplus of between 4% and 5% of GDP[24] – a range in line with OECD estimates discussed above – is needed to achieve the government's objective of balancing the public debt ratio. Achieving such an improvement will require increased government revenue. Indeed, the same government projection expects that between 4.6% and 5.9% of GDP in additional tax revenue is needed for this goal, while an even larger amount is required to reduce the debt ratio beginning in the mid-2010s. However, the government's medium-term fiscal plans do not suggest any concrete measures to raise revenue. While this may have been an appropriate strategy to focus attention on expenditure cuts during the initial stage of fiscal consolidation, the serious fiscal situation now requires a comprehensive tax reform to achieve the government's fiscal objectives. Chapter 4 analyses Japan's tax system and proposes a comprehensive reform plan.

Box 3.2. **Summary of recommendations for medium-term fiscal consolidation**

Improve the framework for fiscal consolidation

- Make the spending cut targets in the *Direction and Strategy* more ambitious by aiming at a further reduction in the share of government spending relative to GDP.

- Make sure that the economic assumptions underlying the *Reference Projections* are not overly optimistic.

- Ensure the sustainability of the social security fund, which is not included explicitly in the *Direction and Strategy*. The government's budget target for central and local governments should not be achieved through a deterioration in the balance of the social security fund.

- Set targets for the primary balance of general government that are large enough to stabilise, and eventually reduce, the debt to GDP ratio in the mid-2010s, in line with the government's stated objective.

Pursue policies to contain spending

- Focus future reforms of the pension system on raising the pension eligibility age rather than on cutting benefits or increasing premiums, which are already set to rise significantly.

- Strengthen market forces and incentive mechanisms in healthcare and long-term nursing care to limit cost increases.

- Reduce healthcare costs by increasing the use of generic medicines, and nursing care costs by providing care managers with incentives to curb the expenditures of their clients.

- Make greater use of information technology in medical bills to reduce management costs and strengthen oversight.

- Further reduce public investment, while emphasising a more efficient allocation to boost its impact on economy-wide productivity.

- Develop a comprehensive plan to close inefficient public infrastructure in the context of population ageing and urbanisation to limit renewal and maintenance costs that would crowd out important new public investment.

- Expand the plan to cut the central government wage bill to include the entire public sector and make it more binding on local governments.

- Focus on reducing the government wage bill by increasing productivity in the public sector rather than on across the board cuts in employment.

- Promote greater use of market testing to outsource government activities to the private sector.

Notes

1. On a cyclically-adjusted basis, the general government deficit adjusted for one-off factors declined by 3.1% of GDP during the period 2002-07, some three-quarters of the 4.1% fall in the deficit (Table 3.1).

2. Given shrinking interest payments, the primary budget deficit – which excludes interest payments – has fallen by less than the overall budget deficit over the period 2002-2007. In 2007, it was around 3% of GDP on a general government basis, excluding one-off factors.

3. While net debt may provide a better indicator of the economic burden, there are several factors that make gross debt a more appropriate measure. *First*, government assets are largely held by the social security system and are thus earmarked for future obligations. *Second*, the quality of some government assets, such as credits to Fiscal Investment and Loan Programme institutions, is doubtful. Only about a third of government assets are in the form of liquid instruments, such as bonds or cash. *Third*, both net and gross measures of debt exclude contingent liabilities, such as loan guarantees for quasi-government institutions, and may thus understate the government's eventual obligations. Gross debt, which is higher as it excludes government assets, may thus provide a more realistic picture of the government's obligations. Indeed, the government's medium-term fiscal objectives are framed in terms of stabilising gross debt relative to GDP.

4. The *Direction and Strategy* replaces the *Reform and Perspective*, which had earlier set the target of a primary budget surplus in the early 2010s. Like its predecessor, the *Direction and Strategy* will be revised annually based on a Cabinet decision. One of its key features is a formal review mechanism to check outcomes with the target.

5. This target was first set by the *Basic Policies 2006*, which included the *Integrated Expenditure and Revenue Reform*, published in July 2006 (see the 2006 *OECD Economic Survey of Japan*).

6. The gap between the primary deficit of 3.2% of GDP for the general government in calendar year 2007 estimated by the OECD (Table 3.1) can be reconciled with the 0.7% primary deficit for central and local governments in the 2008 *Reference Projection* as follows: i) the OECD estimate excludes a one-off factor of 0.6% of GDP. The overall deficit was thus 2.5% of GDP; ii) the *Reference Projection* excludes the social security fund, which had a primary deficit estimated at 1.2% of GDP in FY 2007 (Table 3.2). Including social security thus raises the deficit estimated by the *Reference Projection* to 1.9% of GDP. The remaining gap of 0.6% of GDP is explained by the difference between calendar and fiscal years, which begin in April of each year. Over the past ten years, the primary budgets of calendar and fiscal years have differed by an average of 0.4% of GDP.

7. The 0.4 percentage improvement in the social security fund is projected to reduce its deficit, on a primary budget basis, by a similar amount, from an estimated 1.2% of GDP in FY 2007 to 0.8% in FY 2011.

8. This includes the 0.6% of GDP decline in the primary budget deficit of central and local governments (from 0.7% of GDP to 0.1%) and the 0.4% of GDP improvement in the social security fund.

9. The 2008 *Reference Projection* for FY 2011 (based on the "growth scenario") shows a primary budget deficit of 0.1% of GDP for central and local governments in FY 2011 (Table 3.2). Given the projected deficit in the social security fund as well, as noted above, the primary balance in the general government is likely to be negative.

10. A 1% surplus would stabilise gross debt – the government's objective – at its current level of around 144% of GDP, according to the government's definition.

11. An effective interest rate that is higher than the nominal growth rate is also the norm in the OECD area (see the 2006 *OECD Economic Survey of Japan*).

12. The 2007 and 2008 *Reference Projections* assume the expenditure path in the *Integrated Reform of Expenditure and Revenue* of July 2006, which targets cuts relative to a baseline of 3% nominal output growth. Consequently, it has a smaller amount of expenditure cuts than the 2006 *Reference Projection*.

13. In addition, there was a temporary change in the indexation of pension benefits to prices. During the years 1999 to 2001, the decline in the consumer price index (CPI) was not reflected in pension benefits. To bring benefits back into line with the CPI, it was decided to adjust the growth of pension benefits in line with changes in the CPI when it declines but not when it rises. When the cumulative increase in the CPI relative to 2005 reaches 1.7%, the adjustment of pension benefits in line with increases in the CPI would resume.

14. Without macroeconomic indexation, the sustainability of the pension system over 100 years (as shown in Table 3.6) cannot be assured.

15. In FY 2008, the eligibility age for receiving the flat-rate portion of the pension was 64 for men and 62 for women, respectively. It is to be raised to 65 years in 2013 for men and in 2018 for women.

16. The government requires all insurers to support medical exams for their insurees above age 40.

17. These are identified as obesity, high blood pressure and elevated levels of cholesterol and insulin.

18. The share of generic medicine in Japan is 17% in terms of quantity and 5% in terms of value. In contrast, the shares are 56% and 13% in the United States, 49% and 21% in the United Kingdom and 41% and 23% in Germany. The Ministry of Finance estimates that greater use of generic medicines could save 1.3 trillion yen per year.

19. Indeed, domestic demand growth slowed from 2% in 2004 to 1% in 2007, while export growth remained buoyant at more than 8% over that period.

20. The FTC has been engaged in a strong effort against bid-rigging, which accounted for six of 13 legal measures taken in FY 2006 (see Chapter 5).

21. The successful bid rate – the bid price as a per cent of the assumed price – for public investment by the Ministry of Land, Infrastructure and Transport dropped from a simple average of 97% in FY 2000 to 90% in FY 2006.

22. This objective was included in the 2006 Law for the Promotion of Administrative Reform, which includes: *i)* scaling back public financial institutions; *ii)* reforming independent administrative agencies; *iii)* reforming the special accounts; *iv)* cutting the total compensation of public-sector workers, including a 5% cut in the number of central government employees over five years; and *v)* sales of government assets.

23. This may also reflect the fact that the skills of public-sector workers are similar across regions while there are large differences in the private sector.

24. Assuming economic growth of 1.7%, a rate somewhat above the OECD's estimate of potential growth of 1.4%.

Bibliography

Cabinet Office (2004), *Annual Report on the Japanese Economy and Public Finance 2003-2004*, Tokyo.

Cabinet Office (2006), *Reference Projection*, January, Tokyo (in Japanese).

Cabinet Office (2007a), *Annual Report on National Accounts 2007*, Tokyo.

Cabinet Office (2007b), *Annual Report on National Accounts by Prefecture 2007*, Tokyo.

Cabinet Office (2007c), *Reference Projection*, January, Tokyo (in Japanese).

Cabinet Office (2008), *Reference Projection*, January, Tokyo (in Japanese).

Carlin, Wendy and David Soskice (2005), *Macroeconomics: Imperfections, Institutions and Policies*, Oxford University Press.

Council on Economic and Fiscal Policy (2007a), *On the Reform of Public Investment*, a paper submitted by the expert members, 8 May 2007, Tokyo (in Japanese).

Council on Economic and Fiscal Policy (2007b), *On the Menu of Burden and Provision*, a paper submitted by the expert members, 17 October 2007, Tokyo (in Japanese).

Council on Economic and Fiscal Policy (2007c), *On the Promotion of Integrated Reform of Social Security and Taxation – For the Safe and Sustainable Social Security System and Taxation in the 21st Century*, a paper submitted by the expert members, 17 October 2007, Tokyo (in Japanese).

EU Commission (2006), "The Long-term Sustainability of Public Finance in the European Union", *European Economy*, No. 4, European Union, Brussels.

Fátas, Antonio (2005), "Is there a case for sophisticated balanced-budget rules?", Economics Department Working Paper No. 466, OECD, Paris.

Fiscal System Council (2007), *On the Analysis of Fiscal Sustainability*, a paper submitted by members of the drafting committee, 26 October 2007, Ministry of Finance, Tokyo (in Japanese).

Government of Japan (2005), *Structural Reform and Medium-Term Economic and Fiscal Perspectives – FY 2004 Revision*, Tokyo (in Japanese).

Government of Japan (2006a), *Basic Policies 2006*, Tokyo (in Japanese).

Government of Japan (2006b), *Structural Reform and Medium-Term Economic and Fiscal Perspectives – FY 2005 Revision*, Tokyo (in Japanese).

Government of Japan (2007a), *Basic Policies in 2007*, Tokyo (in Japanese).

Government of Japan (2007b), *Direction and Strategy of the Japanese Economy*, Tokyo (in Japanese).

Government of Japan (2008), *Direction and Strategy of the Japanese Economy*, Tokyo (in Japanese).

Ministry of Finance (2007a), *On Public Investment*, a reference paper submitted to the Fiscal System Council on 22 October 2007, Tokyo (in Japanese).

Ministry of Finance (2007b), *On the Wage Bill of Central Government Employees*, a reference paper submitted to the Fiscal System Council on 26 October 2007, Tokyo (in Japanese).

Ministry of Finance (2007c), *On the Wage Bill of Local Government Employees*, a reference paper submitted to the Fiscal System Council on 26 October 2007, Tokyo (in Japanese).

Ministry of Finance (2007d), *On Social Security*, a reference paper submitted to the Fiscal System Council on 5 November 2007, Tokyo (in Japanese).

Ministry of Health, Labour and Welfare (2005), *Actuarial Revaluation in 2004*, Tokyo (in Japanese).

Ministry of Health, Labour and Welfare (2006), *Projection on Social Security Payments and Contributions*, May 2006, Tokyo (in Japanese).

Ministry of Health, Labour and Welfare (2007), *The Effect of Changes in Population Estimates and Other Factors on Pension Balance – Tentative Projection*, a paper submitted to the Pension Committee in the Social Security Council on 6 February 2007, Tokyo (in Japanese).

Ministry of Land, Infrastructure and Transport (2005), *White Paper on Land, Infrastructure and Transport in Japan, 2005*, Tokyo (in Japanese).

OECD (2003), "Identifying the determinants of regional performances", Working Party on Territorial Indicators, June 2003, OECD, Paris.

OECD (2006a), *OECD Economic Survey of Germany 2006*, OECD, Paris.

OECD (2006b), *OECD Economic Survey of Japan 2006*, OECD, Paris.

OECD (2006c), "Projecting OECD Health and Long-term Care Expenditures: What are the Main Drivers?", Economics Department Working Paper No. 477, OECD, Paris.

OECD (2007a), *Health Data 2007*, OECD, Paris.

OECD (2007b), *Social Expenditure Database 2007*, OECD, Paris.

Van den Noord, Paul (2002), "Automatic Stabilisers in the 1990s and Beyond", in *The Behaviour of Fiscal Authorities: Stabilisation, Growth and Institutions*, edited by M. Buti, J. Von Hagen and C. Martinez-Mongay, European Communities.

ANNEX 3.A1

"Growth scenario" and "risk scenario" of the 2008 Reference Projection[1]

Fiscal year		2005	2006	2007	2008	2009	2010	2011
A. Macroeconomic indicators (per cent change from proceeding year)								
Real GDP	2008a	2.4	2.3	1.3	2.0	2.3	2.5	2.6
	2008b	2.4	2.3	1.3	2.0	1.6	1.3	1.1
Nominal GDP	2008a	1.1	1.6	0.8	2.1	2.5	2.9	3.3
	2008b	1.1	1.6	0.8	2.1	1.8	1.6	1.6
GDP deflator	2008a	−1.3	−0.7	−0.5	0.1	0.2	0.4	0.7
	2008b	−1.3	−0.7	−0.5	0.1	0.1	0.3	0.5
CPI	2008a	−0.1	0.2	0.2	0.3	0.6	1.0	1.4
	2008b	−0.1	0.2	0.2	0.3	0.6	0.9	1.1
Nominal long-term interest rate (per cent)	2008a	1.4	1.7	1.6	1.7	2.1	2.4	2.9
	2008b	1.4	1.7	1.6	1.7	1.9	2.1	2.3
B. Fiscal Indicators (per cent of GDP)								
General government fiscal balance	2008a	−4.3	−3.3	−2.8	−3.0	−2.7	−2.4	−2.2
	2008b	−4.3	−3.3	−2.8	−3.0	−2.8	−2.7	−2.7
of which:								
Central government	2008a	−4.1	−3.4	−2.8	−2.9	−3.0	−3.0	−2.9
	2008b	−4.1	−3.4	−2.8	−2.9	−3.0	−3.2	−3.2
Local government	2008a	−0.4	0.2	0.2	0.5	0.3	0.4	0.5
	2008b	−0.4	0.2	0.2	0.5	0.3	0.4	0.4
Social security fund[2]	2008a	0.3	−0.1	−0.2	−0.6	0.0	0.2	0.2
	2008b	0.3	−0.1	−0.3	−0.6	0.0	0.1	0.1
Primary balance of the general government[2]	2008a	−3.6	−2.7	−1.9	−2.1	−1.6	−1.2	−0.9
	2008b	−3.6	−2.7	−1.9	−2.0	−1.7	−1.5	−1.5
of which:								
Central and local government	2008a	−2.9	−1.7	−0.7	−0.5	−0.6	−0.4	−0.1
	2008b	−2.9	−1.7	−0.7	−0.5	−0.7	−0.7	−0.6
Social security fund[2]	2008a	−0.7	−1.0	−1.2	−1.6	−1.0	−0.8	−0.8
	2008b	−0.7	−1.0	−1.2	−1.5	−1.0	−0.8	−0.9

1. The figures are from the scenarios 1-A (2008a) and 2-A (2008b). While both scenarios assume that the fiscal consolidation programme announced in 2006 is implemented, the macroeconomic assumptions are different. In the case of the "growth scenario" (shown in 2008a), the positive effects of supply-side reforms and favourable global economic conditions will boost growth (this scenario is also shown in Figure 3.2). However, in the absence of these positive factors, growth will be lower in the "risk scenario" shown in 2008b.

2. The figures are calculated by the OECD based on the figures in the *Reference Projection and the OECD Economic Outlook,* No. 82 Database.

Source: Cabinet Office (2008) and OECD calculations.

ISBN 978-92-64-04306-0
OECD Economic Surveys: Japan
© OECD 2008

Chapter 4

Reforming the tax system to promote fiscal sustainability and economic growth

Tax reform is an urgent priority, as Japan needs as much as 5% to 6% of GDP of additional government revenue just to stabilise public debt, which has risen to 180% of GDP. In addition to raising revenue, tax reform should promote economic growth, address the deterioration in income distribution and improve the local tax system. Additional revenue should be obtained primarily by increasing the consumption tax rate, currently the lowest in the OECD area, while broadening the personal and corporate income tax bases. The corporate tax rate, now the highest in the OECD area, should be cut to promote growth, while eliminating aspects of the tax system which discourage labour supply and distort the allocation of capital. Japan should also consider introducing an Earned Income Tax Credit to promote equity. The local tax system should be simplified, increasing reliance on existing taxes on property, income and consumption.

The Japanese tax system is facing one of the most difficult and complicated challenges of any OECD country: raising tax revenue to stem the steep run-up in public debt and finance higher social spending resulting from rapid population ageing, while also promoting economic growth, addressing the deterioration in income distribution and increasing the gains from fiscal decentralisation. There is much scope for raising additional tax revenue in Japan, in particular by raising the consumption tax rate, which is the lowest among OECD countries at 5%, and by broadening the base of direct taxes. Given the increasing urgency of the fiscal situation, the government's medium-term fiscal plan calls for a "fundamental reform of the tax system". While raising additional tax revenue is important, the already low potential growth rate and declining labour force reinforce the need for tax reform to enhance productivity and output growth. In addition, the tax system should address the problem of widening income inequality and rising relative poverty, while reforms in local government taxes are needed to increase the gains from decentralisation.

This chapter begins by presenting the key challenges facing the Japanese tax system – raising the necessary revenue, supporting economic growth, reversing the increase in inequality and improving fiscal relations between central and local governments. The following section analyses the major tax issues from the perspective of meeting these challenges. The chapter concludes with recommendations for a comprehensive tax reform, which are summarised in Table 4.2.

Major challenges facing the Japanese tax system

Japan's tax system stands out among OECD countries in a number of ways (see Box 4.1). *First*, the ratio of total tax revenue to GDP is one of the lowest in the OECD area (Figure 1.9).[1] *Second*, the reliance on direct taxes – personal and corporate income taxes and social security contributions – is relatively high compared to other OECD countries. *Third*, the local tax system is exceptionally complicated. Given these features of Japan's tax system, resolving the challenges outlined below will require a major overhaul of the system.

Challenge 1: restoring fiscal sustainability

The counter-cyclical fiscal policies implemented to support economic growth following the collapse of the bubble economy in the early 1990s resulted in unsustainably high budget deficits and a run-up in government debt. On the expenditure side, an increase in public investment and social security outlays boosted government spending. On the revenue side, the government introduced a series of tax cuts that were partially offset by a hike in the consumption tax rate in 1997. Tax revenue fell from a peak of 30% of GDP in 1990 to 26% in 2003, before rebounding slightly with the economic expansion (Figure 4.1). The fall in revenue since 1990 is explained by a 5 percentage-point decline in direct taxes on households and firms (as a share of GDP), which more than offset a 2.5 percentage-point rise in social security contributions. Overall, the decline in revenue

Figure 4.1. **Trends in Japanese tax revenue, 1990-2005**

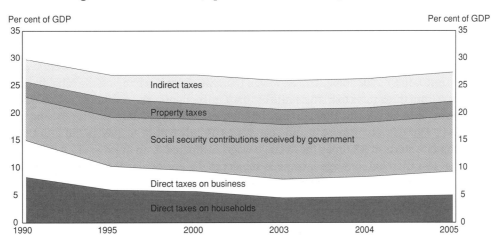

StatLink ⟨≋≋⟩ http://dx.doi.org/10.1787/277475731725

Source: OECD (2007c), Revenue Statistics 1965-2006, OECD, Paris (http://dx.doi.org/10.1787/366725334503).

accounted for almost a quarter of the increase in the fiscal deficit between 1990 and 2005. Although the deficit has been on a decreasing trend since its peak of 8% in 2002, the accumulated amount of debt, at 180% of GDP in gross terms, makes the fiscal situation vulnerable to interest rate fluctuations. The need for additional revenue is illustrated by the fact that bond issuance accounts for 30% of general account revenues, about half of the 60% share of tax revenue.

The task of restoring fiscal health is heightened by a number of factors, notably the unprecedented speed of ageing. Indeed, the share of the population over age 65 increased from 7% in 1970 to 20% in 2006 (Box 1.2). In contrast, a similar transition is projected to take at least 80 years in the other major industrialised countries. As a share of the working-age population (aged 20 to 64), the over 65 age group is projected to rise from 28% in 2000 to 72% in 2050, the second highest in the OECD area (Figure 1.7).

Ageing affects fiscal policy through its impact on both expenditures and revenues. On the expenditure side, the government plans to limit the rise in public social spending to 1% of GDP, from 17.5% of GDP in 2006 to 18.4% in 2015 (Table 3.5). Outlays are to be contained by measures to reduce pension benefits and encourage healthier lifestyles. However, achieving this target will be difficult, as the effectiveness of policies to contain healthcare spending is uncertain (see Chapter 3).[2] On the revenue side, personal income tax receipts are likely to fall relative to GDP due to a decline in the share of the working-age population as well as a further erosion of the personal income tax base caused by the generous income deductions targeted at elderly people. It is estimated that demographic changes will reduce personal income tax revenue by 10% between 2000 and 2020, and by 40% between 2000 and 2050 under the current tax structure (Cabinet Office, 2002b). Rapid ageing thus implies that tax reform is needed simply to maintain the current amount of revenue.

In the Direction and Strategy in 2007, the government set three targets to help restore fiscal sustainability; i) limiting the expansion in the size of the government; ii) a primary budget surplus in the combined central and local governments by FY 2011; and iii) a steady reduction in the debt to GDP ratio in the mid-2010s. Although the government's priority is on expenditure cuts, the plan also calls for fundamental reform of the tax system. The

Box 4.1. **Major features of the Japanese tax system**

National taxes

At 18% of total tax revenue, *direct taxes on households* are below the OECD average of 25% (Figure 4.2). The four rates in the personal income tax system in FY 2006 – ranging from 10% to 37% – were replaced by six rates from 5% to 40% in FY 2007 (Table 4.1). However, this was offset by changing the inhabitant tax (a local government tax) from three rates to a single rate of 10%. Consequently, the combined tax rate on household income – personal income tax plus the local inhabitant tax – still ranges from 15% to 50% and the rates are identical to the FY 2006 level for most income categories. Nearly 60% of taxpayers fall into the lowest tax rate and the top rate starts at 3.6 times the average wage, compared to an average of 2.4 times in the OECD area. Given that less than half of wage income is subject to the personal income tax (see below), a worker would have to earn more than seven times the average wage to be subject to the 50% rate. Consequently, less than 1% of taxpayers fall into the 50% tax rate, which is high by international standards, while 3% are in the 43% rate. About a quarter of salaried employees do not pay any personal income tax. Retirement income receives preferential treatment, as it is reduced by a special deduction for older persons and then only half of the remaining income is taxed. Financial income, including interest, dividends and capital gains, is taxed separately at a 20% rate. However, in an effort to boost the stock market, the rate has been temporarily reduced to 10% on dividends (until the end of March 2009) and on capital gains on listed stocks and equity investment trusts (until the end of December 2008). Capital gains from the sale or transfer of land, buildings, and securities are also taxed separately. Capital gains on real estate are taxed at 39% for short-term gains (when the property is held less than five years) and 20% for long-term gains.

Direct taxes on households fell from 8% of GDP in 1990 to 5% in 2005 (Figure 4.1). A salaried employee with a wife and two children earning the average salary of around 5 million yen ($46 000) per year paid an average tax rate of 4.0% in 2007 compared to 7.8% in 1986 (Ministry of Finance, 2007). For a salary of 30 million yen, the rate declined from 45% to 30.6% over that period. The relatively low effective income tax reflects generous allowances and deductions, notably for wage income. The wage deduction is 0.65 million yen on wages of up to 1.63 million yen and rises with income, though at a diminishing rate.[1] There are a number of other exemptions and deductions, including those for spouses and dependent relatives, widows, the handicapped, working students, social insurance payments, premiums for life and casualty insurance, casualty losses and medical expenses, in addition to the basic exemption for all taxpayers. These deductions and exemptions add up to more than half of wage earnings.

Figure 4.2. **The tax mix in OECD countries**
Per cent of total tax revenue in 2005[1]

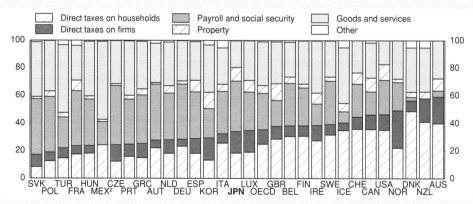

StatLink http://dx.doi.org/10.1787/277826184161

1. Countries are ranked by the share of direct taxes on households and firms in total taxes.
2. For Mexico, the data for direct taxes on households also contains direct taxes on firms.

Source: OECD (2007c), *Revenue Statistics 1965-2006*, OECD, Paris (*http://dx.doi.org/10.1787/366725334503*).

Box 4.1. **Major features of the Japanese tax system** (cont.)

Revenue from the *corporate income tax* fell from 6.7% of GDP in 1990 to 3.7% in 2004, before rebounding to 4.3% in 2005. It accounted for 15% of total tax revenue in 2005, compared to the OECD average of 10%. The tax rate varies by the size of capital and sales, with a lower rate granted to smaller companies. For corporations with capital of more than 100 million yen ($914 thousand), the central government tax rate is 30% (although local taxes boost the overall rate to 40%, the highest in the OECD area). For corporations with capital below 100 million yen, the tax rate is 22% for income up to 8 million yen.

Mandatory *social security contributions* by employees and employers for pensions, heath, long-term care and unemployment are the single largest source of government revenue at 37% of the total in 2005. Under the FY 2004 reform, the pension contribution rate is being raised from 13.6% in FY 2004 to 18.3% by FY 2017. Contributions are imposed on wages up to 0.62 million per month (1.5 times the average wage). Total social security contributions amount to 26% of wages, shared almost equally between employees and employers (Table 4.1, Panel B).

The *consumption tax* (a tax on value added) accounts for half of indirect tax revenue, which provides almost one-fifth of total tax revenue. The consumption tax was introduced in 1989, with a 3% rate that was raised to 5% in 1997. The rate is applied to all businesses with taxable sales of more than 10 million yen, although a simplified system for calculating the tax is available to businesses with taxable sales of up to 50 million yen. In addition, specific indirect taxes are applied to some goods and services, including liquor, tobacco, gasoline, coal, aviation fuel, LPG fuel, and registration and licenses.

Table 4.1. **Personal income tax and social security contributions**

A. Personal income

	Income tax			Local inhabitant tax			Total		
Taxable income (million yen)	2007 (%)	2006 (%)	Taxable income (million yen)	2007 (%)	2006 (%)	Taxable income (million yen)	2007 (%)	2006 (%)
Under 1.95	5		Under 2.0		5	Under 1.95	15	15
From 1.95 to 3.3	10	10				1.95 to 2.0	20	15
						2.0 to 3.3	20	20
From 3.3 to 6.95	20	20	From 2.0 to 7.0	10	10	3.3 to 6.95	30	30
From 6.95 to 9.0	23					6.95 to 7.0	33	30
From 9.0 to 18.0	33	30				7.0 to 9.0	33	33
Over 18.0	40	37	From 7.0		13	9.0 to 18.0	43	43
						Over 18.0	50	50

B. Social security contributions (as of October 2007)

	Employees	Employers	Total	Ceiling on contributions[4]
	(Per cent of wages)			(Yen)
Pension (standard rate)	7.50	7.50	15.00	620 000
Healthcare[1]	4.10	4.10	8.20	1 210 000
Long-term care[2]	0.62	0.62	1.23	
Employment[3]	0.60	0.90	1.50	
Total	12.81	13.11	25.93	

1. The total premium varies between 6.6% and 9.1%.
2. The premium for long-term care paid by those between the ages of 40 and 64.
3. The employment insurance contribution by employers includes a 0.3% charge for employment programmes.
4. Contributions are paid on monthly salaries up to this amount.
Source: Ministry of Finance and Ministry of Health, Labour and Welfare.

Box 4.1. **Major features of the Japanese tax system** (cont.)

Local taxes[2]

Japan has a relatively complex local tax system consisting of 13 major prefectural taxes and ten municipal taxes, which cover personal and corporate income, property and consumption (Figure 4.3). The complicated system results in some duplication and overlapping of tax bases. For example, corporate income is subject to municipal and prefectural inhabitant taxes and to the prefectural enterprise tax, in addition to the central government corporate tax. Some discretionary power has been given to local governments to set rates for a number of taxes, but it has so far failed to promote tax competition and fiscal discipline. Moreover, several local taxes include tax-sharing arrangements with the central government. For example, one percentage point of the 5% consumption tax is levied by prefectures. This revenue is collected by the central government and distributed among prefectures based on objective criteria. In general, local governments tend to take the basic tax system as given by the central government, while competing to provide *ad hoc* tax rebates for specific policy targets, such as attracting firms to industrial parks, and introducing local discretionary taxes, such as those on nuclear waste and hotel stays.

Figure 4.3. **Composition of sub-national government tax revenues**

2005

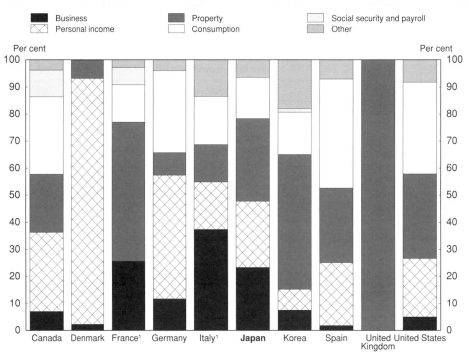

StatLink ᴍ๒๒ http://dx.doi.org/10.1787/277827004437

1. Including other taxes paid solely by business (*Taxe professionnelle* in France and IRAP in Italy).

Source: OECD (2007c), *Revenue Statistics 1965-2006*, OECD, Paris (*http://dx.doi.org/10.1787/366725334503*).

1. For example, employees are allowed to deduct 40% of annual wage income up to 1.8 million yen and 30% plus 180 000 yen from wage income of 3.6 million yen. Thus, for a wage of 1.62 million yen, 40% is deducted from taxable income, but the ratio falls to 35% for wage income of 3.6 million yen.
2. See the 2005 *OECD Economic Survey of Japan* for a detailed description of local government taxes in Japan.

target of a primary balance surplus is just the first step towards restoring fiscal sustainability. According to a projection by the Cabinet Office and estimates by the OECD, an improvement of 4% to 5% of GDP in the primary budget balance is needed to stabilise the debt to GDP ratio (see Chapter 3).[3] The same projection estimates that additional tax revenue, amounting to 4.6% to 5.9% of GDP, is needed to stabilise the debt ratio, assuming that growth is close to Japan's potential rate. Moreover, reducing the debt ratio requires an even larger primary budget surplus and thus a larger increase in tax revenue.

Challenge 2: supporting growth in the context of rapid population ageing and globalisation

The design of the tax system is crucial for output growth, as taxation impinges on most aspects of economic activity. A number of studies, including those by the OECD, suggest that the overall tax burden, and more importantly, a tax structure oriented toward direct taxes, can have a negative impact on growth.[4] The effect thus depends on how tax increases are designed and implemented (Box 4.2), as well as on the use of the extra tax revenue. As noted, the composition of the tax burden influences growth; for a given level of taxes, a higher incidence of direct taxes relative to indirect taxes is detrimental to economic growth. Furthermore, for a given level of direct taxes, a higher proportion of corporate taxes relative to personal income taxes has an additional negative impact on growth. Designing a tax regime that limits the depressing impact of taxes on economic activity is particularly important in Japan, given the effect of rapid ageing on output growth. The decline in the working-age population is expected to keep Japan's potential growth rate at around 1½ per cent over the period 2009-13,[5] well below the OECD average of 2.2% (see Chapter 1). With the increasingly negative contribution from a shrinking labour force, sustaining economic growth requires pro-growth tax reform, as well as reforms in a wide range of other areas to boost labour force participation, raise productivity and improve the allocation of resources (see Chapter 5).

In addition, the tax system needs to adapt as globalisation strengthens the competitive pressure on firms, making them more sensitive to cross-country variations in the corporate tax system. The increasing mobility of resources across borders has prompted international competition to lower tax rates. Despite a cut in 1999, Japan has had the highest statutory corporate tax rate in the OECD area since 2006. Hence, it faces increasing pressure to keep up with international trends and maintain the country's growth potential by providing a tax framework that encourages firms and individuals to stay in Japan.

Challenge 3: coping with widening income disparity

Income inequality has been widening in Japan. Indeed, the Gini coefficient for disposable income rose by 13% between 1985 and 2000, compared to an average increase of 7% in the OECD area, according to cross-country comparisons by the OECD based on national data (Förster and Mira d'Ercole, 2005).[6] While population ageing is boosting income disparity, as in most OECD countries, the key reason has been increasing income inequality among the working-age population in Japan, which is due in turn to two factors (2006 *OECD Economic Survey of Japan* and Tajika and Yashio, 2007). *First*, there has been a marked rise in inequality in market income, reflecting in part the increased proportion of low-paid non-regular workers (see Chapter 6). *Second*, the impact of the tax system on income redistribution has weakened as the personal income tax has become less

Box 4.2. **Principles to guide tax reform**

In meeting the challenges for tax reform, Japan should seek the best possible balance between efficiency, equity and simplicity.

Efficiency

Raising taxes to resolve Japan's fiscal imbalance and to fund higher public spending required by population ageing will impose costs that will tend to slow economic growth. The deadweight costs (sometimes referred to as the excess burden) rise sharply as tax rates increase.[1] Estimates of deadweight costs from taxes typically range from 10% to 100% (Diewert and Lawrence, 1994 and Leibfritz et al., 1997). Tax policies have a major impact on productivity and growth in both the short and long term as they affect all aspects of economic activity through their effect on incentives for savings, investment, employment and technological innovation. To limit distortions, the tax system should avoid introducing discrimination for, or against, any particular economic choices, except in certain cases, such as when there are clear externalities. In practice, this requires broadening tax bases, while minimising differences between tax rates. Understanding the magnitude and nature of the deadweight losses is important for assessing the true cost of increased government spending and for constructing an appropriate tax structure.

The impact of taxes on the behavior of economic agents and ultimately on economic growth varies between different types of taxes. Some taxes have a stronger effect on investment, while others influence incentives to accumulate human capital and accept employment. Other taxes affect technical progress through their impact on R&D, foreign direct investment and entrepreneurship. Consequently, the structure of the tax system is an important factor determining growth.

There is substantial research indicating that, for a fixed amount of tax revenue, relying more on indirect taxes and less on direct taxes has a positive impact on GDP. According to research by the OECD, a stronger reliance on direct taxes, for a given overall tax burden, has a negative and statistically significant effect on GDP per capita (Bassanini and Scarpetta, 2001). The negative impact of direct taxes stems in part from the sensitivity of investment to corporate income taxes (Myles, 2007). In addition, personal income taxes impact employment as high tax wedges distort the labour market.[2] According to one study, a 10 percentage-point reduction in the tax wedge on labour use (including income tax and social security contributions) is estimated to raise female employment and hours worked by 1½ and 3½ per cent, respectively (OECD, 2008). In contrast, a one percentage-point increase in the tax wedge on labour income would lower overall employment by 0.25% (Bassanini and Duval, 2006). While both personal and corporate income taxes are negative for growth, the impact of corporate income taxes is larger. The benefit of relying more on indirect rather than on direct taxes and more on personal income rather than on corporate income taxes is also supported by a study by Baylor (2007). It found that the welfare gain per $1 of reduction in taxes was 40 cents for corporate taxes, 30 cents for personal income taxes and only 10 cents for consumption taxes.

Equity

Tax reform should also take into account equity considerations, even if this entails costs in terms of economic efficiency. Tax systems usually aim to achieve two forms of equity. *Horizontal equity* requires that taxpayers in equal situations should be taxed in an equal manner, suggesting that the tax on a given level of total income should be the same regardless of how that income is generated. Horizontal equity thus favours a comprehensive definition of income for tax purposes. Moreover, tax allowances and tax credits that are not directly linked to the generation of that income conflict with the objective of horizontal equity.

Box 4.2. **Principles to guide tax reform** *(cont.)*

Vertical equity requires the "fair treatment" of individuals in different situations. It is a normative concept that depends on the definition of fair. One view of vertical equity is that taxpayers in better circumstances should bear a larger part of the tax burden as a proportion of their income, implying a more equal distribution of income after taxes than before. Achieving such an outcome requires progressive tax rates on income. Another definition of vertical equity favours proportional income tax (*i.e.* a flat tax rate). The approach to vertical equity depends on the extent to which countries want to diminish variations in income across the population.

Simplicity

The enforceability of tax rules and the cost arising from compliance are important considerations, and have implications for the efficiency of the tax system and public perceptions of its fairness. Tax systems are complicated by attempts to use them to redistribute income and to encourage certain behaviours. Complexity in the tax system also encourages tax planning, which imposes deadweight losses for an economy.

1. According to Creedy (2003), deadweight losses rise with the square of the tax rate.
2. The tax wedge measures the difference between total labour compensation paid by the employer and the net take-home pay of employees, as a per cent of total labour compensation.

---

progressive. The number of rates was reduced from 15 in 1986 to four in 1999, with a cut in the top rate from 70% to 37% (see Box 4.1).

Consequently, the reduction in the Gini coefficient due to the tax system declined from 2.2 percentage points in 1993 to between 1.3 and 1.4 points from 1999 to 2005 (Figure 4.4). The tax system now accounts for only about one-tenth of the difference between the Gini coefficients of market income and disposable income, while the social security system is playing a growing role in income redistribution as the population ages. However, this does little to reduce inequality among the working-age population, as

Figure 4.4. **The impact of taxes and the social security system on income distribution in Japan**

Improvement in the Gini coefficient[1]

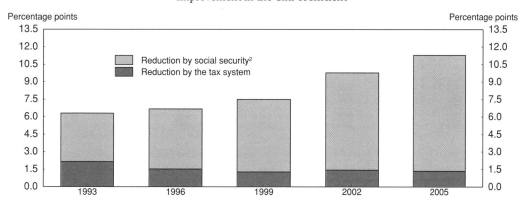

StatLink 🔗 *http://dx.doi.org/10.1787/277843220418*

1. Based on equivalised household income. The Gini coefficient is multiplied by 100.
2. Social security benefits in kind and social security payments minus social security contributions.
Source: Ministry of Health, Labour and Welfare (2005).

only 11% of the working-age population received government benefits, about half of the OECD average of 20% (OECD, 2003). The combined impact of the tax and social security systems on income distribution for the working-age population is the lowest in the OECD area.[7] Rising income inequality was accompanied by an increase in relative poverty, defined as a household income below 50% of the median, to 15% of the total population in 2000, the fifth highest in the OECD.

Rising inequality and poverty in Japan suggest a need to use the tax system, together with social welfare spending, to reverse these trends. However, strengthening the redistributive function of the tax system could weaken work incentives, reducing the potential growth rate of the economy. The challenge is to introduce a tax reform that effectively addresses income inequality while minimising the negative impact on the economy.

Challenge 4: improving the local tax system

Providing greater autonomy to local governments would enhance their ability to innovate and respond to the preferences of local citizens. The "Trinity Reform" launched in FY 2002 transferred a substantial amount of tax resources from the central to local governments, while reforming earmarked grants and block transfers (Box 4.3). While the transfer of tax resources from the central government is a positive step in strengthening local government autonomy, there are a number of issues that should be addressed to improve the efficiency and equity of the local tax system. *First*, the gap between prefectures in per capita tax revenue is large, with the ratio between the richest and poorest remaining above three during the past 20 years (Figure 4.5). *Second*, a number of taxes at the local level duplicate and overlap with central government tax bases, thereby complicating the overall tax system. *Third*, although local governments have some discretionary powers to change tax rates, they have been used in a limited and often distorted way (2005 *OECD Economic Survey of Japan*). *Fourth*, a high reliance on corporate taxation at the local level leads to high volatility in local tax revenues, as profits tend to fluctuate much more than property values

Figure 4.5. **The gap in tax revenue across prefectures**[1]

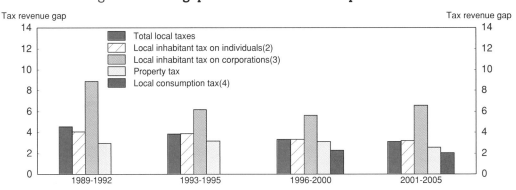

StatLink http://dx.doi.org/10.1787/277863057700

1. The ratio of the prefecture with the highest tax revenue per capita to the lowest. Population data are from the Basic Resident Register, as of 31 March each year.
2. Individual local inhabitant tax revenue is the sum of the individual prefectural inhabitant tax and individual municipal inhabitant tax.
3. Local corporation tax revenue is the sum of the prefectural corporate inhabitant tax, the municipal corporate inhabitant tax and the enterprise tax.
4. Local consumption tax revenue is after inter-prefectural adjustment. This tax was introduced in 1997.

Source: Ministry of Internal Affairs and Communications.

or consumption. The challenge is to create a simpler and more efficient local tax system that can provide sufficient resources and further increase local autonomy.

Analysis of the major taxes in Japan

Meeting the complicated and inter-related challenges discussed in the previous section requires a comprehensive and prompt reform of the tax system. The limited progress in tax reform achieved since 1999 (Box 4.3) demonstrates the difficulty of implementing fundamental changes. However, further delaying reform would only impose higher costs on the economy in the years to come. At the same time, reform should be phased in so as to sustain the current economic expansion.

The consumption tax

Greater reliance on indirect taxes would help achieve the first two goals of restoring fiscal sustainability and supporting economic growth. The value-added tax rate in Japan is the lowest in the OECD area at 5%, and is well below the EU average of 20% (Figure 4.6). As a result, indirect taxes on goods and services account for 19% of total tax revenue in Japan compared to an OECD average of 30%. Substantial increases in revenue thus appear to be possible. Japan's consumption tax has a broad base, as reflected in its C-efficiency ratio, which was the sixth highest in the OECD area in 2003 (Panel B). The base of the consumption tax was further broadened in 2004, when preferential treatments for SMEs were scaled back (Box 4.3). Each 1 percentage-point hike in the tax rate would add about 2.5 trillion yen (0.5% of GDP) of extra revenue. Raising the tax rate from 5% to 11%, for example, would thus provide sufficient revenue to balance the primary budget on a general government basis (see Chapter 3). While the revenue-raising capacity of the consumption tax, along with its other advantages noted below, make a hike in the consumption tax rate a key element of tax reform, it should not mask the necessity for base broadening of direct taxes, as well as for spending cuts.

Consumption taxes may have a negative impact on labour supply, as they reduce the return on labour by boosting the prices of goods and services. Nevertheless, a revenue-neutral move towards a consumption tax that raises the share of indirect taxes in total tax revenue would have a positive effect on growth, as noted in Box 4.2. In addition, it would increase consumption possibilities over the life cycle by lowering distortions on saving decisions. Indeed, the shift to a consumption tax makes taxation more neutral between present and future consumption, as income taxes are usually levied on a base that includes savings and income from savings. Another advantage is that indirect taxes are simple and relatively difficult to avoid or evade in Japan.

Regarding the third objective of improving income equality, a higher consumption tax rate would increase the effective taxation of the elderly, thereby contributing to a more equitable sharing of the tax burden across generations. However, the regressive nature of indirect taxes has negative implications for equity among the working-age population. Proposals to boost the consumption tax rate raise the issue of whether to introduce a multiple rate, an approach used in a number of countries, in order to limit its regressive impact by excluding food and other necessities. However, the tax rate in Japan is unlikely to approach the level in Europe, which goes as high as 25%, weakening the argument for multiple rates. Moreover, such an approach should be avoided as it has several drawbacks. *First*, it would result in higher administrative costs and induce lobbying. *Second*, it would have to be compensated by a higher standard rate. *Third*, it would reduce the neutrality of

---

Box 4.3. **Recent progress in tax reform in Japan: a follow-up of the 1999 Economic**
Survey of Japan

The 1999 *OECD Economic Survey of Japan* pointed out a number of challenges in the tax system and called for a comprehensive reform. Despite some progress since then, many of the problems identified in 1999 remain unresolved, partly due to political obstacles and the complexity of the problems. In the meantime, the need for wide-ranging tax reform has become even more urgent with the further deterioration in the fiscal situation, accelerated population ageing and widening income inequality. The major recommendations in the 1999 *Survey* included:

i)   Tax reform should cover a sufficiently broad range of measures (a "package approach") to make all groups contribute to the inevitable tax increases.

ii) Tax bases should be broadened substantially.

iii) Increasing the consumption tax rate gradually over a number of years should be one of the key financing mechanisms for the costs related to ageing.

iv) Taxation of pension savings should be stepped up in effective terms, at a minimum perhaps by reducing the indexation of retirement and annuity income allowances.

v)   Social security contributions should be increased as projected in the draft 1999 pension reform.

vi) Corporate taxation is not in need of substantial reform but could be enhanced with a view to improving neutrality across financing and investment instruments.

vii) Tax administration should step up the efforts to control evasion – in particular among the self-employed.

viii) Local government taxes – in particular at the prefectural level – should be made less volatile and more equitable between firms that pay taxes and those that do not.

The most important step to boost tax revenue was the phasing out of the 1999 fixed-rate temporary tax cuts in the personal income and local inhabitant taxes in FY 2006-07. There have also been some measures to broaden the base of the personal income tax. Most importantly, the exemptions for spouses and elderly people were scaled back in 2004 and 2005, respectively. As for financial income taxation, a uniform tax rate of 20% was introduced in FY 2003 for interest, dividends from listed stocks and investment trusts and capital gains on listed stocks, while rates on dividends and capital gains on listed stocks are temporarily reduced to 10%, as explained in Box 4.1. As for the consumption tax, the base was broadened by reducing the threshold for exempting small retailers from 30 million yen in taxable sales per year to 10 million yen. In addition, the scope for using the "simplified tax scheme" to calculate the tax was reduced from 200 million yen to 50 million yen.

In contrast, the corporate tax base was narrowed by the introduction of R&D and investment incentives in FY 2003 for three years, which resulted in an estimated 1.1 trillion yen (0.2% of GDP) of foregone tax revenue per year. Although the temporary measures were largely terminated in FY 2006 as scheduled, the R&D incentive for small and medium-sized enterprises (SMEs) was extended for another two years, while new measures, including a temporary tax incentive for acquiring information infrastructure, were introduced. Meanwhile, a part of the tax base for the local enterprise tax was changed in FY 2004 from profits to a "pro-forma" scheme that is based on capital and other value-added items such as wages.

The "Trinity Reform" launched in FY 2002 reformed earmarked grants and block transfers and transferred around 3 trillion yen (0.6% of GDP) of tax revenue from the central to local governments. This was accomplished by changing the tax rate schedule for the personal income tax to make it more progressive and replacing the three tax rates in the local inhabitant tax by a flat rate of 10% in 2007 (Table 4.1). Finally, the 2004 pension reform is boosting the pension contribution rate gradually each year from 13.6% in FY 2004 to 18.3% in FY 2017.

Figure 4.6. **Value-added taxes in OECD countries**

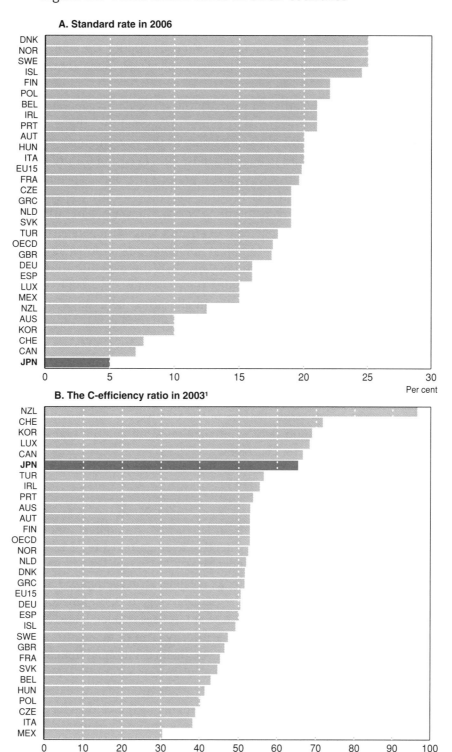

StatLink ᴍᴍᴸ *http://dx.doi.org/10.1787/277865051510*

1. The C-efficiency measure is the ratio of value-added tax revenue to consumption spending divided by the standard tax rate. 2003 is the most recent year for which complete data are available.

Source: OECD (2006a), *Consumption Tax Trends*, OECD, Paris.

the consumption tax, thus distorting consumption decisions and decreasing welfare. *Fourth*, it does little to reduce inequality, as high-income households that buy more goods in general tend to benefit most from lower rates on some items (OECD, 2006c). It is important to keep the simplicity of the current consumption tax while addressing income distribution objectives through better-targeted policy tools, such as an Earned Income Tax Credit (see below).

A second issue is whether to earmark the tax revenue generated from raising the consumption tax rate. For example, it is often proposed that the additional revenue be earmarked for financing the scheduled hike in the government's subsidy rate for the basic pension from one-third to one-half in FY 2009 (a cost of 0.4% of GDP) and financing additional social spending (the government projects that social spending will rise by 0.9% of GDP by 2015). Earmarking the revenue for social security spending may make it politically easier to raise the consumption tax rate.[8] However, earmarking is generally not an efficient way to manage public finances from a long-term perspective. *First*, it reduces the flexibility of policy makers to adjust spending programmes as needs change over time. *Second*, if revenues are more buoyant than the expenditure for which they are targeted, it is difficult to avoid extending the programme beyond its original objectives. Therefore, Japan should retain flexibility in allocating the additional revenues from tax reform.

As noted in Box 4.1, the local consumption tax rate (1%) is set at a quarter of the national consumption tax (4%). If the current scheme is maintained, an increase in the overall rate would thus boost the rate of the local consumption tax. In addition, 29.5% of national consumption tax revenue is currently transferred to local governments through the grant system.[9] Increasing the role of the relatively stable consumption tax in local government revenue would reduce reliance on more volatile taxes, notably the local taxes on the corporate sector (see below).

Corporate taxation

Raising more revenue

The statutory corporate tax rate in Japan was the highest among OECD countries in 2006 (Figure 4.7). Moreover, the effective average tax rate of 32% and the effective marginal tax rate of 28% were well above the OECD averages of 24% and 20%, respectively. Despite high statutory rates, corporate tax revenue, at an average of 3.6% of GDP during the first half of the 2000s, was close to the OECD average of 3.3%, reflecting a number of tax expenditures in Japan and a high share of enterprises making losses and thus not paying tax. Broadening the tax base is thus a priority. The number of tax expenditures fell from 80 in FY 2000 to 61 in FY 2007. However, their cost jumped from 5% of total corporate tax revenue in FY 2002 to 18% in FY 2003 when temporary tax subsidies on R&D and investment incentives were introduced (Figure 4.8). Although these measures were largely terminated as scheduled in FY 2006, the additional R&D incentive for SMEs was extended for another two years, while new measures, including a temporary tax incentive for acquiring information infrastructure, were introduced (see the 2006 *OECD Economic Survey of Japan*).

The rate of tax subsidy for R&D expenditures in Japan is relatively generous, ranking in the upper half of OECD countries (Figure 4.9). Some studies suggest that tax relief for R&D can have a positive impact on R&D spending.[10] Such policies can be justified on the

Figure 4.7. **Statutory corporate income tax rates**

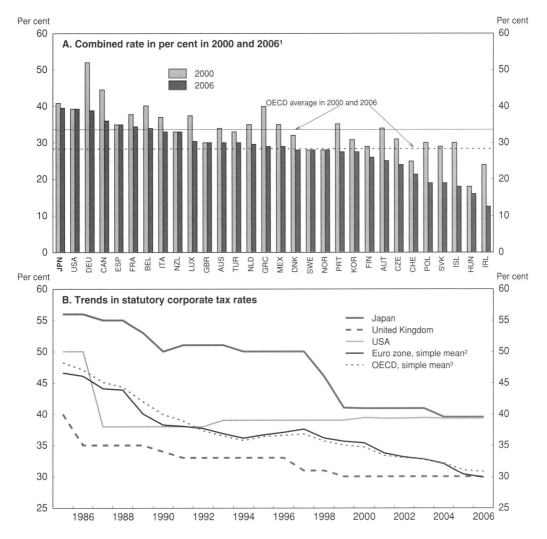

StatLink ⟡ http://dx.doi.org/10.1787/278008265144

1. Basic combined central and sub-central (statutory) corporate income tax rate. Averages are un-weighted.
2. Excludes Luxembourg.
3. Includes 17 OECD countries.

Source: OECD (2007e), *Tax Database*, OECD, Paris (*www.oecd.org/ctp/taxdatabase*); European Commission (2006), *Structures of the Taxation Systems in the European Union*; and OECD (2007b).

grounds that without it, investment in R&D would fall short of the socially optimal level due to spillover effects, with negative consequences for growth. However, some countries such as Finland and Sweden, which are generally seen as front-runners in innovation, do not provide any tax relief for R&D. If Japan wants to have such tax incentives, it should ensure that the benefits of additional R&D spending resulting from tax expenditures outweigh the cost of those expenditures. If tax expenditures are in fact effective, it is questionable then why the additional special tax treatment is granted only to SMEs. With total tax expenditures amounting to 7% of corporate tax revenue – well above the average during the 1990s – further efforts are needed to reduce the number and amount. Many of the tax expenditures were introduced several decades ago and have continued without any

Figure 4.8. **Tax expenditures in the corporate tax system**

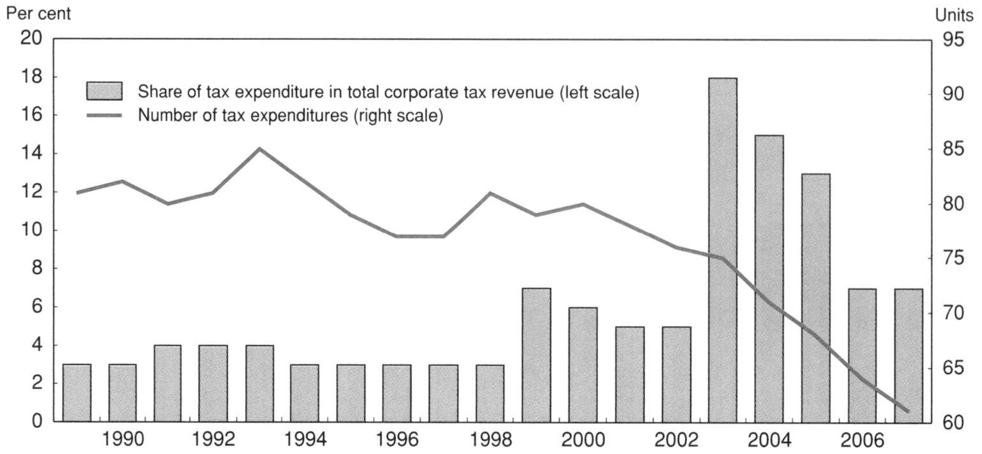

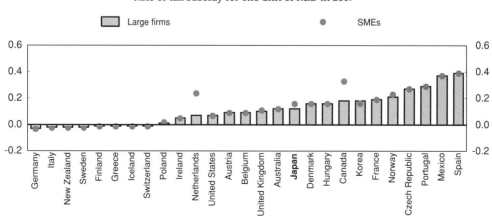

StatLink ᵃᵐˢ￫ http://dx.doi.org/10.1787/278020862024

Source: Tax Commission and Ministry of Finance.

rigorous quantitative assessments of the cost and benefits. Broadening the tax base by reducing tax expenditures would make the system more efficient, thereby promoting growth.

A large number of companies report losses according to the tax code and thus are not subject to corporate taxes (except for some local corporate taxes). The share rose to nearly 70% in 1999 before falling slightly in recent years (Figure 4.10). The proportion is higher for small companies with capital of less than 100 million yen. The high corporate income tax rate gives family companies an incentive to use the generous deduction for employee expenses under the corporate tax code to shift profits to personal income, which is taxed at a lower rate for most taxpayers. However, this may discourage successful small companies from expanding, as that would presumably make it more difficult to shift

Figure 4.9. **Tax treatment of R&D in OECD countries**
Rate of tax subsidy for one unit of R&D in 2007[1]

StatLink ᵃᵐˢ￫ http://dx.doi.org/10.1787/278027158847

1. For example, the score of 0.12 for large firms in Japan means that 100 yen of R&D spending resulted in 12 yen of tax relief for them.

Source: OECD (2007d), Science, Technology and Industry Scoreboard, OECD, Paris.

Figure 4.10. **Proportion of firms making losses according to the national tax code**

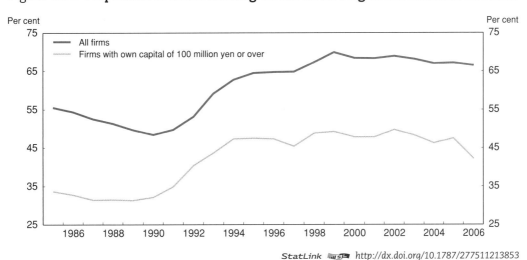

StatLink http://dx.doi.org/10.1787/277511213853

Source: National Tax Agency, *Results of the Corporation Sample Survey.*

profits into personal income. Even among large companies (more than 100 million yen of capital), the proportion not paying corporate tax has been close to half since the mid-1990s, reflecting issues related to the size of deductions, depreciation and the length of loss carryover.[11] The introduction of pro-forma taxation in the local enterprise tax (see below) was intended in part to require companies reporting losses to pay taxes. However, taxation based on the size of the company has drawbacks. The government should instead aim at boosting the share of firms paying taxes by changing the tax code to reduce generous deductions and by introducing measures to improve compliance. At the same time, it is important to maintain loss carryover provisions, which help to encourage risk-taking.

Promoting economic growth

In addition to reducing tax expenditures, cutting corporate income tax rates would also promote the broadening of the tax base. The objective should be to shift the composition of direct taxes away from corporate income and towards personal income, which would also have a positive impact on growth, as noted in Box 4.2. This is based on evidence that a lower corporate tax rate leads to higher investment and faster economic growth.[12] This has encouraged a downward trend in corporate income tax rates in the OECD area since the early 1980s, reducing the average statutory rate from 48% to 31% in 2006 (Figure 4.7, Panel B). Japan's rate has also fallen during the past few decades, notably in 1999, when the central government basic rate was lowered from 34.5% to 30%. The worldwide fall in corporate tax rates has been motivated in part by the aim of attracting foreign direct investment (FDI) in a world of increasingly mobile global capital flows. There is evidence showing that differences in corporate tax rates affect international flows of capital and profits and the location decisions of firms. In addition, an OECD study (Hajkova *et al.*, 2006) found that a one percentage-point increase in the effective corporate tax rate reduces the stock of FDI by between 1% and 2%. Another study reported that a similar decline in the rate can raise the stock of FDI by about 3.3% (de Mooij and Ederveen, 2003). Consequently, the ability to raise revenues through high tax rates on an internationally mobile tax base may be constrained in the context of an increasingly globalised economy and shifting attitudes toward tax compliance. However, economies with a large market potential, such as Japan, may be better able to sustain a higher tax rate than smaller countries.

International differences in corporate tax rates also create incentives for more aggressive use of transfer pricing by multinationals, which shift profits to subsidiaries in countries that have lower tax rates and costs to countries with higher tax rates, and this may be the case in Japan as well. Such transfers are facilitated by the increasing proportion of intangible assets, such as patents, in corporate assets. Indeed, intangible assets account for 75% of the total net assets of Fortune 500 companies, making it easier to relocate activities and tax bases around the world.

For Japan, the importance of additional government revenue should be balanced against the risk that high corporate tax rates will reduce economic activity and Japan's potential growth rate, in the context of growing international tax competition. Given the serious fiscal situation, the government has thus far resisted pressure from domestic business groups, such as Nippon Keidanren (2006), to reduce statutory corporate tax rates. However, the impact of lower tax rates on government revenues is likely to be limited by positive supply-side effects. Indeed, in some OECD countries, revenue was boosted by lower tax rates, thanks to higher profitability and the increased size of the corporate sector (2007 *OECD Economic Survey of the United Kingdom*). Indeed, the amount of taxable income in the corporate sector tends to be higher in countries with low corporate tax rates (Figure 4.11). Consequently, corporate income tax receipts show less variation across countries as the impact of higher tax rates is negated by the lower level of taxable income. As a result, there is almost no correlation between the statutory corporate tax rate and corporate tax receipts as a share of GDP (Panel B).

Improving the local tax system

One way to lower the corporate tax rate and improve the local tax system would be to phase out local taxes on enterprises, while increasing other local taxes, notably on personal income, property and consumption. A unique feature of Japan's corporate tax system is the significant amount that is imposed at the local level through the prefectural enterprise tax and the local inhabitant tax on corporations. Corporate taxation at the local level has various drawbacks such as the large revenue gap between jurisdictions – tax revenues per capita in Tokyo were nearly seven times higher than in the poorest prefecture between 2001 and 2005 (Figure 4.5) – and high volatility in revenue. These problems could be reduced by the pro-forma scheme introduced in 2004, which determines the enterprise tax on the basis of assets and value-added, as well as income. Such an approach can be justified by the benefit principle – even firms that are not profitable should pay for the services they receive. However, many OECD countries have phased out this type of taxation as it tends to discourage job creation and business investment. Moreover, it may exacerbate enterprise failures during economic downturns by transferring the cyclical risk from local governments to companies (2005 *OECD Economic Survey of Japan*). Given the numerous drawbacks, Japan should shift away from corporate taxation at the local level, which would reduce the overall corporate tax rate toward the OECD average.

Figure 4.11. **International comparison of corporate taxes**
Average 2000-05

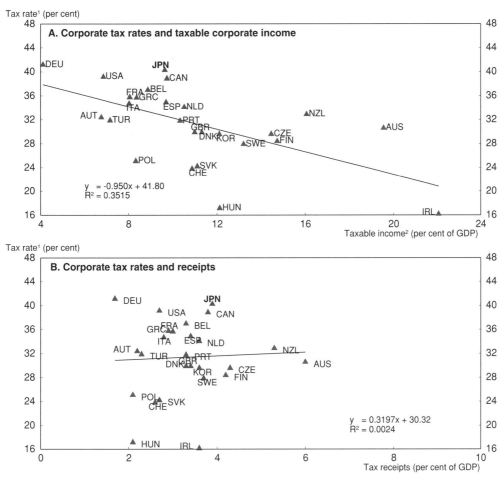

StatLink ᠍᠍᠍᠍ *http://dx.doi.org/10.1787/277527153057*

1. Combined central and sub-central statutory corporate income tax rate.
2. Calculated by grossing up corporate tax revenue and dividing by the tax rate.

Source: OECD (2007e), *Tax Database*, OECD, Paris (*www.oecd.org/ctp/taxdatabase*) and OECD (2007c), *Revenue Statistics 1965-2006*, OECD, Paris (*http://dx.doi.org/10.1787/366725334503*).

Personal income taxation

Raising more revenue

As noted above, the fall in direct taxes on households since 1990 largely explains the downward trend in government revenue (Figure 4.1). The decline was caused by weak economic conditions that depressed personal income and changes in the tax system aimed at revitalising the weak economy. Some other OECD countries have also experienced a decline in personal income tax revenue during the past two decades as tax rates have been reduced.[13] Nevertheless, the proportion of direct taxes in Japan remains well below the OECD average for several reasons. *First*, 60% of Japanese taxpayers are in the lowest personal income tax bracket, with a 5% rate (15% including the local inhabitant tax). *Second*, Japan allows a large number of exemptions and deductions. Despite the efforts to broaden the tax base in recent years, about a quarter of employees are exempted from the personal income tax. Moreover, less than 40% of wage income was subject to personal income tax in

Figure 4.12. **Personal income tax**

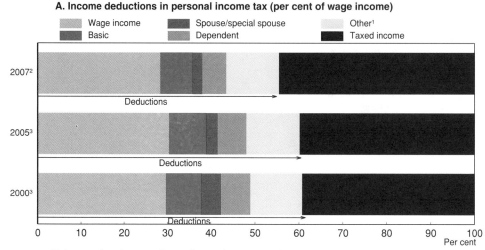

A. Income deductions in personal income tax (per cent of wage income)

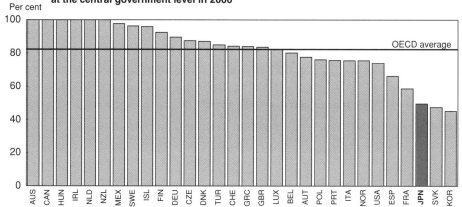

B. International comparison of wage income subject to personal income tax at the central government level in 2006

StatLink ⬚⬚ *http://dx.doi.org/10.1787/277534646512*

1. Primarily ageing-related deductions, such as pension contributions.
2. OECD calculations based on data from the Ministry of Finance, *Explanation of Tax and Stamp Revenues in FY 2007*.
3. OECD calculations based on data from the National Tax Agency, *The Statistical Survey of Actual Status of Salaries in the Private Sector*.

Source: Ministry of Finance, National Tax Agency and OECD (2006f), *Taxing Wages 2005-2006*, OECD, Paris.

FY 2000 and FY 2005, according to the National Tax Agency (Figure 4.12).[14] The Ministry of Finance's budget for FY 2007 assumed that the figure will rise to 45%.[15] According to OECD statistics, the share of wage earnings subject to personal income tax (for a single person earning the average production worker's wage) averaged 82% in the OECD compared to less than 50% in Japan, the third lowest in the OECD (Panel B). The deductions from the personal income tax base reduced tax revenue by 5% of GDP in 2000 (Ishi, 2001).

Reducing deductions on wage income would substantially boost tax revenues. The largest income deduction, accounting for 28% of wage earnings, is for wage income itself (Figure 4.12).[16] This deduction allows employees to exclude a certain proportion of their earnings based on their income level (see Box 4.1). The wage deduction was introduced to improve horizontal equity between wage earners and the self-employed, whose income is difficult to fully capture. Indeed, a number of studies have shown significant differences in tax compliance between types of workers. According to a 2001 study, the proportion of income subject to tax (the "capture ratio") was 40% for farmers and 80% for other self-employed, compared to nearly 100% for salaried workers (METI, 2001). A more recent study concluded that the capture ratio of taxable income for self-employed (excluding farmers) was 70% (Arai, 2007).

The wage deduction for salaried workers helps to level the playing field by subjecting a similar proportion of income (around 45%) to the personal income tax for both employees and the self-employed.[17] However, the wage deduction significantly narrows the tax base. Given that the amount of personal income tax receipts in Japan is low compared with other major economies, there is scope to reduce the wage income deduction, while improving the tax compliance of the self-employed to ensure equal treatment. Although there is no simple way to raise compliance, a package of measures may be effective. It should include the introduction of a taxpayer identification number and more intensive use of information technology, thus freeing up resources of the tax authority to improve enforcement. In addition, stronger penalties for tax evasion are needed.

Promoting economic growth

i) Removing features of the tax code that distort the allocation of capital

Raising personal income tax revenue by lowering deductions, with offsetting declines in direct taxes on the corporate sector, would have a positive impact on growth (Box 4.2). Base broadening of direct taxes also accelerates growth by reducing distortions that result in a misallocation of resources. In addition to raising the share of wage income captured by the personal income tax, it is important, particularly in the context of population ageing and a declining saving rate, to remove features of the tax system that distort the allocation of capital. In principle, this requires eliminating non-neutrality in the tax system by integrating the taxation of all financial income at the same rate, while taxing it separately from other income. In addition, allowing loss carryover between various financial investments encourages risk-taking.

Under the FY 2003 reform, Japan has moved in this direction. The comprehensive income tax, in which financial income (interest, dividends and capital gains from financial assets) was taxed with other income, was replaced by a system in which most financial income is taxed separately at a uniform rate of 20%.[18] As noted in Box 4.1, the rate on dividend income and capital gains on listed securities has been temporarily reduced to 10% for five years in order to re-vitalise the stock market. This rate should be raised to the uniform 20% in FY 2009 for dividend income and in CY 2009 for capital gains, as planned. In addition, the tax code allows capital losses on listed equities and trusts to offset capital gains on those assets, but not to offset interest and dividend income. In sum, it appears impractical and undesirable to return to comprehensive income taxation. Japan should instead maintain the separate taxation of financial income at a unified rate, an approach in line with international trends. Moreover, loss offset should be extended to all financial income, as recommended in the 2004 report of the Tax Commission.

ii) Encouraging the supply of labour

Cross-country research by the OECD suggests that taxes tend to reduce labour supply and demand, as well as saving and capital investment, thereby reducing the growth potential. The tax wedge on labour income in Japan was the seventh lowest in the OECD area in 2006 at 29%, well below the OECD average of 38%, thus encouraging employment and output growth (Figure 4.13). As noted in Box 4.2, an increase in the tax wedge on labour income reduces overall employment. On the other hand, a reduction in the tax wedge has the potential to significantly boost the labour supply of women. However, the decision on whether to cut personal income tax rates needs to take into account its impact on Japan's fiscal situation. While additional revenue should come primarily from a hike in the consumption tax rate, maintaining the amount of direct tax revenue should be an objective of tax reform. The scope for cutting personal income tax rates, while maintaining direct tax revenue, thus depends on the extent to which the broadening of the personal and corporate income tax bases generates additional revenue.

Figure 4.13. **International comparison of tax wedges**
2006

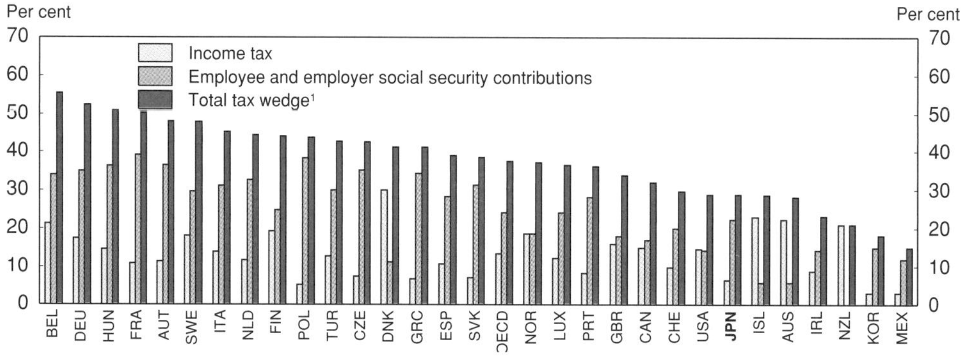

StatLink ⟪ゑ⟫ http://dx.doi.org/10.1787/277540653472

1. The tax wedge measures the difference between total labour compensation paid by the employer and the net take-home pay of employees as a ratio of total labour compensation. The international comparison of tax wedges is based on an individual with an income level of the average worker.

Source: OECD (2006f), Taxing Wages 2005-2006, OECD, Paris.

Even without rate cuts, it is important to address features of the personal income tax system that reduce growth. While the overall labour force participation rate in Japan is among the highest in the OECD area, reflecting a very high rate for men, the tax system appears to significantly discourage labour supply for certain groups, in particular second earners in households. For women in the prime age group of 25 to 54 years, the labour force participation rate is the sixth lowest in the OECD area (Figure 4.14). Moreover, 41% of female employees worked part-time in 2006, the third highest proportion in the OECD area and well above the average of 26% (Panel B). A number of features limit the female labour supply:

● Wages of a secondary earner up to a ceiling of 1.03 million yen per year (around a quarter of the average wage) are exempted from the personal income tax and the local inhabitant tax.[19]

● The main income earner in a household also qualifies for an income tax deduction of 380 000 yen if the second earner makes less than 1.03 million yen per year. The special spouse deduction allows the main earner to take a portion of this deduction if the spouse earns between 1.03 and 1.41 million yen per year.

● The incentive to limit working hours is further reinforced by the fact that secondary earners with an annual income below 1.3 million yen are exempt from social insurance premiums for pensions, healthcare and long-term nursing care.[20]

Figure 4.14. **International comparison of labour force participation rates and part-time employment**

Per cent in 2006

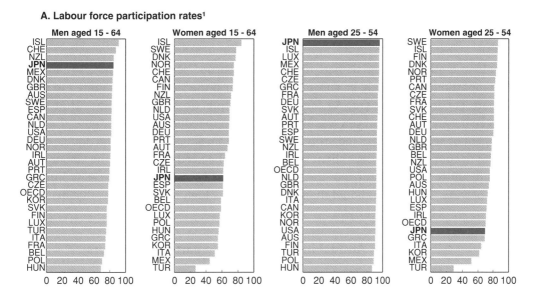

A. Labour force participation rates[1]

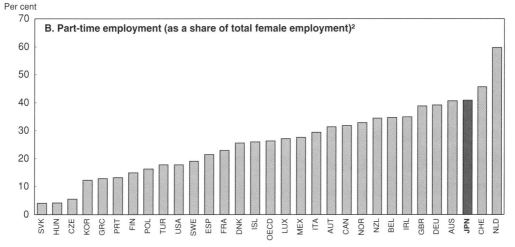

StatLink ⟪⟫ http://dx.doi.org/10.1787/277607225528

1. For Luxembourg, data is only available up to 2005.
2. For Mexico, data is only available up to 2004.

Source: OECD (2007a), *OECD Employment Outlook*, OECD, Paris.

● Many firms provide additional allowances to spouses earning less than a certain threshold, which is generally set at the same level as in the tax and social security systems.

These features helped to ensure equal treatment of wage earners relative to the self-employed, who are able to shift a part of their income to family members and deduct it as a business expense. However, according to a government survey, these aspects of the tax system have a significant impact on female employees: i) 67% limit hours worked to avoid paying taxes imposed above the 1.03 million yen threshold; and ii) 46% limit hours worked so that their spouse can claim the income tax deductions for second earners. In addition, 27% limit hours worked in order to continue receiving company allowances for spouses

(Ministry of Health, Labour and Welfare, 2007). Consequently, earnings of part-time female workers are concentrated near the threshold at which taxes are imposed (Figure 4.15). In 1994, when income up to 1 million yen was tax exempt for secondary earners, 24% of female part-time workers earned between 0.9 and 1.0 million yen. In contrast, only 8% earned between 1.0 and 1.1 million yen in 1994, but the proportion jumped to 15% in 2000, after the threshold for the tax exemption had been increased to 1.03 million yen.[21] In 2005, more than a quarter of female part-time workers earned between 0.9 and 1.1 million yen. The proportion would likely be substantially higher if the sample were limited to women who are secondary earners. As for male part-time workers, the share that earned between 0.9 and 1.1 million yen was 17%. In addition to reducing labour inputs, the special treatment of second earners redistributes income from single workers and double-income couples to couples with a dependent spouse. Given the need to increase the labour supply, it is difficult to justify features of the tax system that encourage employees to limit their hours of work. Tax reform should therefore reduce the high marginal rates that discourage full-time work by second earners.

Figure 4.15. **Annual income of female part-time workers**

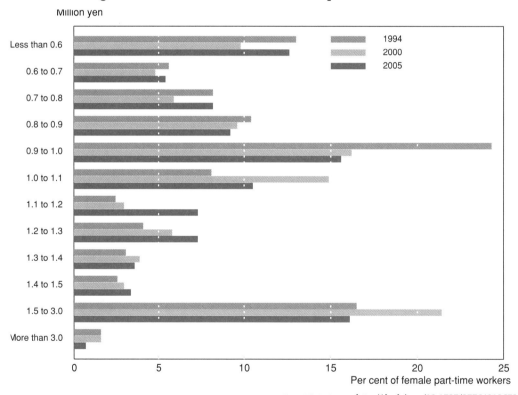

StatLink ᵐˢᴾ http://dx.doi.org/10.1787/277640186736

Source: Ministry of Health, Labour and Welfare (1996, 2002 and 2007).

iii) Improving labour productivity

The retirement allowance system, a lump-sum payment for departing employees that is voluntarily paid by most companies in Japan, is treated favourably by the tax system despite the fact that it discourages labour mobility.[22] Moreover, the amount of the allowance subject to tax is reduced as the length of service increases.[23] For example, the

OECD ECONOMIC SURVEYS: JAPAN – ISBN 978-92-64-04306-0 – © OECD 2008 tax base of a worker who receives a lump-sum retirement allowance of 20 million yen for 30 years of service is 2.5 million yen, resulting in an income tax payment of only 153 thousand yen (an effective rate of 0.8%). For a worker with 15 years of service, the effective tax rate would be almost 5%. The favourable tax treatment of a system that discriminates against workers who change jobs and the fact that the extent of the favourable tax treatment increases with job tenure combine to discourage labour mobility. The tax treatment should be reformed to encourage labour mobility, which needs to be enhanced in Japan to promote innovation and productivity (2006 *OECD Economic Survey of Japan*). Given that the retirement allowance is considered to be part of pension income, its taxation should be harmonised with that on benefits from the pension system.

Average and marginal tax rates on different types of income can affect the internal rate of return to education and thereby the level of human capital and labour productivity. Tax policies can thus be important drivers of investment in education through their effects on opportunity costs (*i.e.* foregone earnings), net wages and unemployment and pension benefits. A recent OECD study shows that a one percentage-point increase in the marginal tax rate reduces the internal rate of return to tertiary education by about 0.1 percentage point (Oliveira Martins *et al.*, 2007). The net effect of raising personal income tax rates to increase progressivity would be to reduce the education premium and thereby discourage human capital formation. In Japan, the degree of progressivity in the tax system is relatively low, suggesting that the negative effect on human capital is limited. Indeed, the ratio of income tax and employee contributions paid by a single person earning two-thirds of the average wage of a production worker was almost 80% of that paid by someone earning two-thirds more than the average, a high ratio compared to other OECD countries (Figure 4.16). The weak degree of progressivity in the personal income tax system thus has a positive impact on both labour inputs and on human capital and labour productivity. Maintaining the relatively low degree of progressivity, or even reducing it further subject to the fiscal constraints, would be beneficial for Japan's growth potential.

Figure 4.16. **Indicators of progressivity in OECD countries**

Ratio of the tax burden for a low-income person relative to a high-income person[1]

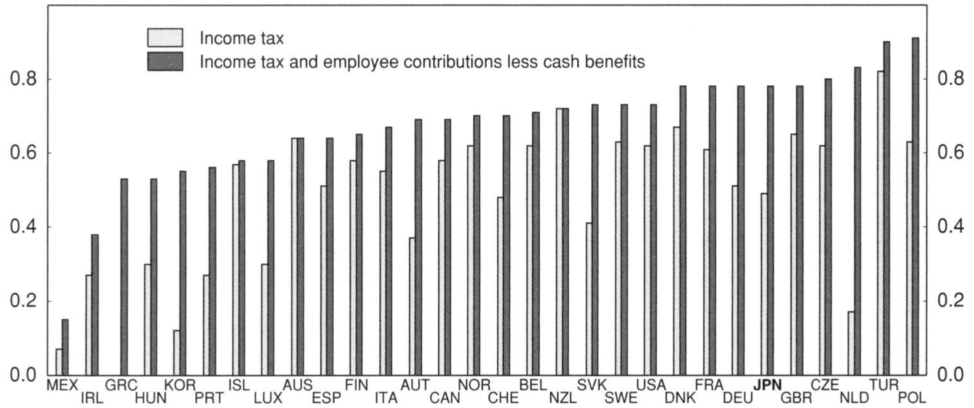

StatLink ⟡ http://dx.doi.org/10.1787/277646018527

1. Progressivity is assessed by comparing the tax burden of a single worker (without children) earning 67% of the average production worker to one earning 167% in 2005.

Source: OECD (2006f), *Taxing Wages 2005/2006*, OECD, Paris.

Figure 4.17. **Tax and social security payments by income decile**
Per cent of income[1]

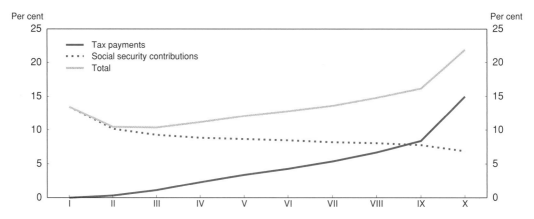

StatLink ⌨ http://dx.doi.org/10.1787/277714862455

1. For households receiving salaries. I represents the lowest-income decile.
Source: Tajika and Yashio (2007).

Coping with widening income distribution

However, the weak progressivity of tax rates, combined with the narrow tax base, limit the redistributive impact of the personal income tax system. While the top rate is 40%, some 60% of taxpayers are in the lowest (5%) tax bracket (15% including the local inhabitant tax). In addition, the progressivity of the tax system is partially offset by the regressivity of social security contributions (Figure 4.17). Currently, the most important tool for income redistribution is the inter-generational transfers that take place through the pension system.

Tax allowances tend to benefit higher-income groups since low-income people are already exempted from income tax. The abolition of the basic allowance, as well as the allowances for dependents, spouses and social security payments, would substantially increase the tax burden of persons with incomes of 5 million yen (the average wage) or more (Figure 4.18). For example, the proportion of taxpayers receiving the spouse

Figure 4.18. **Impact of abolishing personal income tax deductions**
By income category of taxpayer[1]

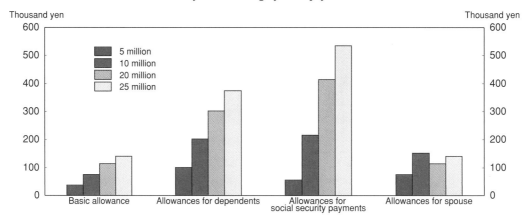

StatLink ⌨ http://dx.doi.org/10.1787/277740207726

1. Per person in each annual income group. Wage earner with a spouse without a job and two children (the employed parent is eligible for the special dependent allowance).
Source: Cabinet Office (2002b).

OECD ECONOMIC SURVEYS: JAPAN – ISBN 978-92-64-04306-0 – © OECD 2008 deduction was more than 70% for those with an income above 10 million yen, compared to only 20% for those with an income between 2 and 3 million yen (Cabinet Office, 2002b). Consequently, abolishing or reducing allowances and deductions would reduce differences in disposable income and could be used to finance targeted (means-tested) transfers or tax credits to low-income groups. It should be noted that broadening the tax base would raise effective marginal rates on labour, thus tending to weaken work incentives. If the base broadening generated sufficient revenue, Japan should thus consider reducing personal income tax rates to offset the impact of base broadening. Another important option to strengthen income redistribution through the tax system is the introduction of an Earned Income Tax Credit (EITC) system (Box 4.4).

One of the most important allowances in the personal income tax system in Japan is for social security payments. In theory, taxation of pensions can take place at three stages: when contributions are made to the pension scheme, on the earnings from the investment

---

Box 4.4. **Earned Income Tax Credit systems in OECD countries**

In-work tax credits can help "make work pay" for the low-skilled, thus encouraging them to enter the labour market and to increase their work efforts. In addition, an Earned Income Tax Credit (EITC) can allow more targeted policies, such as supporting households with children. A number of OECD countries have introduced EITCs:

● The EITC introduced in the United States in 1975 has been especially successful at encouraging the employment of single parents, particularly mothers (2007 *OECD Economic Survey of the United States*).

● In the Netherlands, an EITC was introduced in 2001 by eliminating existing income deductions. The collection of income tax and social security contributions by the same agency makes it possible to give income tax credits through reductions in social security contributions (Tajika and Yashio, 2007).

● Denmark introduced an EITC in 2004 that does not gradually phase out as incomes rise, making the system expensive and increasing the deadweight losses. However, phasing out the EITC as incomes rise, a typical feature of schemes in other countries, would be problematic in Denmark as it would imply a significant rise in the effective marginal tax rates for a large number of workers, given the relatively compressed wage distribution. The EITC will be expanded in 2008 (2008 *OECD Economic Survey of Denmark*).

● In 2007, Sweden introduced an in-work tax credit, which will cost over 1¼ per cent of GDP, partially offset by a reduction in unemployment benefits. The tax credit effectively reduces the marginal effective tax rate by 4 percentage points for those with incomes between 40% and 95% of the average full-time earnings. By increasing the attractiveness of work relative to unemployment, this reform is likely to improve employment rates and lower structural unemployment (2007 *OECD Economic Survey of Sweden*).

● In the United Kingdom, the Working Families Tax Credit for low-income families and single-parent households has been successful in raising the disposable income of the poorest workers relative to the median since 1999. This in-work, means-tested benefit has now been replaced by the Working Tax Credit, which tops up the earnings of low-income persons working more than 16 hours per week who are responsible for children and more than 30 hours for those without children. In addition, the disabled and persons over age 50 who are returning to work after a period of receiving unemployment benefits are also eligible. In 2006, almost 2 million households received the Working Tax Credit (2007 *OECD Economic Survey of the United Kingdom*).

> ### Box 4.4. **Earned Income Tax Credit systems in OECD countries** *(cont.)*
>
> Japan is discussing the costs and benefits of introducing an EITC.[1] The employment effects of such a system depend on the potentially offsetting income and substitution effects and the increase in marginal tax rates as the subsidy fades out. The effectiveness of an employment-conditional tax credit, in terms of increasing total labour supply and decreasing unemployment, depends on the *ex ante* distribution of market earnings, the tax system and the level of benefits for non-employed persons (Bassanini, Rasmussen and Scarpetta, 1999). Not surprisingly, an EITC has better results in countries with a wide earnings distribution, low tax rates on labour and low benefits for the non-employed, such as the United States and the United Kingdom. In contrast, an EITC is costly in countries, such as Denmark and Sweden, with a compressed earnings distribution and high taxes on labour. The criteria noted above suggest that an EITC would be an effective approach in Japan, as it has a relatively unequal income distribution (see above) and low taxes on labour income (Figure 4.13). Moreover, strict eligibility conditions and the short duration of unemployment benefits in Japan reduce the proportion of unemployed receiving benefits to 34% compared to an OECD average of 92%, while the generosity of benefits, with an average replacement rate of 67%, is in line with the OECD average of 62%. Other government transfers are quite limited in Japan. The proportion of the population receiving government benefits is small, as noted above, and benefits to the lowest income decile amounted to only 2.7% of household disposable income in Japan compared to an OECD average of 4.6% (2006 *OECD Economic Survey of Japan*).
>
> In sum, an EITC is likely to have a positive effect on aggregate employment and income distribution in Japan.[2] However, there is a high possibility of fraud, given the difficulties noted above related to the taxation of the self-employed. The introduction of a tax identification number system, proposed above to improve the tax enforcement of the self-employed, would also help to minimise such a risk. In addition, it is important that the EITC be based on individual income, rather than household income, to avoid weakening work incentives of spouses.[3] In any case, the improvement in income distribution and employment through the introduction of an EITC will need to be weighed against the amount of fiscal resources needed to finance such a system.
>
> 1. This was part of the work of the Tax Commission in 2007.
> 2. There is a growing body of evidence suggesting that an EITC has a positive effect on aggregate employment (OECD, 2004).
> 3. The EITC in Belgium is moving from a household to individual income base for this reason (2007 *OECD Economic Survey of Belgium*).

in the scheme and on the benefits that are paid out. In most OECD countries, the first two stages – contributions and interest – are largely tax exempt. When the first two stages are tax exempt, there is a strong case for taxing benefits. The Japanese tax system is generous in its treatment of the public pension system, as contributions and accrued interest are completely exempted and the tax on benefits is only partial, due to the allowances granted to persons over the age of 65.[24] Such allowances were scaled down by the abolition of some special treatments for elderly people as part of the FY 2004 tax reform (see Box 4.3). Nevertheless, the personal income tax threshold for households receiving pension benefits is 30% higher than for wage earners, making benefits from both tiers of the public pension system – a basic pension provided to all insured persons and a second tier linked to individual income – largely exempt from taxes.[25] Given that one-third of the basic pension is financed by the current budget, this implies a significant income transfer from working-age persons to those who are retired. Moreover, the proportion financed by the budget is to be raised to one-half beginning in FY 2009.

Private pension plans also receive favourable tax treatment in many countries, reflecting concern that workers tend to consume too much during their working lives and free ride on the social safety net once they are retired.[26] In Japan, the so-called "third tier" of corporate pension plans includes a number of schemes that receive preferential tax treatment. Depending on the decision of management and the labour union, employees can join the Employees' Pension Fund (EPF, created in 1966), the Tax-Qualified Pension Plan (TQPP, created in 1962 and scheduled to be abolished by the end of FY 2011), Small Enterprise Retirement Allowance Mutual Aid (created in 1959), the defined benefit corporate pension (DB, created in 2002) and/or the defined contribution pension (DC, created in 2001). For the self-employed, the government established the National Pension Fund (NPF) in 1991 to provide fair treatment relative to employees. Self-employed persons are also eligible to join the DC scheme. Contributions to third-tier pensions are usually tax deductible.[27] At the asset management stage, the special corporate tax is supposed to be levied on the assets, although this has been postponed.[28] At the withdrawal stage, the pension deduction is applied to benefits and the deduction for retirement income is applied for lump-sum payments, resulting in weak taxation of benefits.

The benefits from exempting pension plans from taxes should be carefully weighed against the costs, particularly in the context of rapid ageing. There is no solid evidence that preferential tax treatment of savings leads to a higher aggregate level of national savings (Yoo and de Serres, 2004). Such policies to promote pension saving may thus have high deadweight costs while benefiting high-income groups that will earn pension income that is well above the social safety net. While not increasing the total amount of savings, favourable tax treatment of pension plans tends to distort the composition of household savings and reduce government tax revenue. In the case of Japan, tax incentives bias savings toward pension plans and against individual investments, including purchases of equities. To restore neutrality between financial products and promote equity investment, tax subsidies to public and private pension plans should be scaled down.

Another area favoured by the tax system in many countries is home ownership. The favourable treatment of home ownership compared to other types of personal savings is motivated by social policy objectives, such as helping middle-income groups to acquire housing. In Japan, the 2004 mortgage tax credit, which was available to those earning less than 30 million yen (five times the average wage), accounts for the largest amount of foregone tax revenue among all tax subsidies. However, it risks favouring higher-income groups, who face a comparatively high marginal income tax rate and can afford the investment necessary to qualify for the tax subsidy. It also significantly raises the tax exempt threshold for home-owners.[29] Given that home ownership is already high in Japan, this tax credit should be phased out or at least scaled down in its coverage.

Improving the local tax system

Broadening the personal income tax base would provide additional revenue for local governments, which receive a quarter of their revenue from taxes on personal income (the local inhabitant tax). Given the complicated local tax system, boosting local government revenues should focus on existing taxes, such as the local inhabitant tax, rather than on the introduction of new levies. As noted above, local governments have discretion, in principle, in setting the rates of some local taxes, including the local inhabitant tax, but rarely exercise this power due to several factors. First, local governments that cut rates below standard rates are not allowed to issue bonds to finance local public works without permission from the central or prefectural government. *Second*, as central government support is to some extent discretionary, local governments fear that cutting tax rates would result in lower grants from the central government. Such controls on local government autonomy, which are aimed at preventing irresponsible behaviour by local governments, should be removed in the process of local government reform. Instead, local governments should be subject to more financial market discipline. Finally, the key to raising more revenue from the local income tax is to broaden the tax base, which is set at the national level.

Property and inheritance taxes

Property tax as a share of GDP in Japan is higher than the OECD average, although lower than in some other major economies (Figure 4.19). OECD countries experienced a decline in the share of taxes on immovable property, from 8% to 6% of total tax revenue, over the past decade, in part as a result of voter resistance to such highly visible taxes and a failure to update property valuations in line with prices. Nevertheless, since revenues from property tax are relatively evenly distributed between regions (Figure 4.5) and the proceeds are relatively stable over the economic cycle, the dependence of local governments on property tax in Japan should be maintained and perhaps even increased further to offset the phasing out of local taxes on corporations. This could be accomplished by raising the assessed value of property from its current level of 70% of market value. Strengthening the role of property tax would also be effective in reducing inequality.

The burden of the *inheritance tax* has been reduced by an increase in the amount of deductions and the decline in land prices. Consequently, the tax is imposed on only 4% of persons at the time of death and accounted for 1.5% of tax revenue in FY 2005, compared to 5.5% and 2%, respectively, a decade earlier. The number of inheritance tax brackets was reduced from nine to six rates and the top rate was reduced to 50%. Strengthening the role of the inheritance tax, by reducing the basic deduction and raising the top tax rate, would help to promote equality. In FY 2003, the gift tax was reformed to bring it into line with the inheritance tax in an attempt to encourage transfers of assets from older to younger generations at an early stage, thus promoting the more effective use of assets. As a result,

Figure 4.19. **International comparison of immovable property taxes**
Per cent of GDP in 2005

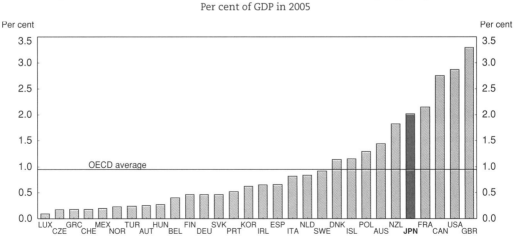

StatLink ⟶ http://dx.doi.org/10.1787/277760281846

Source: OECD (2007c), *Revenue Statistics 1965-2006*, OECD, Paris (*http://dx.doi.org/10.1787/366725334503*).

the total amount of tax is essentially the same whether parents give assets to their children or the assets are inherited after the parents' death.

Directions for tax reform

A comprehensive reform of Japan's tax system is essential to achieve fiscal sustainability. Indeed, as much as 6% of GDP in additional tax revenue is needed to stabilise the government debt to GDP ratio. In addition to fiscal objectives, tax reform should also aim at sustaining Japan's growth potential in the context of rapid ageing, limiting the upward trend in inequality and improving the local tax system. Specific recommendations for tax reform are summarised in Table 4.2.

Table 4.2. **Summary of OECD recommendations**

	Raising revenue	*Promoting growth*	*Reducing inequality*	*Increasing gains from decentralisation*
Consumption tax	● Raise the rate from the current 5%, while maintaining a unified rate.	● Raise the rate from the current 5% to increase reliance on indirect taxes relative to direct taxes.	● Raising the rate increases the tax burden on pension recipients, thus improving inter-generational equity.	● Raising the overall rate would increase the local consumption tax (set at a ¼ of the national rate) under the current system.
Corporate income tax	● Broaden the tax base by reducing tax expenditures and cutting generous deductions.	● Reduce the share of corporate income tax in total direct tax. ● Lower the statutory tax rate on corporations. ● Phase out local taxes on corporations		● Phase out local taxes on corporations, while relying more on taxes on personal income, consumption and property.
Personal income tax	● Broaden the tax base. ● Increase compliance of the self-employed by improving enforcement, in particular by introducing taxpayer identification numbers and stronger penalties for tax evasion.	● Increase the share of personal income tax in total direct tax. ● Remove features that distort the allocation of investment. ● Weaken disincentives for full-time employment of secondary earners in households. ● Reduce the preferential treatment of retirement allowances. ● Consider reducing personal income tax rates if the base broadening of direct taxes provides adequate revenue.	● Scale-down exemptions that favour high-income households. ● Introduce an Earned Income Tax Credit.	● Broaden the base for the local inhabitant tax, thereby offsetting the phasing out of local taxes on corporations.
Property and inheritance taxes	● Bring evaluations closer into line with market prices.		● Bring evaluations closer into line with market prices. ● Strengthen the inheritance tax by scaling back the basic deductions.	● Bring evaluations closer into line with market prices.

The government plans to implement a fundamental tax reform. As a first step, the Tax Commission, a group of private-sector experts that was established by law in 1959, released its report on the direction for tax reform in November 2007. Many of the recommendations by the Tax Commission, which are summarised in Box 4.5, correspond to those proposed in this chapter. However, there are a number of significant differences:

● The Tax Commission proposes a hike in the consumption tax rate to finance social welfare expenditures. The rise in social spending is part of the fiscal challenge facing

Japan: the government projects that it will increase by 1% of GDP over the decade 2005 to 2015 (Table 3.5). However, the need for additional revenue extends beyond social spending. From a long-term perspective, earmarking the rise in the tax revenue could weaken efforts to control social spending, while limiting flexibility in expenditures.

- The Tax Commission favours expanding the pro-forma local government tax on enterprises. However, such taxes, which are based on the size of firms, are negative for growth and increase the risk of company failures during downturns. For this reason, a number of OECD countries have abolished or sharply reduced such taxes in recent years.

- The Tax Commission supports continued tax expenditures for activities, such as R&D, that promote productivity. Such incentives should only exist if rigorous cost-benefit analysis reveals that they expand productivity-enhancing activities to levels that are socially optimal.

- To enhance the role of the personal income tax system in income redistribution, the Tax Commission recommends that a number of policies be examined; i) changes in tax brackets and rates, including the top rate of 50%; ii) replacing personal deductions by tax credits; and iii) introducing an Earned Income Tax Credit, following an in-depth analysis of costs and benefits. Given that increasing the progressivity of tax rates risks discouraging the supply of labour and the acquisition of human capital, this chapter favours achieving greater redistribution through an Earned Income Tax Credit that is financed through a broadening of the personal income tax system.

The main challenge from a political economy perspective is how to gain a consensus for a comprehensive tax reform that achieves the four objectives outlined in this chapter. Fundamental tax reform is never easy, particularly when the reform must be revenue-enhancing as in Japan. In particular, the recommendation to lower corporate tax rates while raising the consumption tax rate and broadening the personal income tax base may be unpopular. It is important to point out that the corporate tax is borne not only by shareholders, but also by workers through reduced wages and possibly lower employment, suggesting that a cut in the corporate rate would boost household income and consumption. Indeed, a study of the United Kingdom found that workers bear about half of the corporate tax burden in the short run and all of it in the long run (Arulampalam, Devereux and Maffini, 2007).

Implementing a comprehensive tax reform requires clear communication of the plan and its objectives, based on transparent and well-articulated principles, so that taxpayers understand what the government is trying to achieve. This should include the following points:

- The government should demonstrate its commitment to improving the efficiency of spending before asking the public to pay higher taxes. Further efforts in this regard, such as the on-going cuts in public investment, the planned reduction in the government wage bill and the market-testing initiative (see Chapters 3 and 5), would decrease public opposition to higher taxes.

- It is important to recognise that tax revenue in Japan is one of the lowest in the OECD area and well below the OECD average of 36% of GDP. If Japan, one of the most aged societies in the OECD area, wishes to maintain its social welfare system, higher tax revenues are unavoidable.

- The reform must be fair to the extent possible across different segments of the population. In particular, it is essential that the broadening of the tax base also includes the self-employed, thus avoiding an unfair burden on salaried workers.

- Nearly all OECD countries have launched substantial reforms of their tax systems in recent years, driven by the need to provide a fiscal environment that is more conducive to investment, risk-taking and work incentives (OECD, 2004). Failure to do so in Japan would risk letting the country fall behind in an increasingly integrated and competitive world economy.

- The proposed tax reform should address emerging concerns about inequality, such as through the introduction of an Earned Income Tax Credit and a strengthening of inheritance and property taxes, as proposed in this chapter. Such an approach would avoid increasing personal income tax rates, which tends to discourage human capital formation and labour supply.

Box 4.5. **A comparison of the OECD recommendations with those of the Tax Commission**

	OECD recommendations	Tax Commission recommendations
Consumption tax	• Boost the consumption tax rate from its relatively low level of 5% to raise additional revenue to achieve fiscal targets and thereby increase the share of indirect taxation. • Maintain a single consumption tax rate to avoid the complications inherent in multiple-rate systems. • Retain flexibility in allocating additional tax revenue. • As the consumption tax rate is increased, maintain the share that is allocated to local governments, allowing them to reduce their reliance on more volatile taxes.	• Hikes in the consumption tax rate, both at the national and local government levels, should be considered as an option to finance social welfare expenditures. • Maintain a single tax rate, which is preferable for neutrality and simplicity.
Corporate taxation	• Reduce the statutory tax rate by phasing out local taxes on corporate income. • Broaden the corporate tax base by reducing the number and size of tax expenditures, particularly those that target specific industries and regions, thereby improving the allocation of resources. Maintain incentives only if rigorous cost-benefit analysis demonstrates that they expand productivity-enhancing activities to socially optimal levels. • Increase the proportion of firms that pay the corporate income tax by modifying generous exemptions allowed in the tax code, while retaining loss carryover provisions, which encourage risk-taking.	• A large number of the Commission's members insisted that the effective tax rate on corporations should be reduced in line with current international trends. • Lower tax rates should be combined with consideration of measures to expand the tax base. • Preferential treatment of activities that promote productivity and sustainable growth, such as R&D investment, should be continued. • Local taxation of corporations based on the pro-forma approach should be expanded in light of the benefit principle.
Personal income tax	• Raise additional revenue by broadening the income tax base. The key priority is to reduce the deduction for wage income, while increasing the tax compliance of the self-employed so as to enhance fairness between employees and the self-employed. • Reform the deductions and allowances in the personal income and local inhabitant taxes that encourage secondary earners to limit their hours of work in order to keep income below certain thresholds. • Reduce the preferential tax treatment of retirement allowances (the lump-sum payments) in order to promote labour mobility.	• The wage income deduction should reflect actual expenses and working conditions. • The deduction for self-employed business income should be examined more strictly, while considering the use of a lump-sum method of estimating the deduction. • The spouse deduction should be examined in terms of its impact on the labour supply of spouses and the fairness of the double deduction (spouse deduction by the primary income earner and basic deduction by the secondary income earner). • The retirement allowance system should be examined with the goal of reducing distortions in job choice and encouraging labour mobility.

Box 4.5. **A comparison of the OECD recommendations with those of the Tax Commission** (cont.)

	OECD recommendations	Tax Commission recommendations
	● Address income inequality primarily through the introduction of an Earned Income Tax Credit, financed through broadening the base of the personal income tax system, while avoiding increasing its progressivity. ● Reduce exemptions, which tend to benefit high-income households, such as the mortgage deduction, to help reduce income inequality. ● Strengthen pension taxation by reducing the deduction on pension benefits and by taxing corporate-based pensions more strictly.	● The structure of rates and brackets should be examined from the perspective of enhancing the redistributive role of the tax system. ● The level of the top rate (50%), which has been reduced in past reforms, should be examined from the perspective of improving income distribution. ● Replacing income deductions by tax credits should be discussed as a way of strengthening the income redistribution function of the income tax system. ● Further discuss the introduction of an EITC with due considerations of its costs and benefits. ● Examine the merits of setting the deduction for dependents based on the age of the dependents and making it a tax credit to encourage fertility. ● The pension deduction for high-income persons should be examined as a way of promoting intra- and inter-generational fairness.
Local inhabitant tax	● The base of the local inhabitant tax should be broadened.	● The various deductions on the income part of the tax should be amended to allow the tax to follow the benefit principle. ● The amount of the per capita levy (fixed amount per household) should be increased.
Financial income	● Continue to move in the direction of a unified tax on financial income at a uniform rate to reduce distortions in the allocation of capital, while expanding the scope of loss offsets between various financial investments.	● Abolish the temporary reduction of the tax on dividends and capital gains from listed securities that was introduced in FY 2003. ● Expand possibilities for loss offsets in financial income.
Property and inheritance taxation	● Strengthen property taxation as a revenue source for local governments by bringing the assessment of property values used for tax purposes closer to market prices. ● Strengthen the role of the inheritance tax by reducing the basic deduction and raising the top tax rate, to promote equality.	● Pursue measures to equalise the tax burden across properties. ● To limit disparities in wealth, the role of the inheritance tax should be enhanced by scaling back the basic deduction, which was increased in the context of rising land prices, and raising the top rate.

Notes

1. Excluding social security, tax payments in Japan in 2005 were the lowest in the OECD area after Mexico at 17.3% of GDP.

2. An OECD study (OECD, 2006e) estimated that economic and demographic factors will boost public spending on healthcare and long-term nursing care from 7% in 2005 to between 9% and 13% by 2050.

3. The Cabinet Office projection included two different assumptions for growth (Table 3.4). Under the high-growth assumption of 2.4%, the necessary improvement in the primary budget surplus is lower at 1.5% to 2.7% of GDP. However, such a growth rate is well above Japan's potential growth rate for the period 2007-11, which is estimated at 1.4% by the OECD, a rate close to the current estimate by the Japanese government. Under the low-growth assumption of 1.7%, which is more line with estimates of potential growth, the necessary improvement in the primary budget surplus is 3.9% to 4.9% of GDP.

4. An increase of about one percentage point in the tax to GDP ratio could be associated with a direct reduction of about 0.3% in output per capita in the long run. If the investment effect is taken into account, the overall reduction would be about 0.6-0.7% (Bassanini and Scarpetta, 2001).

5. This is a about the same as during the period 2004-08, despite the acceleration in the potential rate of labour productivity growth in Japan from 2.0% to 2.2% in the 2009-2013 period. However, the

larger contribution from productivity is more than offset by the faster decline in the working-age population.

6. The Gini coefficient in 2005 was identical to that in 1999 according to calculations by the Japanese government. Internationally-comparable data through 2005 will be published by the OECD in 2008.

7. According to an OECD calculation of Gini coefficients, the tax and social security systems reduced the coefficient by 5 percentage points for the working-age population in Japan, the lowest of any of the 14 OECD countries for which data are available (Förster and Mira d'Ercole, 2005).

8. The *Basic Policy for Economic and Fiscal Management and Structural Reform* in July 2006 stated: "To ensure a stable revenue source for social security benefits, the government will consider whether to clearly designate the consumption tax as a revenue source, taking into account the link between the benefit recipients and the revenue source" (see the *2006 OECD Economic Survey of Japan*).

9. While the consumption tax is a convenient source of additional revenue for local governments, its impact on local autonomy would be limited as local governments cannot change the rate nor the base.

10. A permanent 10% increase in the tax subsidy for R&D was estimated to raise the level of R&D spending by over 8% (Jaumotte and Pain, 2005).

11. The aggregate operating revenues of loss-making corporations, at 474 trillion yen (95% of GDP) in 2005, amounted to 33% of the aggregate operating revenues of all corporations (1 455 trillion yen, 290% of GDP).

12. For instance, Uemura and Maekawa (2000) estimated that the cut in corporate tax and enterprise tax rates from 46.4% to 40.9% in 1999 resulted in an increase in business investment by 3%. In addition, the high statutory tax rate makes the bias in favour of debt finance especially strong in Japan.

13. The share of personal income tax in total tax revenue in the OECD area fell slightly from an average of 27% in 1990 to 25% in 2005, compared to a drop from 28% to 18% in Japan over the same period.

14. The tax base of salaried workers expanded slightly from 39.4% in FY 2000 to 39.8% in FY 2005 as a result of the reduction of the special spouse deduction (2.0 percentage points), and the abolition of the deduction for the elderly (0.3 percentage points). However, this was offset by a negative 1.2 percentage-point contribution from the fall in the average salary and a negative 0.7 percentage-point contribution from higher social security premiums resulting from a hike in the contribution rate and population ageing.

15. However, it should be noted that the Ministry's estimate that 43.5% of wage income was taxed in FY 2002 was above the share of 40% calculated from National Tax Agency data.

16. Another major deduction is the category of "other deductions" (Figure 4.12), which includes ageing-related spending, such as pension contributions. With population ageing and hikes in the pension contribution rate, the amount of such deductions rose from 10% to 10.7% of total wage income between FY 2000-05 and is likely to continue rising. In contrast, the deduction for dependents has fallen substantially following a drop in the number of children per household, while the reform in the special spouse deduction lowered the size of this deduction.

17. Excluding the wage income deduction, the remaining deductions (basic, spouse, dependent and "other" shown in Figure 4.12) exempted 27% of wage income in 2007. For self-employed, those deductions excluded 35% of income. However, if only 70% of the income of the self-employed is captured by the tax system, then only 46% of their true income is subject to tax, well below the 73% for employees. The wage income deduction, which exempted an additional 28% of wage earnings in 2007, brings the ratio down to 45%, thus providing equal treatment of employees and the self-employed.

18. Under the Income Tax Law, taxable income is classified into the following ten categories and taxed on a comprehensive basis with some exemptions noted below: 1) interest; 2) dividends; 3) real estate; 4) business; 5) employment; 6) retirement; 7) timber; 8) capital gains; 9) occasional; and 10) miscellaneous. Retirement income and timber income are taxed separately from the other categories of income. Under the split-income model, interest, dividends and capital gains are also taxed separately.

19. The local inhabitant tax consists of a per capita levy (kinto-wari) and an income-based levy (shotoku-wari). The exemptions apply to the latter. The per capita levy is a fixed amount imposed on those earning above a ceiling, which is around 0.98 million yen but varies between jurisdictions.

20. To qualify for the exemption, the second earner must work less than three-quarters of the working hours or days of regular workers and have a spouse that is covered by the insurance scheme.

21. The threshold was increased in 1995. Presumably, a substantial proportion of those were in the 1.0 to 1.03 million yen range.

22. More than 95% of companies with over 100 employees pay a lump-sum retirement allowance, and 63% of them use a system in which the allowance rises more than proportionally with tenure (Ministry of Internal Affairs and Communications, 2001). Such an approach tends to discourage labour mobility.

23. The number of years multiplied by 0.4 million yen is deducted for a length of service of up to 20 years, and the number of years times 0.7 million yen is deducted for service beyond 20 years.

24. Japan is among the 12 OECD member countries where pensions are partially taxed at the withdrawal stage but exempt at the contribution and accrual stages – a so-called EEpT regime (Yoo and de Serres, 2004).

25. The personal income tax threshold for a couple receiving a pension is 2.05 million yen, 30% higher than the 1.57 million yen threshold for a working couple without children (Miyauchi, 2006).

26. The Workers' Property Accumulation System is another tax preferred savings scheme for three types of savings; general, pension and housing savings. Interest is tax-deductible up to a certain combined amount for the three types of savings. Despite the favourable tax treatment, both the number of contracts and amounts have been falling. The number of contracts fell from 14.2 million in 2001 to 10.8 million in 2007 while the amount declined from 19 trillion yen (3.8% of GDP) to 17.5 trillion yen over the same period.

27. In the EPF, the contribution of the employer is deductible as an expense and that of the employees is deductible as a social insurance premium. In the TQPP and DB, employer contributions are deductible as an expense, while employee contributions are deductible by the same amount as the deduction for private life insurance premiums. In the DC scheme, employer and employee contributions are deductible, although there are deduction limits. Similarly, contributions to the NPF are deductible up to a certain level.

28. Private investors argue that the treatment of interest on third-tier schemes should match the tax exempt status applied to the public pension system. One concern is that the tax rate – 1% of outstanding assets – is inappropriate in the current low interest rate environment.

29. For a couple with two children, the mortgage tax credit raises the income tax threshold from 3.68 million yen to 9.3 million yen.

Bibliography

Arai, H. (2007), "Problems with estimation of income tax compliance rate based on SNA – focusing on the tax compliance rate of the self-employed", Reference No. 675, April 2007, the National Diet Library, Tokyo (in Japanese).

Arulampalam, W., M. Devereux and G. Maffini (2007), "The Incidence of Corporate Income Tax on Wages", Oxford University Centre for Business Taxation Working Paper 07/07, Oxford.

Bassanini, A. and R. Duval (2006), "The determinants of unemployment across OECD countries: reassessing the role of policies and institutions", OECD Economic Studies, No. 42, OECD, Paris.

Bassanini, A., J. Rasmussen and S. Scarpetta (1999), "The Economic Effects of Employment Conditional-Income Support Schemes for the Low-Paid: An Illustration from a CGE Model Applied to Four OECD Countries", OECD Economics Department Working Paper No. 224, OECD, Paris.

Bassanini, A. and S. Scarpetta (2001), "The driving forces of economic growth: panel data evidence for the OECD countries", OECD Economic Studies, No. 33, OECD, Paris.

Baylor, M. (2007), "Estimating the excess burden of taxation through general equilibrium modelling", paper presented at the OECD Workshop on Tax and Growth, Paris, 30 March 2007.

Cabinet Office (2001), "Impact of income tax reforms in the 1990s", Policy Analysis Report No. 9, Tokyo (in Japanese).

Cabinet Office (2002a), Annual Report on the Japanese Economy and Public Finance (2001-02), Tokyo.

Cabinet Office (2002b), "The tax base and the tax burden of personal income tax", Policy Analysis Report No. 15, Tokyo (in Japanese).

Cabinet Office (2005), *Annual Report on the Japanese Economy and Public Finance (2005-06)*, Tokyo.

Creedy, J. (2003), "The Excess Burden of Taxation and Why It (approximately) Quadruples when the Tax Rate Doubles", Treasury Working Paper No. 03/29, Wellington.

De Mooij, R.A. and S. Ederveen (2003), "Taxation and Foreign Direct Investment: A Synthesis of Empirical Research", *International Tax and Public Finance*, No. 10.

Diewert, E. and D. Lawrence (1994), "Measuring New Zealand's Productivity", Treasury Working Paper No. 94/5, Wellington.

European Commission (2006), *Structures of the Taxation Systems in the European Union,* Brussels.

Förster, M. and M. Mira d'Ercole (2005), "Income Distribution and Poverty in OECD Countries in the Second Half of the 1990s", OECD Social, Employment and Migration Working Paper No. 22, OECD, Paris.

Hajkova, D., G. Nicoletti, L. Vartia and K. Yoo (2006), "Taxation, Business Environment and FDI Location in OECD Countries", Economics Department Working Paper No. 502, OECD, Paris.

Ishi, H. (2001), *The Japanese Tax System*, Oxford: Oxford University Press.

Ishi, H. (2004), *How will the tax burden change?*, Chuo Koron Shinsha, Tokyo (in Japanese).

Ishi, H. (2006), "Moving towards a Dual Income Tax", *Asia-Pacific Tax Bulletin*, July/August 2006, IBFD, Washington, D.C.

Jaumotte, F. and N. Pain (2005), "Innovation in the business sector", OECD Economics Department Working Paper No. 459, OECD, Paris.

Leibfritz, W., J. Thornton and A. Bibbee (1997), "Taxation and Economic Performance", OECD Economics Department Working Paper No. 176, OECD, Paris.

Ministry of Economy, Trade, and Industry (2001), *Study Group Report on Basic Taxation Issues for Economic Vitalisation,* Tokyo (in Japanese).

Ministry of Finance (2007), *Let's talk about taxes*, Tokyo.

Ministry of Health, Labour and Welfare (1996, 2002 and 2007), *General Research on the Condition of Part-time Workers*, Tokyo (in Japanese).

Ministry of Health, Labour and Welfare (2005), *Survey on Income Redistribution*, Tokyo (in Japanese).

Ministry of Internal Affairs and Communications (2001), *Survey on the Retirement Allowances of Private Companies,* FY 2001, Tokyo (in Japanese).

Mintz, J. (2007), *2007 Tax Competitiveness Report*, C.D. Howe Institute, Toronto, Canada.

Miyauchi, Y. ed. (2006), *The Japanese Tax System Illustrated, FY 2006*, Tokyo (in Japanese).

Morinobu, S. (2002), *A study on the Japanese income tax base*, Japan Tax Association, Tokyo (in Japanese).

Morinobu, S. (2003), *Tax reform for the rebirth of Japan*, Chuo Koron Shinsha, Tokyo (in Japanese).

Myles, G.D. (2007), "What do we know about the effects of taxes on growth", paper presented at the OECD Workshop on Tax and Growth, Paris, 30 March 2007.

Nippon Keidanren (2006), *Recommendations concerning the FY 2007 tax reform*, Tokyo (in Japanese).

OECD (1999), *OECD Economic Survey of Japan*, OECD, Paris.

OECD (2003), *OECD Employment Outlook*, OECD, Paris.

OECD (2004), "Recent Tax Policy Trends and Reforms in OECD Countries", OECD Tax Policy Studies No. 9, OECD, Paris.

OECD (2005), *OECD Economic Survey of Japan*, OECD, Paris.

OECD (2006a), *Consumption Tax Trends*, OECD, Paris.

OECD (2006b), "Fundamental Reform of Personal Income Tax", OECD Tax Policy Studies No. 13, OECD, Paris.

OECD (2006c), *Getting it Right: OECD Perspectives on Policy Change in Mexico*, OECD, Paris.

OECD (2006d), *OECD Economic Survey of Japan*, OECD, Paris.

OECD (2006e), "Projecting OECD Health and Long-Term Care Expenditures: What are the Main Drivers?", OECD Economics Department Working Paper No. 477, OECD, Paris.

OECD (2006f), *Taxing Wages 2005/2006*, OECD, Paris.

OECD (2007a), *OECD Employment Outlook*, OECD, Paris.

OECD (2007b), *OECD Economic Survey of New Zealand*, OECD, Paris.

OECD (2007c), *Revenue Statistics*, OECD, Paris (*http://dx.doi.org/10.1787/366725334503*).

OECD (2007d), *Science, Technology and Industry Scoreboard*, OECD, Paris.

OECD (2007e), *Tax Database*, OECD, Paris (*www.oecd.org/ctp/taxdatabase*).

OECD (2008), "Explaining Differences in Hours Worked across OECD Countries", *Growing for Growth*, OECD, Paris.

Ohta, H., H. Tsubouchi and T. Tsuji (2003), "Horizontal equity of income tax", Economic Assessment and Policy Analysis Discussion Paper DP/03-1, Cabinet Office, Tokyo (in Japanese).

Oliveira Martins, J., R. Boarini, H. Strauss, C. de la Maisonneuve and C. Saadi (2007), "The Policy Determinants of Investment in Tertiary Education", OECD Economics Department Working Paper No. 576, OECD, Paris.

Tajika, E. and H. Yashio (2007), "Addressing widening disparity through the tax system: utilising reimbursable tax credits", *Zeikeitsushin* 07.4, Tokyo (in Japanese).

Tax Commission (2002), "Policy guidance on the establishment of a desirable tax system", Tokyo (in Japanese).

Tax Commission (2003), "A sustainable tax system for Japan's ageing society", Mid-term report by the Tax Commission, Tokyo (in Japanese).

Tax Commission (2004), "Basic view on the integration of financial income taxation", Sub-Committee on the Taxation of Financial Assets, Tokyo (in Japanese).

Tax Commission (2005), "Issues concerning personal income taxation", Sub-Committee on Fundamental Issues, Tokyo (in Japanese).

Tax Commission (2006a), "Main issues based on discussions so far", Sub-Committee on Fundamental Issues, Tokyo (in Japanese).

Tax Commission (2006b), "Towards further discussion on tax reform", a remark by Hiromitsu Ishi, Chair of the Commission, Tokyo (in Japanese).

Tax Commission (2007), "Basic view toward fundamental tax reform; a report to the inquiry from the prime minister", Tokyo (in Japanese).

Uemura, T. and S. Maekawa (2000), "Industrial Investment Behavior and Corporate Income Tax: Tax-adjusted Q Approach Using Japanese Firm", Japan Center for Economic Research No. 41, Tokyo (in Japanese).

Yoo, K.-Y. and A. de Serres (2004), "Tax treatment of private pension savings in OECD countries and the net tax cost per unit of contribution to tax-favoured schemes", OECD Economics Department Working Paper No. 406, OECD, Paris.

ISBN 978-92-64-04306-0
OECD Economic Surveys: Japan
© OECD 2008

Chapter 5

Enhancing the productivity of the service sector in Japan

Labour productivity growth in the service sector, which accounts for 70% of Japan's economic output and employment, has slowed markedly in recent years in contrast to manufacturing. The disappointing performance is associated with weak competition in the service sector resulting from strict product market regulation and the low level of import penetration and inflows of foreign direct investment (FDI). Reversing the deceleration in productivity growth in the service sector is essential to raise Japan's growth potential. The key is to eliminate entry barriers, accelerate regulatory reform, upgrade competition policy and reduce barriers to trade and inflows of FDI. Special attention should be given to factors limiting productivity growth in services characterised by either low productivity or high growth potential, such as retail, transport, energy and business services. Finally, it is essential to increase competition in public services, such as health and education, where market forces have been weak.

Boosting productivity in the service sector is a key priority for promoting long-term growth. Services account for a dominant share of economic activity in Japan; its share of output increased from 66% in 1993 to 70% in 2003, matching the OECD average. The disappointing productivity performance in Japan's service sector – which has lagged far behind the manufacturing sector in recent years – is thus a source of major concern. At the same time, the globalisation of service industries is creating more opportunities for domestic firms, while exposing them to stronger competition. This chapter addresses the challenges of fostering a more dynamic and competitive business environment that encourages service-sector firms to enhance productivity, offer new services and create new employment. After an overview of Japan's service sector, the chapter discusses the main factors hindering its growth. The following sections analyse policies to improve the overall productivity of the service sector as well as the major issues in key service industries. This chapter concludes with recommendations, which are summarised in Box 5.4.

The role of the service sector in the Japanese economy

The upward trend in the share of the service sector in GDP and total employment in Japan is expected to continue in the context of rapid population ageing and intense competition with low-cost manufacturers in Asia.[1] Another factor boosting services is the increased outsourcing from manufacturing, accelerated by the modularisation of that sector. Consequently, the competitiveness of manufactured goods in Japan depends increasingly on the performance of the service sector.[2] The growing size of the service sector and its impact on other parts of the economy makes it all the more important to promote efficiency in services and thereby boost economy-wide labour productivity, which was only 70% of the US level in 2006 (Figure 5.1). Japan ranks only 18th among OECD economies in terms of labour productivity.

The service sector is largely responsible for low aggregate productivity in the Japanese economy. The growth of labour productivity per hour worked in services decelerated from an annual rate of 3.5% between 1976 and 1989 to 0.9% between 1999 and 2004, with both market and non-market services recording significant slowdowns (Figure 5.1). Moreover, labour productivity in non-market services declined in absolute terms, while Information and Communication Technology (ICT) services recorded a marked slowdown from a 3.9% annual rate between 1989 and 1999 to less than 2% from 1999 to 2004. In contrast to the across-the-board deceleration in services, labour productivity growth in the manufacturing sector has remained fairly constant at around 4% over the past 30 years. Productivity growth in the service sector was thus less than a quarter of that in manufacturing between 1999 and 2004, a much larger gap than in the United Kingdom and the European Union.[3] Consequently, the contribution of the service sector to overall productivity growth between 1990 and 2002 in Japan was the eighth lowest among the 24 countries surveyed (OECD, 2005a). In sum, the slowdown in the service sector has brought down labour productivity growth in the entire economy from more than 4% in the 1976-89 period to less than 2% from 1999 to 2004.

Figure 5.1. **Labour productivity by sector**

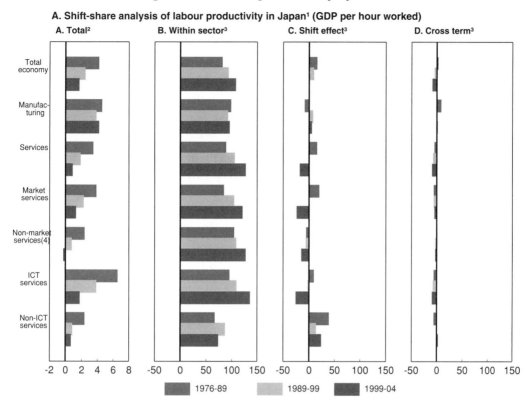

A. Shift-share analysis of labour productivity in Japan[1] (GDP per hour worked)

1976-89   1989-99   1999-04

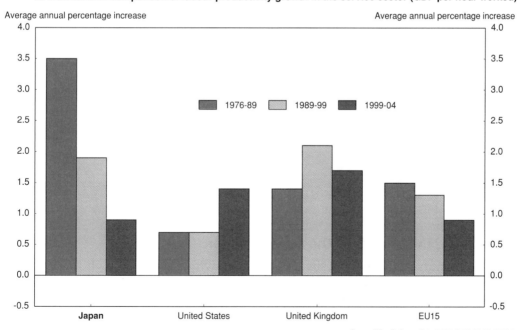

B. International comparison of labour productivity growth in the service sector (GDP per hour worked)

StatLink http://dx.doi.org/10.1787/278034845532

1. See endnote 4 in the text for an explanation of shift-share analysis.
2. Annual increase in GDP per hour worked.
3. Per cent of total increase.
4. Includes activities such as public administration and defence; compulsory social security; education, health and social work.

Source: EU KLEMS Database (2007).

As in most OECD countries, productivity growth in the service sector was driven primarily by growth within each service industry (the "within-sector" effect shown in Figure 5.1).[4] In contrast, the effect of shifting labour from less to more productive service industries (the "shift effect") has been small or even negative. In particular, in market services and ICT services, labour has been reallocated from more to less productive industries in recent years, in contrast to the 1970s and 1980s. The fact that labour productivity benefited little from a reallocation of labour to more productive service sectors indicates the need for further structural change that promotes the development of the more dynamic service industries.

Breaking down the performance of the service sector by industry shows an across-the-board deterioration in "within industry" productivity growth between the periods 1990-99 and 1999-2004 (Table 5.1). Wholesale and retail trade recorded the largest decline, while transport and storage reported negative productivity growth. Overall, these finding are consistent with other studies. According to OECD indicators, the growth of value added per person employed in Japan's transport and storage sector was one of the lowest among 18 OECD countries (OECD, 2006b). Another study (Fukao and Miyagawa, 2007) also reported that the largest declines in total factor productivity growth between 1995 and 2004 were observed in distribution and personal and social services. In terms of levels, this study also found significant gaps in labour productivity between Japan and the United States in wholesale and retail trade, transport and finance and insurance.

Table 5.1. **Labour productivity growth in the service sector by industry**
Within-industry contributions to labour productivity growth in percentage points per year

Industry	ISIC code	1990-99	1999-04	Change
Electricity and gas	40	0.08	0.06	−0.02
Wholesale and retail trade	50 to 52	0.42	0.02	−0.40
Hotels and restaurants	55	0.03	0.02	−0.01
Transport and storage	60 to 63	0.03	−0.02	−0.05
Post and telecommunications	64	0.17	0.15	−0.02
Financial intermediation	65 to 67	0.21	0.18	−0.03
Business services	71 to 74	0.34	0.29	−0.05
Education	80	0.17	0.14	−0.03
Health and social work	85	0.08	0.06	−0.02
Market services	40 to 74	1.55	0.76	−0.79
Non-market services	75 to 99	0.39	0.30	−0.09
Total services	40 to 99	1.94	1.06	−0.88
Total economy	1 to 99	2.41	1.46	−0.95

Source: EU KLEMS Database (2007).

Factors hindering the growth of the service sector

The manufacturing sector sustained productivity growth through the 1990s, as international competition drove increases in efficiency. The service sector, in contrast, has been relatively sheltered from both international and domestic competition, as reflected in the low level of import penetration and inflows of foreign direct investment in the service sector (see below), thus weakening competition and incentives to boost efficiency. The lack of competition in non-manufacturing is reflected in mark-ups that are three times higher than in manufacturing and relatively high compared to other OECD countries (Figure 5.2).

Figure 5.2. **Mark-ups in manufacturing and non-manufacturing**[1]

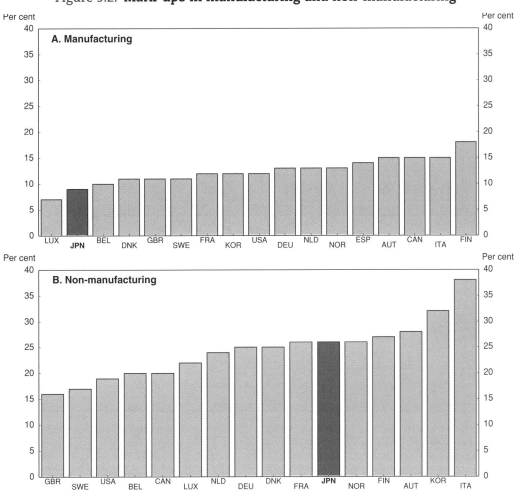

StatLink 🛢️ http://dx.doi.org/10.1787/278207510603

1. Mark-ups are calculated for individual two-digit ISIC sectors and aggregated over all sectors using country-specific final sales as weights.

Source: Hoj et al. (2007).

Market-unfriendly regulations in product markets have been found to disproportionately damage entrepreneurial initiative in services (Nicoletti, 2001). The OECD's indicator of product market competition in seven non-manufacturing industries in 2003 ranks Japan in the middle of member countries, and well below the top performers (Figure 5.3). This indicator compares regulations that affect competitive pressures, including barriers to entry, public ownership, market structure, vertical integration and price controls (Table 5.2). For the indicators of public ownership and market structure, Japan has a better score than the OECD average, while for entry barriers, Japan is close to the average. The main problem for competition is vertical integration, where Japan has the worst score among member countries.[5] Moreover, in all areas (except price controls), Japan lags behind the leading countries. In sum, the indicator approach suggests considerable scope to reform market-unfriendly regulations, a conclusion supported by other studies of the Japanese service sector (Ono, 2000). The potential gains from regulatory reform are significant, as illustrated in Panel B of Figure 5.3. Countries with less restrictive regulations

Figure 5.3. **Product market regulation and productivity growth**

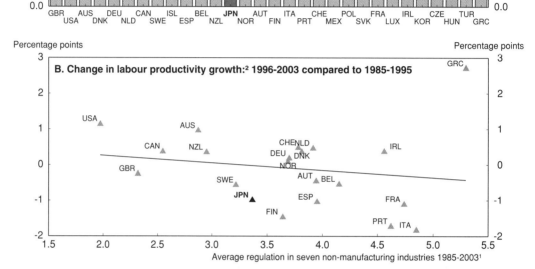

StatLink ⬛⬛⬛ http://dx.doi.org/10.1787/278213016646

1. The indicator ranges from 0 (least restrictive) to 6 (most restrictive). The seven non-manufacturing sectors are gas, electricity, air transport, railways road freight, post and telecom.
2. Percentage-point change in the annual average growth rate of labour productivity in the total economy between the periods 1985-1995 and 1996-2003.

Source: Conway *et al.* (2006a) and Conway *et al.* (2006b).

Table 5.2. **Product market regulations in the non-manufacturing sector in the OECD area**

In 2003[1]

	Entry barriers[2]	Public ownership[3]	Market structure[4]	Vertical integration[5]	Price controls[6]
Highest score	3.6	5.6	5.5	6.0	6.0
Average score	1.8	3.2	3.5	3.2	0.5
Lowest score	0.5	0.7	0.2	1.1	0.0
Japan's score	1.9	1.7	2.1	6.0	0.0

1. The indicators range from zero (least restrictive) to six (most restrictive). The seven non-manufacturing sectors are gas, electricity, air transport, railways, road freight, post and telecom.
2. Covers all seven non-manufacturing industries.
3. Covers all seven non-manufacturing industries except road freight.
4. Covers gas, railways and telecom.
5. Covers gas, electricity and railways.
6. Covers road freight.

Source: Conway *et al.* (2006a).

over the period 1985-2003 tended to have a greater acceleration of labour productivity growth over the period 1996-2003.

Within the regulatory framework, regulations that limit entrepreneurship tend to be especially harmful for productivity growth, particularly in sectors where firms are dynamic and better placed to adopt new technology. Entrepreneurship in Japan is discouraged by administrative burdens on start-ups, which are slightly above the OECD average (Conway *et al.*, 2005). According to a study by the World Bank, starting a business in Japan is relatively complicated, costly and time-consuming: Japan ranks 18th overall in the OECD (Table 5.3).[6] Indeed, Japan's weakness in entrepreneurship and new business creation has been a critical disadvantage to enhancing service sector productivity, according to some studies (Ono, 2000). In sum, reducing the administrative burdens on start-ups would strengthen competition by promoting entrepreneurship.

Table 5.3. **Time and cost of starting a new business**

Countries shown by their overall rank from least to most restrictive

	Rank in the world	Number of procedures	Time (days)	Cost (% of income per capita)	Minimum capital (% of income per capita)
Australia	(1)	2	2	0.8	0.0
Canada	(2)	2	3	0.9	0.0
New Zealand	(3)	2	12	0.1	0.0
United States	(4)	6	6	0.7	0.0
Ireland	(5)	4	13	0.3	0.0
United Kingdom	(6)	6	13	0.8	0.0
France	(12)	5	7	1.1	0.0
Iceland	(14)	5	5	2.7	14.1
Finland	(16)	3	14	1.0	7.7
Denmark	(18)	4	6	0.0	40.7
Belgium	(19)	3	4	5.3	20.1
Sweden	(22)	3	15	0.6	31.1
Norway	(28)	6	10	2.3	23.4
Switzerland	(35)	6	20	2.1	13.9
Portugal	(38)	7	7	3.4	34.7
Netherlands	(41)	6	10	6.0	52.9
Turkey	(43)	6	6	20.7	16.2
Japan	**(44)**	**8**	**23**	**7.5**	**0.0**
Italy	(65)	9	13	18.7	9.8
Hungary	(67)	6	16	17.7	65.1
Germany	(71)	9	18	5.7	42.8
Slovak Republic	(72)	9	25	4.2	34.1
Mexico	(75)	8	27	13.3	11.6
Austria	(83)	8	28	5.4	55.5
Czech Republic	(91)	10	17	10.6	34.9
Korea	(110)	10	17	16.9	296.0
Spain	(118)	10	47	15.1	13.7
Poland	(129)	10	31	21.2	196.8
Greece	(152)	15	38	23.3	104.1
Average		6.5	15.6	7.2	38.6

Source: World Bank (2007), *Doing Business 2008*.

Moreover, a number of studies have found that increased investment in ICT products results in a pick up in labour productivity growth (Nicoletti and Scarpetta, 2005). Such investment is particularly important for innovation in the service sector, as it enables firms to engage in process innovation through the value chain, develop new applications and raise productivity. In the United States, a large proportion of the acceleration in labour productivity achieved since the mid-1990s originated in services that use ICT intensively (Figure 5.4). In contrast, the contribution of ICT using services to labour productivity was relatively low in Japan and it has declined significantly since 1995. Moreover, as shown in Figure 5.1, the rate of labour productivity growth in ICT services, which includes both ICT using and ICT-producing services, has slowed markedly in recent years.

The small contribution to labour productivity from ICT-using services in Japan reflects, in part, the low level of investment. Indeed, investment in ICT accounted for only 14% of non-residential investment in Japan over the period 1995-2003, one of the lowest figures in

Figure 5.4. **The role of ICT-using services in labour productivity growth**

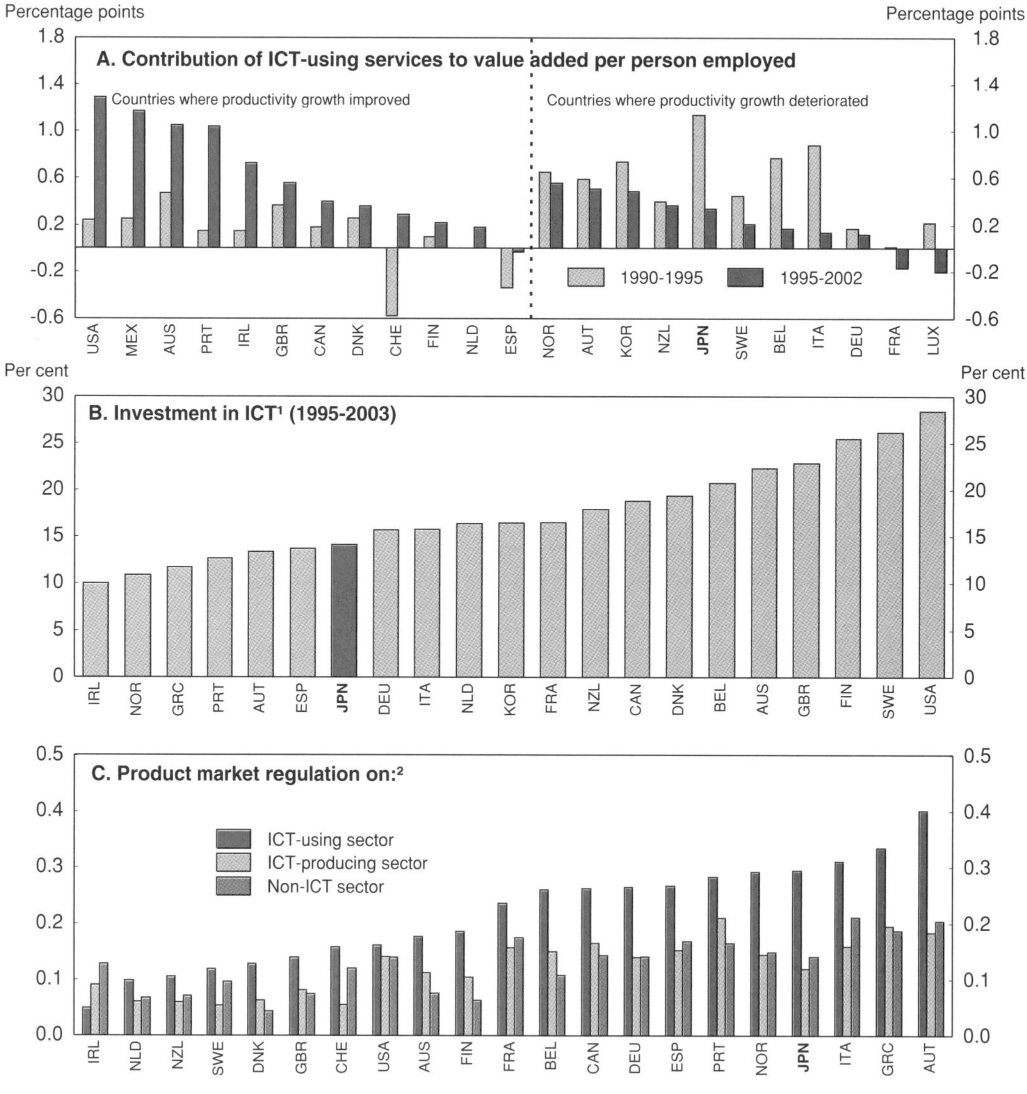

StatLink 🔗 http://dx.doi.org/10.1787/278258247386

1. As a share of non-residential investment.
2. In 2003. The indicators range from 0 (least restrictive) to 1 (most restrictive).

Source: OECD, Productivity Database and Conway et al. (2006b).

the OECD area (Figure 5.4, Panel B). Moreover, ICT services account for only 2% of R&D spending in Japan. The level of investment in ICT-using services is sensitive to the degree of regulation; countries with stringent regulation tend to have lower levels of investment (Conway *et al.*, 2006b). In Japan, product market regulation in ICT-using sectors was the fourth highest in the OECD in 2003 (Panel C), suggesting scope for liberalising restrictions and thereby promoting investment and labour productivity. Easing overall product market regulation to the level of the least restrictive OECD country would have boosted annual productivity growth by 0.7% in ICT-intensive sectors and 0.6% in other sectors over the period 1995 to 2003.[7] Such a gain would have significantly accelerated labour productivity growth from the 1.1% annual rate recorded over that period.

Another factor hindering the growth of the service sector is the legacy of an industrial policy that focused on exports and the manufacturing sector. The lower priority accorded to services reflected the perception that they are non-tradable and merely an appendage to manufacturing. The emphasis on manufacturing is also reflected in its dominant share of R&D spending, while the service sector accounted for only 12% of the total, compared to 43% in the United States and an OECD average of 25%. In addition to policies aimed at promoting manufacturing, excessive government assistance to small and medium-sized enterprises (SMEs) has dampened competitive pressure in the non-manufacturing sector, which accounts for 90% of SMEs. There are 14 special government programmes for SMEs, including tax breaks and subsidies, while the regulatory framework provides preferential treatment and entry barriers in the service sector. According to the OECD's product market regulation index, the level of restrictiveness in Japan in the sub-category "barriers to competition", which includes entry barriers and anti-trust exemptions, lagged behind top performers in the OECD in 2003.

Polices to promote higher productivity in the service sector

A number of studies show that relaxing the strictness of regulations, promoting competition and lowering barriers to trade and foreign direct investment (FDI) have increased the level and rate of growth of productivity by stimulating business investment and promoting innovation and technological catch-up (Nicoletti and Scarpetta, 2005). According to a study by the Japanese government, regulatory reform in the service sector had a particularly strong impact on productivity: a 10% decline in the index measuring the stringency of regulation in the non-manufacturing sector (see below) boosted total factor productivity (TFP) growth by 0.2 percentage point, an impact 1.4 times greater than a similar easing of regulations in all industries (Cabinet Office, 2006).

Recognising the importance of services for the overall performance of the Japanese economy, the government has introduced a number of policy initiatives. *First*, it has launched policies to accelerate the development of the service sector (Box 5.1). *Second*, it has taken steps to level the playing field by harmonising the tax treatment of the service sector with that of the manufacturing sector, including accelerated depreciation on facility investment and reduced acquisition taxes on real estate. The government has also encouraged M&As between manufacturing and service firms by granting the same preferential tax treatment given to M&As within sectors. *Third*, it has accelerated privatisation and the outsourcing of public services through the market testing initiative (see below). Given the diversity of service activities, this sector is affected by a wide range of government policies. This section will focus on the scope for further progress in the key priorities of regulatory reform, competition policy and international competition, which

Box 5.1. **Government initiatives to boost productivity in the service sector**

The "New Industry Development Strategy 2005" selected seven priority areas for development, including four service sectors; business services, software contents, health/welfare and environment/energy. The Ministry of Economy, Trade and Industry (METI) has drawn up detailed action plans for the priority areas. In July 2006, METI announced another programme to develop the service industry as part of a comprehensive initiative, entitled the "New Strategy for Economic Growth". This programme selected six priority areas for development; health/welfare, childcare, tourism, business services, software contents and distribution/logistics. The specific target was to increase their market size by 70 trillion yen (14% of GDP) by 2015, based on a detailed action plan, entitled "Toward Innovation and Productivity Improvement in Service Industries", that focuses on the following priorities:

● Adopting a scientific and engineering approach and utilising information technology.

● Building a framework to provide information to enhance consumer credibility.

● Improving quality assurance and measures to support recognition, while encouraging standardisation.

● Developing human resources.

● Facilitating entry into the service sector.

● Encouraging expansion into foreign markets.

● Revitalising regional economies through service industries.

● Improving the statistical infrastructure to evaluate the current situation.

These plans were followed by the "Program for Enhancing Growth Potential" presented by the Council on Economic and Fiscal Policy (CEFP) in 2007. Its goal is to boost productivity growth, as measured by value-added per worker, by 50% for all industries over five years. Achieving this objective requires raising the annual productivity growth rate in the service sector, which averaged 1.6% over the past decade, to 2.4% by 2011. The action plan includes:

● Fostering Japan's growth potential through the development of human capital, supporting job placement and raising the competitiveness of SMEs.

● Pursing service innovation through reform of the government-controlled service market, promoting innovation in IT and improving regional growth potential.

● Expanding the growth frontier by focusing on areas with high potential, reforming the university system and promoting the diversification of investment.

In addition, the "SME Productivity Improvement Project" was included in "Basic Policies 2007". This project aims at enhancing productivity of SMEs through IT utilisation, corporate revitalisation and the promotion of business start-ups. Major policy tools include providing financial support and R&D assistance and developing human resources.

However, government policies targeted at services raise some concerns. *First*, the action plans of the three initiatives (two by METI and one by the CEFP) contain many similarities. It is, therefore, important to ensure the integration of the plans and avoid any overlap, which would potentially undermine their effectiveness and encourage redundant spending. *Second*, additional government intervention to protect SMEs, on top of the broad array of programmes already in place, might further distort resource allocation. For example, the "SME fund" to promote investment in SMEs, which was included in the action plan "Toward Innovation and Productivity Improvement in Service Industries", and the financial support under the "SME Productivity Improvement Project", need to be reconsidered.

have an important impact on service sector productivity. Labour market flexibility, which is essential to facilitate adjustment in the service sector, is discussed in Chapter 6.[8]

Pursuing regulatory reform

Reforming the regulatory framework, including restrictions on entry and operations, is the key to promoting competition and investment. In addition to the policy measures specifically targeted at the service sector (Box 5.1), other reforms have been undertaken as part of Japan's policy of regulatory reform. According to the government, more than 6 000 regulatory reform measures have been implemented during the past decade. These measures helped to reduce the government's regulation index, which reflects the overall strength of regulations, from 100 for all industries in 1995 to 30 in 2005 (Figure 5.5).[9] The weighted averages by sector indicate a larger fall for the manufacturing sector, although the non-manufacturing sector has been catching up since 1999. However, as noted below, the impact of reforms on consumer surplus has been larger in non-manufacturing, reflecting its lower level of productivity and the greater stringency of regulation.

Figure 5.5. **Overall progress in regulatory reform in Japan**
1995=100

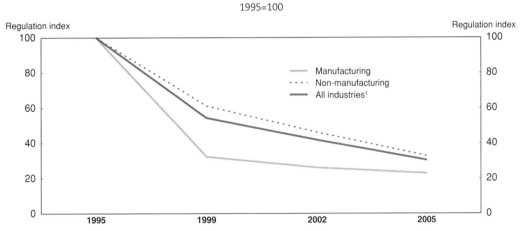

StatLink ⊞ᵍ⊒ http://dx.doi.org/10.1787/278273504076

1. The "All industries" index is a weighted sum of the manufacturing and non-manufacturing indices, based on value added.
Source: Cabinet Office (2006) and OECD calculations.

The total economic benefits of regulatory reform, measured by the increase in consumer surplus, are estimated at 17.6 trillion yen (3.5% of GDP) between 1995 and 2005 (Table 5.4). The largest benefits were achieved in service industries that have experienced significant deregulation since 2000, notably electricity, trucking and telecommunications. Each of these industries recorded large price declines and sharp increases in demand. For example, electricity prices fell by 39%, while consumption rose by 19%. The large consumer surplus gain in telecommunications is due to a twenty-fold increase in the use of mobile telephones accompanied by a 61% drop in the price.

Regulatory Reform Programme

Japan's regulatory reform policies have been presented annually since 2001 in the three-year Programmes for Regulatory Reform based on detailed reports and actions plans from the Council for the Promotion of Regulatory Reform. In June 2007, the Cabinet decided

Table 5.4. **Benefits of regulatory reform**

Gains in consumer surplus in trillion yen

	1995	1996	1997	1998	1999	2000	2001	2002	2003	2004	2005	Total
Electricity	0.2	0.7	0.1	0.6	0.0	0.3	0.1	0.6	0.2	1.0	1.8	5.7
Trucking	0.6	0.7	−0.1	0.3	0.8	0.4	0.4	−0.2	−0.1	0.2	0.2	3.1
Telecommunications	0.3	0.4	0.6	0.4	0.3	0.2	0.3	0.2	0.1	0.0	0.0	2.7
Petroleum products	0.6	0.6	0.3	0.3	0.3	−0.2	0.0	0.4	−0.1	−0.2	0.2	2.1
Car registration and inspection system	0.2	0.2	0.1	0.1	0.0	0.1	0.1	0.0	0.0	0.0	0.0	0.9
Rice	0.0	0.1	0.1	0.1	0.0	0.1	0.1	0.0	−0.3	0.1	0.3	0.6
Liquor sales	0.1	0.1	−0.1	0.1	0.1	0.1	0.0	0.2	−0.1	0.0	0.0	0.6
Railways	0.0	0.0	0.0	0.1	0.1	0.1	0.0	0.1	0.1	0.2	0.0	0.5
Consignment fee for stock transactions	0.0	0.0	0.1	0.0	0.1	0.2	0.0	0.0	0.0	0.0	0.0	0.5
Urban gas	0.0	0.0	0.0	0.0	0.0	0.1	0.0	0.1	0.0	0.1	0.1	0.5
Damage insurance	0.0	0.0	0.0	0.0	0.0	0.1	0.1	0.0	0.0	0.0	0.1	0.3
Cosmetics and pharmaceuticals	0.0	0.0	0.0	0.0	0.0	0.0	0.0	0.0	0.0	0.0	0.0	0.1
Domestic airlines	0.0	0.0	0.0	0.0	0.0	0.0	0.0	0.0	−0.1	−0.1	0.0	0.1
Taxis	0.0	0.0	0.0	0.0	0.0	0.0	0.0	0.0	0.0	0.0	0.0	0.0
Total	2.0	2.9	1.2	2.0	1.6	1.4	1.1	1.5	−0.2	1.3	2.7	17.6

Source: Cabinet Office (2006).

on a new Regulatory Reform Programme, focusing on 15 priority areas, including a number of services, such as education, IT, distribution and energy (Table 5.5). The new three-year programme calls for upgrading public administration, in part by improving the "Public Comment Procedure", the "No-Action Letter" scheme and "Regulatory Impact Analysis" (Box 5.2). Such a focus is appropriate, as some studies have found a significant correlation between the degree of burden imposed by administrative regulations[10] and the acceleration of catch-up in multi-factor productivity growth (Nicoletti and Scarpetta, 2003). Administrative regulations in the OECD area tend to be concentrated in certain non-manufacturing industries, such as public utilities, telecommunications, financial intermediation, business services and the retail sector. Indeed, the stringency of administrative regulations in Japan was higher than in the top performers in the OECD in 2003.

Special zones for structural reform

The programme for "Special Zones for Structural Reform" began in 2002; it marked the start of a fundamentally new approach in Japan, based on local initiatives to advance nationwide regulatory reform. The special zone approach allows geographically limited areas to act as a testing ground for reforms that can be later introduced at the national level, while helping to revitalise regional economies through deregulation. All interested parties, such as local governments, private firms and citizens, are allowed to submit regulatory reform proposals, which are then reviewed by a committee of cabinet ministers chaired by the prime minister ("the Headquarters for the Promotion of Special Zones"). As of the end of 2006, 581 reform measures had been accepted, of which 211 were implemented in 963 special zones and 370 introduced on a nationwide basis (Table 5.6). Proposals implemented in special zones are reviewed, after one year or so, by an Evaluation Committee composed of experts from the private sector, including academia. This Committee assesses whether specific regulatory reforms should be: i) implemented

Box 5.2. **Regulatory reform in public administration**

The transparency of administrative measures is essential to establishing a stable and accessible regulatory environment that promotes competition. However, the opacity and unpredictability of public administration has been cited as one of the major obstacles to doing business in Japan. For example, Keidanren (representing the Japanese corporate sector), the European Union and the United States have voiced concerns about the continued prevalence of administrative guidance, both written and oral, and about the absence of efficient reviews of administrative decisions (OECD, 2004b). In light of these concerns, the 2007 Council for the Promotion of Regulatory Reform chose "evaluating and improving government regulations, including ministerial decree orders, administrative notification and guidelines" as one of its priority areas in 2007. In addition, several tools to increase the transparency and predictability of public administration have undergone major changes to make them more effective.

First, the "Public Comment Procedure" introduced in 1999 requires central government entities to give advance public notice of proposed regulations in order to provide opportunities for public comment and to take those comments into account in preparing the final regulations. The system was strengthened in 2006 by incorporating it into the Administrative Procedure Act, expanding its coverage* and establishing a standardised minimum comment period of 30 days. However, further steps are needed to make the public comment procedure an integral part of the regulatory process. In particular, it is important to strictly enforce the minimum comment period, given that about one-half of public comment periods before FY 2005 fell short of 30 days. In addition, the public should be able to comment on draft laws in their entirety rather than on excerpts or summaries. The coverage of the public comment procedure, which is applied on a discretionary basis to internal orders, communication notes, administrative guidance and negotiations for international agreements, needs to be expanded further.

Second, the "No-Action Letter" system allows a business entity with concerns about the interpretation of regulations, or about whether its proposed business plan would require a license or official approval, to seek advance clarification from the regulator. This system was introduced in 2001 in response to the lack of transparency and predictability in the implementation and enforcement of regulations. However, there were only 11 no-action letters as of FY 2006. The government made several reforms in FY 2004 and FY 2007 to encourage more active use of the system, such as expanding its coverage and enhancing the confidentiality of both the requests and the responses. To further improve the system, the government should strengthen the role of no-action letters by incorporating their use into the Administrative Procedure Act, thus making them legally binding on the issuing administrative body, while also making the letter public to create an easily accessible data base of no-action letters. Moreover, its scope should be expanded to include local government regulations. In addition, the limit on who is eligible to use the system needs to be relaxed further.

Third, Regulatory Impact Analysis (RIA) was introduced in 2004 on a trial basis to carry out objective assessments of the impact of regulatory measures. In 2007, RIAs were made mandatory for all regulations incorporated in laws and cabinet orders. The RIAs need to become an integral part of the regulation-making process by closely monitoring whether regulations actually reflect the outcome of the relevant RIAs, making public the results of RIAs and extending its coverage whenever possible.

---

* However, a number of activities, including advisory council reports and recommendations and the development of bills that are to be considered by the Diet, are excluded.

Table 5.5. **The three-year Regulatory Reform Programme in 2007**

Priority areas	Major issues
1. Improving the horizontal regulatory framework	Improving public administration, including ministerial orders and administrative guidelines
	Encouraging the effective use of the Regulatory Impact Analysis and No-Action Letter schemes
2. Improving public services	Upgrading the operation of independent public corporations
3. Education and research	Expanding choice for schools and establishing a performance evaluation system for teaching staff and schools
4. Information technology, energy and transport	Reforming the governance structure of NHK and softening the principle of prohibiting concentration in the media
	In electricity, pursuing accounting separation and encouraging transactions in the Wholesale Power Exchange
	Liberalising international air traffic and expanding capacity in the Tokyo metropolitan area by allowing international flights at Haneda
5. Housing and land	Creating highly efficient cities
	Realising a safe and secure living environment
6. Welfare, childcare and long-term care	Creating a childcare environment that responds well to the needs of families and facilitating the use of childcare leave
	Actively implementing the law for "Supporting measures to promote the nurturing of the next generation"
7. Medical	Allowing on-line applications for the receipt of medical services
	Facilitating the use of generic medicines
	Encouraging greater co-operation between doctors and medical assistants, such as nurses and medical technicians
8. Living environment and distribution	Improving the regulation of wastes to promote recycling
9. International co-operation	Improving procedures for exports and imports through ports
	Strengthening the monitoring of foreigners after their entry in Japan
10. Standardisation, law and certificates	Reforming commercial and civil laws governing interest rates
	Strengthening the disclosure of information to increase the quality of professional service providers
11. Competition policy and finance	Reviewing the firewall regulation between banking and securities
	Reforming the framework for co-operative financial institutions
12. Agriculture, fishery and forest	Reviewing the agricultural land system
	Supporting the system of providing nutrition information in fish products
	Improving the system for indicating the type of rice
13. Revitalising regional economies	Promoting voluntary transport service by non-profit organisations
	Supporting the location of companies in regional areas
	Allowing outdoor advertisement to support firms in regional areas
14. Labour	Reforming the regulation on dispatched workers
15. Employment and hiring	Relaxing the eligibility requirement on the academic background needed to be licensed as a hairdresser
	Reviewing raising the age ceiling for the exam to become central government officials

Source: Council for the Promotion of Regulatory Reform.

nationwide; ii) continued in the special zone only; or iii) discontinued. Of the 83 special zone reforms considered by the Committee, 69 were expanded nationwide. An additional 51 special zone reforms were approved for nationwide use by the responsible ministry. The extension of 120 measures initially accepted for special zones to nationwide use has reduced the number of special zones to around 400.

The special zones are intended to play a strong role in reforming key industries, such as healthcare and education as well as distribution, research and development and agriculture, where the progress in implementing regulatory reforms is slowed by special interests. Indeed, most special zones are related to areas covered by the Ministry of Health, Labour and Welfare, reflecting a growing demand for higher quality social services, followed by METI and the Ministry of Land, Infrastructure and Transport (Table 5.6, Panel B). In 2007, the special zone initiative was extended through 2012, with new incentives added to encourage local governments to participate more actively. For

Table 5.6. **The special zone initiative**

A. Reforms proposed and implemented

	Total number of proposals	Total number of reforms implemented	Of which: those implemented in special zones	Of which: those implemented nationwide
2002	426	204	93	111
2003	1 269	222	83	139
2004	642	80	18	62
2005	539	41	12	29
2006	643	34	5	29
Total	3 519	581	211	370

B. Special zones by the responsible ministry (2002-2006)

Ministry or agency	Accepted in special zones	Accepted nationwide	Total
National Public Safety Commission	4	4	8
National Personnel Authority	3	0	3
Financial Services Agency	2	11	13
Ministry of Internal Affairs and Communications	13	44	57
Ministry of Justice	15	20	35
Ministry of Foreign Affairs	2	10	12
Ministry of Finance	7	19	26
Ministry of Education, Culture, Sports, Science and Technology	36	36	72
Ministry of Health, Labour and Welfare	35	92	127
Ministry of Agriculture, Forestry and Fisheries	10	20	30
Ministry of Economy, Trade and Industry	54	48	102
Ministry of Land, Infrastructure and Transport	20	56	76
Ministry of the Environment	9	8	17
Cabinet Office	1	1	2
Ministry of Defence	0	1	1
Total	211	370	581

Source: Office for the Promotion of Special Zones for Structural Reform.

example, local governments will retain exclusive use of the special zone reforms for a longer time period before they are extended nationwide.

The success of this programme depends on the creativity and knowledge of local authorities and private entities in identifying and removing obstacles to growth and circumventing vested interests that have blocked reforms at the national level. Despite the government's continued commitment to developing special zones, momentum is slowing; the number of proposals fell from 1 269 in 2003 to 643 in 2006, while the number of reform proposals accepted declined from 222 to 34 over the same period. To some extent, the decrease was inevitable as easier reforms were implemented first. However, it is also due to diminishing interest by local governments and private participants. One reason is that reforms may not go far enough to make them attractive. For example, although the management of hospitals by for-profit corporations was allowed in the special zones in 2004, only one for-profit hospital has been opened thus far, partly due to remaining regulations, such as the rule limiting their services to non-insured treatments.

Perhaps a more important drawback from the perspective of local governments is the focus of the special zone plan on nationwide reform. Not surprisingly, local governments prefer that reforms be limited to special zones for an extended period of time, as expanding the coverage of the measures nationwide diminishes their impact on the local economy. The recent decision to allow local governments to retain special measures for a longer period of time is intended to encourage them to submit more special zone proposals. However, if the fundamental goal is to advance nationwide regulatory reform, measures accepted in special zones should be implemented nationwide as quickly as possible. To accomplish that goal, a maximum time period for reforms in special zones should be set in order to limit any distortions stemming from the uneven application of regulations across the country. In sum, the special zone initiative should place more emphasis on improving the nationwide regulatory framework rather than on promoting regional development. This orientation would be facilitated by changing the organisational structure, under which the same chief secretary is responsible for both the special zones and regional development policies. Moreover, organisational links between the special zone initiative and the Regulatory Reform Programme should be strengthened. Finally, it is important that the establishment and evaluation of special zones be carried out in a transparent manner.

Upgrading competition policy

In recent years, the Japan Fair Trade Commission (JFTC) has increased its efforts to combat anti-competitive practices that stem in part from the legacy of government guidance of investment and industry-wide co-ordination that was permitted by numerous exemptions from the Antimonopoly Act (AMA). The JFTC's role was further enhanced by the 2005 revision of the AMA, which strengthened its enforcement power and increased the penalties for anticompetitive activities.[11] *First*, the surcharge rate on large manufacturing enterprises was increased from 6% to 10% of firms' sales of the affected product for up to three years for violations such as price fixing and output restrictions.[12] The surcharge rate for large enterprises in retail and wholesale industries also increased from 2% to 3% and from 1% to 2%, respectively. *Second*, the JFTC was granted stronger criminal investigative power – compulsory search and seizure based on a warrant issued by a judge – which should improve its capacity to investigate cases that may call for criminal penalties. Previously, search and seizure to obtain evidence was only possible with the consent of the firm being investigated or by referring the case to the prosecutor. *Third*, a leniency programme was introduced in 2006. For firms confessing before the start of a JFTC investigation, it provides 100% immunity from surcharges for the first applicant in addition to immunity from criminal accusation, a 50% reduction for the second applicant, and 30% for the third applicant. Once the investigation is launched, a 30% reduction is granted. In both cases, the maximum number of firms eligible for leniency is three. Since the introduction of the leniency programme, there have been 105 applicants as of the end of FY 2006, primarily in cases of cartels and bid-rigging in the construction industry. *Fourth*, the "recommendation system" was abolished to facilitate administrative measures. In proceedings for cease and desist orders, respondents are now provided an opportunity to be heard before the introduction of administrative measures. Finally, the 2005 revision of the AMA required the government to examine the surcharge system and the procedure for cease and desist orders and take measures to improve them within two years.

The revision of the AMA resulted in stronger actions against violations of the competition law (Table 5.7). The total amount of surcharges jumped from 3.9 billion yen in FY 2003 to 18.9 billion yen in FY 2005, despite a slight decline in the number of cases to 20 (Panel C). The JFTC has been engaged in a strong effort against bid-rigging, which accounted for six of 13 legal measures in FY 2006. In addition, four criminal cases have been filed by the JFTC since the 2005 revision, compared to just one between FY 2000 and

Table 5.7. **JFTC enforcement activity**

Fiscal year	2000	2001	2002	2003	2004	2005	2006
A. Cases resolved	71	79	103	114	104	75	98
Legal measures	18	38	37	25	35	19	13
Recommendations or cease and desist orders	18	37	37	25	35	19	12
Surcharge payment orders[1]	0	1	0	0	0	0	1
Others	53	41	66	88	69	54	83
Warnings	17	15	17	13	9	7	9
Cautions	36	26	49	75	60	47	74
Criminal accusations	0	0	0	1	0	2	2
B. Cases in which legal measures were taken	18	38	37	25	35	19	13
Private monopolisation	0	0	0	1	2	0	0
Cartels	12	36	33	17	24	17	9
Price cartels	1	3	2	3	2	4	3
Bid-rigging	10	33	30	14	22	13	6
Other types of cartels	1	0	1	0	0	0	0
Unfair trading practices[2]	6	2	3	7	8	2	4
Others	0	0	1	0	1	0	0
C. Surcharge payment orders							
Number of cases	16	15	37	24	26	20	13
Surcharge amount (billion yen)	8.5	2.2	4.3	3.9	11.2	18.9	9.3
D. Cases newly initiated	69	90	111	121	101	88	141
E. Hearings initiated	8	44	30	77	27	19	16

1. Cases in which surcharge payment orders were given without a recommendation or cease and desist order.
2. Includes mainly resale price restrictions, other restrictive exclusionary dealings and abuse of dominant bargaining power.
Source: Japan Fair Trade Commission.

FY 2004. The increased enforcement activity partly reflects the enhanced resources available for enforcing competition policy. Indeed, the JFTC's budget grew 6.6% between FY 2004 and FY 2006 in a context of falling government spending in nominal terms, while the number of staff increased from 672 to 737, reflecting a commitment to strengthen competition policy.

However, there is still a need to strengthen the legal framework and enforcement of competition policy in Japan. Indeed, Japan ranked only 21st in terms of both the legal framework and enforcement in 2003 according to the OECD indicator (Hoj, 2007). In particular, legal measures by the JFTC in response to M&As have been rare, with only one merger formally rejected in more than 35 years. Moreover, the JFTC has taken no legal actions regarding M&As since 2000, even though nearly 100 mergers per year were reported to the JFTC during the period 2003-05.[13]

A number of measures are needed to strengthen the legal framework and enforcement of competition policy. *First*, the deterrent effect of surcharges and criminal penalties is still inadequate and they need to be raised further. According to estimates by the JFTC, the average rate of illegal profits from cartels was 16.5% of sales and, in 90% of the cases, it was 8% or more.[14] International comparisons also suggest that the surcharge rate in Japan is still low.[15] Furthermore, limiting the maximum period of turnover used in calculating surcharges to three years significantly restricts the deterrent effect. Instead, surcharges should be applied to sales during the full period during which violations occurred. In addition, criminal penalties should be increased and applied more frequently in order to strengthen the deterrence effect. Indeed, there has been no case in which a representative of a firm guilty of violating the AMA was subject to criminal punishment.[16] The highest possible fine, 500 million yen ($5 million), is substantially lower than fines imposed in many other major jurisdictions (OECD, 2004b). Unfair trade practices are subject to only cease and desist orders.[17] Given the prevalence of unfair trade practices in the retail sector, the JFTC issued orders to prohibit certain practices by large-scale retailers (see below). In addition, "private monopoly of exclusionary type"[18] is also subject to only cease and desist orders. The JFTC has proposed that this practice should be subject to surcharges. Strengthened sanctions would also make the leniency programme an even more effective tool. At the same time, increasing the number of firms allowed to benefit from the leniency programmes from the current number of three per violation of the AMA may facilitate its use.

Second, reducing explicit exemptions from the AMA that are aimed at achieving other policy goals is a prerequisite for the active enforcement of competition policy. Although the number of exemptions has been reduced from 89 in 1996 to 21, the exemptions cover a wide range of areas such as insurance, the liquor business, hair cutting, agricultural co-operatives, air transport (international and domestic) and maritime transport. These exemptions are contained in 15 laws, including the AMA. For example, SMEs in personal services, such as hair cutting, benefit from an exemption that permits agreements to prevent "excess competition" and similar agreements are allowed in the liquor business. In particular, the lower sanctions imposed on SMEs for anti-competitive behaviour should be lifted unless there is a clear rationale. For example, SMEs are subject to less than half of the surcharge rate imposed on large firms.[19] In addition, the AMA explicitly allows SMEs to form cartels aimed at providing mutual aid for their members. Consequently, measures to enforce the competition law against SME co-operatives have been very rare. Although co-ordination among smaller firms could in theory improve efficiency, such exemptions may reduce competitive pressures.

Third, the role of trade associations should be limited to norm setting, information sharing and provision of administrative information. Japan has a large number of such associations.[20] When the activities of the trade associations interfere with the operation of firms, there is a risk that they will curb competitive forces. For example, the Japanese Habour Transport Association significantly influences the business operations of firms in this sector (see below).

Fourth, it is important to ensure the neutrality and independence of hearing procedures for firms appealing cease and desist orders or surcharge payment orders. Such hearings are presided by the JFTC commissioners or by independent hearing examiners.[21] Relying more on hearing examiners would help ensure fairness and build confidence in the JFTC. In this regard, the JFTC should look to the private sector to recruit more hearing examiners with necessary expertise and experience. Moreover, the full hearing process, which can take two years or more, needs to be resolved more quickly, especially for time sensitive matters.

Strengthening international competition

The globalisation of services has been driven by technological advances such as the development of broadband networks and the growing scope for digitalisation, supported by regulatory reform and trade liberalisation. Indeed, the proportion of jobs in the service sector that can be outsourced was estimated to be as high as 20% in OECD countries in 2003 (OECD, 2005a). However, competitive pressure from international trade and FDI in the service sector is surprisingly weak in Japan. Its trade in services remains under-developed compared to other OECD countries; Japan had the lowest import penetration rate for services in 2003 (Figure 5.6)[22] and the lowest growth rate of service imports between 1997 and 2005. Consequently, trade in services as a share of GDP is relatively low in Japan (Panel B). Regarding inward FDI, the share of foreign affiliates in total service turnover in Japan was also the lowest among countries surveyed (Panel C), reflecting a low level of FDI in services. In wholesale and retail trade, an area of low productivity growth in Japan, the share of turnover of foreign affiliates in Japan was the lowest in the OECD area (see below). Moreover, the share of service turnover in the total turnover of foreign affiliates is the lowest in the OECD at 40% (Panel D). In most OECD countries, in contrast, services account for more than half of the total turnover of foreign affiliates. As a result, the turnover generated by Japan's outward investment in the service sector was nine times higher than that from its inward investment, the largest difference in the OECD area (OECD, 2005b).

Figure 5.6. **International competition in the service sector**

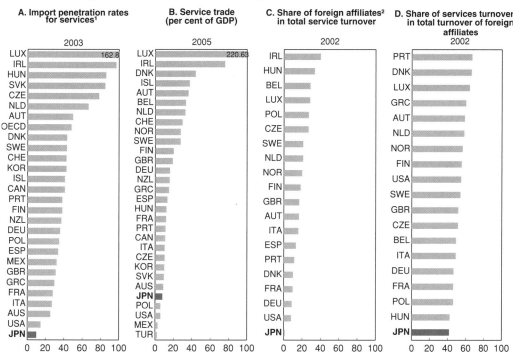

StatLink http://dx.doi.org/10.1787/278283673847

1. As a per cent of domestic demand.
2. Majority-owned affiliates under foreign control.

Source: OECD (2005b), *Economic Globalisation Indicators*, OECD, Paris, and *Service Trade Database*, 2007.

Given the low presence of foreign affiliates in services, the scope for increasing FDI in Japan's service sector appears large. The limited number of foreign affiliates in Japan's service sector have reported a stronger performance than domestic firms: their labour productivity was 1.8 times higher than the national average during the period 1997 to 2000 (Figure 5.7),[23] and they accounted for a third of total productivity growth between 1995 and 2001 (Panel B). However, the absolute size of the contribution was small, reflecting the limited role of foreign affiliates. Increasing the presence of foreign affiliates to a level in line with the OECD average would thus have a significant impact on overall productivity, given the large gap in productivity between domestic and foreign-affiliated firms.

Figure 5.7. **Contribution of foreign affiliates in the service sector in OECD countries**

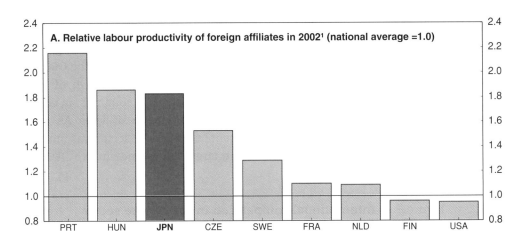

A. Relative labour productivity of foreign affiliates in 2002[1] (national average =1.0)

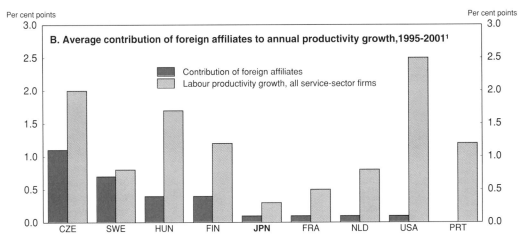

B. Average contribution of foreign affiliates to annual productivity growth, 1995-2001[1]

Contribution of foreign affiliates
Labour productivity growth, all service-sector firms

StatLink ⬛⬛ http://dx.doi.org/10.1787/278307762540

1. See the source for exact years.
Source: OECD (2005b), Economic Globalisation Indicators, OECD, Paris.

The low penetration of foreign affiliates reflects explicit FDI restrictions and product market regulations. Explicit restrictions are higher than the OECD average in telecom (due to regulations on fixed lines) and transport (due to regulations on air travel), according to the OECD's indicator of FDI regulatory restrictiveness (Golub and Koyama, 2006). According to another index measuring the degree of protection from inward FDI in the service sector, Japan was found to be the most protective among OECD countries (Francois et al., 2007). As for product market regulations, they tend to have a larger negative impact on foreign players, who are not familiar with the regulatory environment in Japan. Given the small presence of foreign affiliates in the service sector and the large potential contribution to labour productivity, Japan should further open up its services market to global competition through trade liberalisation, including unilateral measures and both multilateral and bilateral agreements, and encourage FDI in the service sector by lifting explicit restrictions and relaxing product market regulations. It is important that trade liberalisation in services and regulatory reform go hand in hand. Trade liberalisation alone could increase international market concentration, while lowering entry barriers through regulatory reform would tend to reduce such concentration. In trade agreements, harmonisation or mutual recognition of licences, standards and qualification requirements would substantially enhance market integration by significantly reducing trade costs. Indeed, trade costs as a percentage of delivered service prices in Japan were estimated at 14.4%, one of the highest in the OECD area (Francois *et al.*, 2007). Moreover, a country's rating on the indicator "communication and simplification of rules and procedures" was found to have a significant impact on trade. Countries with a poor rating on this index had reduced exports and imports of services, as well as low levels of inward FDI in services and outward FDI in business services. Therefore, enforceable horizontal rules on transparency are likely to help stimulate trade and FDI in services (OECD, 2007a).

Selected issues at the sectoral level

This section focuses on specific regulatory issues in major service industries that are characterised by either low productivity or high growth potential. Retail and transport are industries with low productivity while public services and business services are increasingly important in the context of population ageing and globalisation.

Retail distribution

Labour productivity growth in the retail sector in Japan has been one of the lowest in the OECD since 1990 due to a lack of competition stemming from regulations, especially on large stores, weak application of the competition law and the prevalence of unfair trade practices, notably vertical restraints.[24] The retail sector is characterised by an exceptionally large number of small stores and a corresponding lack of large stores. Indeed, Japan had 100 stores per 10 000 inhabitants compared to 43 in the United Kingdom and an average of 73 in the European Union (Table 5.8). Food supermarkets averaged 832 m^2 in area in 1999, roughly a fifth the size of the typical supermarket in the United States (Flath, 2002). In other OECD countries with more than 100 stores per 10 000 inhabitants, the average number of employees per store was about half that in Japan, suggesting a low level of labour productivity in Japan. The large number of small stores in Japan is partially explained by a relatively low rate of car ownership in the past and small houses, which favour shopping in local stores despite higher prices. However, it also reflects the legacy of the "Large-scale Retail Store Law", which strictly controlled the establishment of stores in an effort to balance supply and demand.[25] In practice, this law gave considerable power to existing retailers in setting the conditions under which large stores could be opened.

The Large-scale Retail Store Law was replaced in 2000 by the "Large-scale Retail Store Location Law" (LSRSL), which is aimed at protecting the local living environment. Consequently, it shifts the responsibility for regulating large stores from the central government to the municipalities, while expanding the coverage of the law by lowering the threshold to stores of more than 1 000 m^2. In addition, the objective of balancing supply and demand was eliminated. Under the new law, a firm that wishes to open a large store begins by notifying the local government and holding a public hearing to explain its plans. The local government reviews the plan and considers the comments of local residents and interest groups from the viewpoint of whether the new store would have an adverse effect on the local living environment. The process usually lasts about four to eight months if the local government is satisfied with the plan. Otherwise, it makes a "presentation of views"[26] and the company proposing the new store is required to submit a "voluntary co-ordination

Table 5.8. **Key structural features of the retail distribution sector**

2002-03

	Outlet density[1]	Employees per store
Austria	52	7.5
Belgium	74	4.0
Czech Republic	137	3.0
Denmark	45	8.4
Finland	44	5.7
France	70	4.1
Germany	30	9.9
Hungary	114	3.0
Ireland	47	8.7
Italy	124	2.5
Luxembourg	60	6.6
Netherlands	49	8.9
Norway	65	6.3
Poland	113	3.0
Portugal	138	2.6
Slovak Republic	9	15.0
Spain	125	3.1
Sweden	64	4.5
United Kingdom	43	15.4
European Union	73	4.4
Japan	**100**	**6.1**

1. Number of stores per 10 000 inhabitants.
Source: Ministry of Economics, Trade and Industry, *Census of Commerce* and OECD (2007b).

plan" taking into account those views. Since the law came into effect, there have been about 4 000 filings, with a "presentation of views" by the local government in 448 cases. In this situation, the process can take up to one year and the firms must delay construction until they have complied with the views of the local government. If the local government finds that its views are not fully reflected in the co-ordination plan submitted by the firm, it publicly issues "recommendations" to pressure the firm to conform to the local government's wishes. However, this has occurred only once so far. The fact that there has been only one case of public "recommendations" out of 4 000 filings suggests that it is practically impossible to open a store without fully complying with the views of local governments.

A key concern is the uncertainty and opacity of the procedure for opening large stores. The requirement to protect the local living environment is a vague and subjective standard for judging applications, which *de facto* relies on the discretionary decisions of local governments. Large store applicants thus still face a high degree of uncertainty. For example, some local authorities have imposed vague and subjective conditions, notably on the issue of parking space and traffic noise, which differ from the minimum requirements set by the central government.[27] Such uncertainty puts foreign retailers in a disadvantageous position relative to domestic firms, as they are new to the market and have less experience and fewer contacts at the local level. This helps to explain the 1% share of foreign affiliates in total turnover in wholesale and retail trade, an extremely low level compared to other OECD countries (Figure 5.8).

Another concern is regulations on construction, such as the building permit system and environmental impact assessments in major cities, which overlap with the LSRSL in controlling the establishment of large stores. The lack of co-ordination and the overlap

Figure 5.8. **Turnover of foreign affiliates as a share of wholesale and retail trade**
ISIC 50 to 52 in 2002[1]

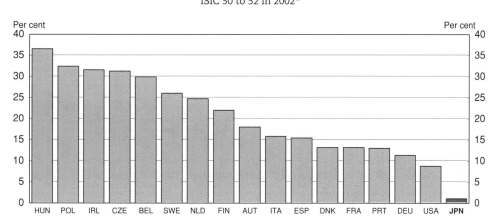

StatLink http://dx.doi.org/10.1787/278312537318

1. 2001 for Austria, Finland, France, Germany, Italy, Japan, the Netherlands and Portugal; 2000 for Sweden and 1999 for Denmark.

Source: OECD (2005b), *Economic Globalisation Indicators*, OECD, Paris.

among these regulations further complicates the application procedure for opening large stores. For example, the objective of environmental impact assessments is to "maintain the local living environment", the same objective as the LSRSL. Furthermore, in 2006, the City Planning Law was revised to introduce stricter zoning regulations on facilities larger than 10 000 m[2], including stores, in order to limit suburbanisation and revitalise central urban areas. Under the revised law, developers of large facilities must go through several procedures that involve the local authorities, shops and residents in the initial planning process. The strengthened City Planning Law thus has the potential to act as an entry barrier to large-scale stores, distorting competition and offering considerable advantages and rents to established retailers.

The regulations on large stores appear to have become more binding in recent years, as the proportion of sales by department stores and general merchandise stores subject to the LSRSL (or its predecessor) fell from 21% of total sales in 1997 to 16% in 2004. Moreover, their share of the total number of shops also declined from 13.1% to 11.7% over the same period, although this partly reflects the popularity of convenience stores in recent years. The small number of large-scale outlets has been identified as a key factor behind the low level of productivity in the retail sector (Aoki *et al.*, 2000). Research shows that regulations to protect small shops from competition from large-scale outlets tend to increase incumbents' market power and price margins, pushing up retail prices. At the same time, such regulations fail to maintain employment, while discouraging investment and modernisation (Bertrand and Kramarz, 2002 and McGuckin *et al.*, 2005). According to another study, easing restrictions on outlet size, opening hours and product selection increases both overall sales and employment (Nicolletti and Scarpetta, 2003). The OECD's product market regulatory indicators in retail distribution show that the degree of restrictiveness in Japan fell significantly from 1998, when it was the highest among member countries, to the OECD average in 2003, reflecting the repeal of the "Large-scale Retail Store Law" (Figure 5.9). However, Japan still lags behind the top performers, leaving scope for further liberalisation, particularly in the sub-category of "price control". Moreover, the lack of transparency concerning the application of the LSRSL and the

Figure 5.9. **OECD indicators of regulation in retail distribution**[1]

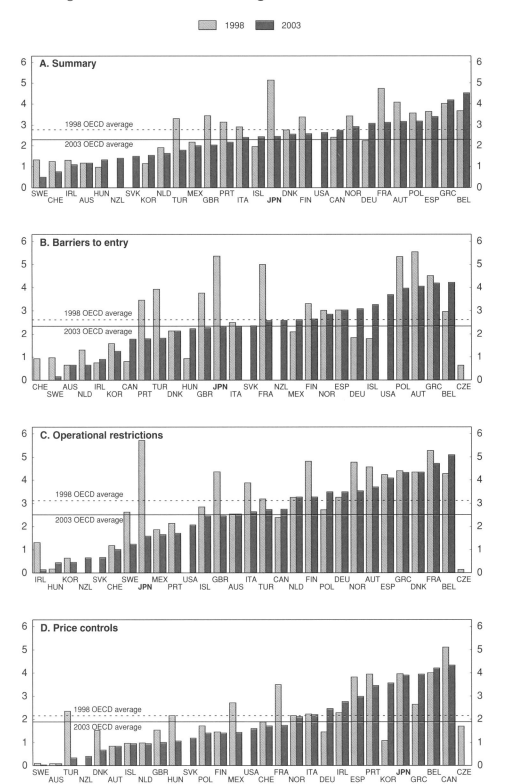

StatLink ⟶ http://dx.doi.org/10.1787/278318135473

1. The indicators range from 0 (least restrictive) to 6 (most restrictive). OECD is a simple average.

Source: Conway et al. (2006a).

subjective nature of the criteria used by local governments in the review process are not fully reflected in the product market indicator, which therefore does not fully capture the actual degree of restrictiveness. Improving productivity of the retail sector requires a relaxation of large-store regulation, more transparency in its application and strong enforcement of the competition law by the JFTC.

The energy sector: electricity and gas

Electricity is generated primarily by ten private "General Electricity Utilities" (GEUs) that have integrated generation, transmission, distribution and retail supply and enjoy near monopoly status within their respective regions.[28] The generation of electricity by the GEUs is supplemented by two wholesale electricity utilities and numerous in-house power producers, such as steel makers and chemical companies. The high electricity price in Japan relative to other OECD countries at the end of the last decade (Figure 5.10) was a major impetus driving deregulation to strengthen competitive pressures.

Figure 5.10. **Trends in electricity prices in major OECD countries**[1]

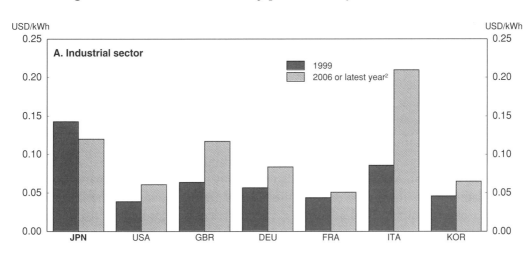

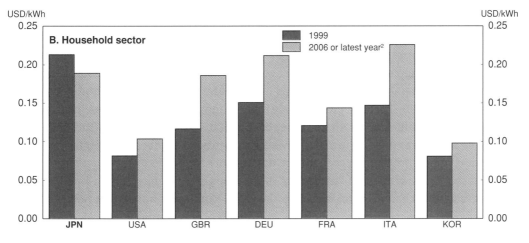

StatLink http://dx.doi.org/10.1787/278088100474

1. Including taxes, except for the United States.
2. 2005 for Japan and Germany.

Source: OECD/IEA, Energy Prices and Taxes, 1Q2007, OECD, Paris.

The 2000 revision of the Electricity Utilities Law allowed free supplier choice for large customers using more than 2 000 kW, resulting in the liberalisation of a quarter of the retail market. The threshold was further cut to 500 kW in 2004 and 50 kW in 2005, increasing consumer choice to 63% of the retail market. Prices in the liberalised market can be freely negotiated between consumers and suppliers. A proposal for full liberalisation, covering all customers including households, is now under consideration. The 2000 reform also allows new entrants – "Power Producer and Suppliers" (PPS) – in the liberalised sector following notification of METI. Third-party access (TPA) to transmission networks was opened to all suppliers, with the tariffs set by the owners of the transmission network in accordance with the ministerial ordinance of METI. In addition, the "pancaking" system[29] was abolished in 2005 to promote inter-regional sales of electricity. A neutral organisation, the Electric Power System Council of Japan (ESCJ), which includes incumbent market players and new entrants, was established to handle electricity transmission and distribution issues. Moreover, the Wholesale Power Exchange for trading excess electricity was established in 2005, thus reducing the reliance of new entrants on bilateral contracts for supply. Finally, one of the two wholesale electric utilities was privatised in 2003.

Reform in the electricity market has been significant. Japan's regulation index in this sector fell by 72% between 1995 and 2005 (Figure 5.11, Panel A), while the OECD measure (Panel B) also showed improvement. The impact of liberalisation was significant, reducing the price of electricity by 16% in the industrial sector and 11% in the household sector between 1999 and 2005, in contrast to rising prices in other major countries (Figure 5.10).[30] As noted above (Table 5.4), electricity showed the largest increase in consumer surplus of any sector in Japan, with a gain of 5.7 trillion yen between 1995 and 2005.

While liberalisation has narrowed the gap with other OECD countries, the electricity price (excluding taxes) in Japan was the fourth highest for both the industrial and household sectors in 2006 (Figure 5.12). High electricity prices in Japan are partially a result of the capital costs for generation and the costs of transmission, distribution and fuel, particularly for natural gas. In addition, electricity prices are boosted by high land costs, the remote location of nuclear power stations,[31] Japan's mountainous terrain, high technical standards for equipment and strict safety regulations on construction and maintenance to withstand earthquakes and typhoons.

While special factors partially explain high electricity prices, additional reform is needed to reduce prices toward the OECD average. The OECD's indicator of product market regulation ranked Japan below the OECD average in 1995 and above it in 2003, suggesting that the pace of liberalisation in Japan has lagged behind that in other member countries (Figure 5.11, Panel B). The key problem is weak competition, which makes it difficult for new entrants to gain market share. Indeed, the share of new entrants (the PPS) in the liberalised sector was only 2% in 2006.[32] Weak competition reflects a high degree of vertical integration,[33] resulting in high costs to use the network for new entrants, in addition to the burden associated with strict "balancing requirements".[34] Indeed, Japan has the worst score among OECD countries according to the OECD's indicator of network policies, which measures legal restrictions on entry, the degree of vertical integration and the independence of sectoral regulators (Figure 5.13). To facilitate competition in the electricity market, unbundling is crucial to prevent vertically-integrated incumbents from impeding the functioning of the market through cross-subsidisation and discrimination in network access (Gönenç et al., 2001). Accounting separation and information firewalls were introduced in 2003 in Japan and enforced from 2005. However, numerous studies argue

Figure 5.11. **Regulatory reform in key service industries**

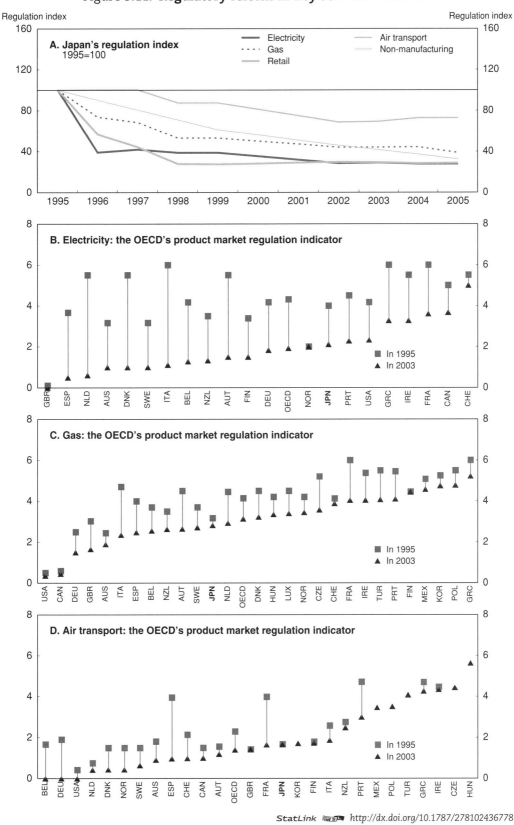

StatLink 🔗 http://dx.doi.org/10.1787/278102436778

Source: Cabinet Office (2006) and Conway *et al.* (2006a).

Figure 5.12. **Electricity prices in OECD countries**

US$/kWh, 2006 or latest year[1]

A. Industrial sector

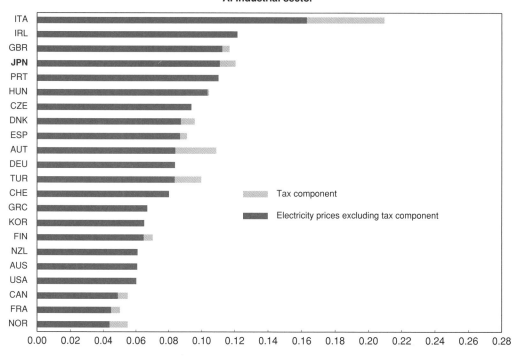

B. Household sector

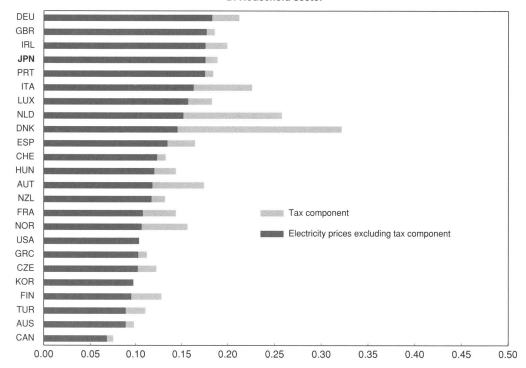

StatLink ᗧᔍᖘ *http://dx.doi.org/10.1787/278110736601*

1. Countries are ranked in order of prices excluding the tax component. For the United States, the price excludes taxes, while for Korea, no tax information is available. For some OECD countries (Ireland, Portugal, Czech Republic, Germany, Switzerland, Greece, New Zealand and Belgium), taxes on electricity are zero for the industrial sector. See the source for the specific year.

Source: OECD/IEA, *Energy Prices and Taxes*, 1Q2007, OECD, Paris.

Figure 5.13. **The OECD indicator of network policies**

0 to 6 scale from most to least favourable to competition[1]

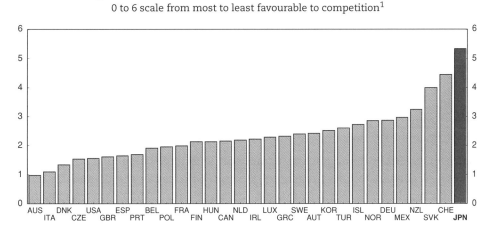

StatLink http://dx.doi.org/10.1787/278121774418

1. This indicator measures network access and the independence of sectoral regulators.

Source: Hoj *et al.* (2007).

that management and accounting unbundling is not sufficient and that legal separation is necessary (Newbery, 2002a and 2002b and Pollitt, 2007). If market liberalisation is to be extended to smaller consumers, unbundling of the retailing and distribution activities of the GEUs will become a more urgent issue. Meanwhile, it is essential to ensure the independence of the ESCJ, which sets the rules for transmission network access and arbitration, from dominant market participants, interest groups and the government. It is important that large market incumbents do not have more power within the ESCJ than new entrants.

As market liberalisation increases the scope for trade across Japan, it is important to expand transmission networks and open access to interconnection capacity, which is a prerequisite for effective market integration.[35] In the past, interconnection capacity was determined on the basis of self-sufficiency in each region without consideration for third-party access, thus leading to low interconnection capacity between regions, even in the same frequency area. In this regard, adopting a capacity auctioning mechanism, as in European countries, would be an attractive option to make transmission capacity available to all users. In sum, in promoting competition in the electricity market, METI should continue to develop an appropriate pro-competition framework in collaboration with the JFTC[36] to avoid the abuse of market positions by GEUs, while ensuring fairness and transparency in network access. Such a strategy would be promoted by the creation of a single independent sectoral regulator, as is the case in most OECD countries.

In parallel with the reform of the electricity sector, Japan has introduced significant changes in the gas sector, which is characterised by many, mostly private, vertically-integrated regional companies with little interconnection capacity between regions. The 2003 revision of the Gas Utilities Law included several initiatives to strengthen competition. Most importantly, large industrial consumers with annual usage of more than 0.5 million m³ were allowed to choose suppliers freely, and the threshold was further reduced to 0.1 million m³ in 2007, thus including most commercial users. As a result, the liberalised sector accounts for 60% of total sales, boosting the number of consumers free to choose their supplier by three times between 2004 and 2007. Moreover, rules and procedures for TPA to pipeline and Liquefied Natural Gas (LNG) terminals were established and non-discriminatory access was increased through accounting separation, information firewalls and a prohibition against discrimination. On the other hand, to stimulate investment in pipelines, new capacity will be exempted from the TPA obligation or will be allowed a higher rate of return in their TPA tariff for a limited time period.

These reforms reduced Japan's regulation index in the gas sector by 61% (Figure 5.11, Panel A) and kept the OECD's indicator of the stringency of regulation below the average (Panel C).[37] Reforms encouraged greater competition, which allowed new entrants in the liberalised sector to increase their market share from 2% in 2001 to 7.6% in 2004. Intensified competition resulted in a 36% fall in prices and a 19% rise in consumption between 1995 and 2005, boosting consumer surplus by 0.5 trillion yen (Table 5.4).

However, given the dominance of incumbents with large bargaining power, additional measures are needed to encourage competition. One key is the establishment of an independent regulator, as found in the gas sectors of other OECD countries, such as the United States, the United Kingdom, Germany and Italy, prior to the effective unbundling of vertically-integrated gas utilities. The expansion of an inter-connected pipeline network is another important task. In addition, TPA to pipelines and LNG terminals should be closely monitored to ensure that it does not act as an entry barrier to new suppliers. The client notification requirement, under which gas suppliers are obliged to notify METI when they acquire a client from another gas company's supply area, is unnecessary. Similar problems in other countries are dealt with through licenses to distributors, stipulating transparent and equal conditions for all players.

The transport sector: harbours and air transport

Harbour charges are high in Japan (Figure 5.14). Although the rental cost of infrastructure that is administratively determined by local governments was not far out of line with other ports, the cost of cargo handling, tugging and pilotage by private providers is much higher than in other countries (Table 5.9). The government introduced reforms for nine major ports in 2000, including the removal of the "demand and supply adjustment scheme", which required potential new entrants to prove that there was surplus demand. The licensing system for entering and leaving the industry was changed to a permission system, which is less strict and allows less room for discretion, and the permission requirement for setting prices was replaced by a prior notification system. These reform measures were expanded to all ports by 2006. Furthermore, the government launched a "Super Hub-Port Initiative" in 2004 aimed at reducing costs and providing services comparable to other major ports in Asia by 2010 through better management and economies of scale. The initiative included specific targets, such as cutting costs by 30% and reducing lead time from three days to one day, the level of Singapore. Ports designated as super-hub ports have been given priority in government support.[38]

Despite these reforms, prices remain high, partly reflecting the lack of competition within and among Japanese harbours (OECD, 2007c). Although the exemption from the competition law was abolished in the late 1990s, the Japanese Harbour Transport Association (JHTA) wields discretionary power over business operations through the "Prior Consultation" process between shipping companies and the labour unions of harbour service providers. The JHTA is an incorporated association under the regulatory authority of the Ministry of Land, Infrastructure and Transport (MLIT) that includes all major port service providers, except shipping lines. Although its participation is not mandatory, the JHTA usually assumes an intermediary role in the prior consultation process between labour unions and shipping companies whenever there are proposals that would cut jobs

Figure 5.14. **International comparison of harbour charges**
Index with Busan port = 100 in 2000[1]

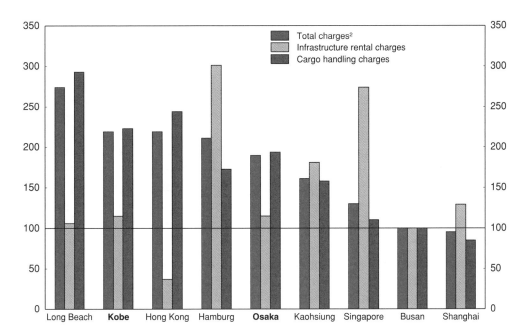

StatLink ⫘⫘ http://dx.doi.org/10.1787/278142481120

1. Based on charges for ships with capacity of 4 000 TEU.
2. Includes pilotage and tugging charges.

Source: Kim *et al. (2000).*

or adversely affect working conditions. In such cases, the JHTA consults with the relevant parties and issues recommendations that all parties are effectively bound to respect. The shipping companies are thus required to obtain advance approval from the JHTA for even minor changes, such as the time of arrival, port or pier designation or substitution of vessels. While the Port Transport Business Law allows competitive bidding at confidential rates, the prior consultation process prevents such bidding for harbour services, including cargo-handling, thus raising the cost of doing business (European Business Council in Japan, 2006).[39] The prior consultation process and the role of the JHTA should thus be reformed to promote greater competition in the harbour industry.

Such anti-competitive practices are further compounded by entry regulations. When the "demand and supply adjustment scheme" was abolished in 2000, the regulation setting the minimum number of workers was revised. Specifically, existing and new firms must have employment that is 50% higher than before 2000 (for the same scale of operations). This regulation makes it difficult for new entrants to gain market share based on higher

Table 5.9. **Comparison of major service charges in international ports**[1]
In thousand yen

	Singapore	Hong Kong	Kaohsiung	Busan	Tokyo
Tugging charge	216	262	457	361	570
Pilotage charge	60	239	131	169	1 044

1. Based on charges for a container ship of 50 thousand tonnes.
Source: Tokyo Metropolitan Harbor Bureau (1999).

efficiency and lower costs. The number of harbour business firms fell from 1 019 to 953 between FY 1999 and FY 2005 despite the liberalisation of entry barriers in 2000, in part reflecting depressed economic conditions and mergers between existing firms. No foreign companies have established terminal operations in Japan.

Another reason for high harbour charges is the additional fees for cargo-handling during weekends and at night, which is as high as 60% to 120% in Tokyo port, compared to 0% to 50% in other major ports in Asia. As a result of the high charges, Japanese ports are losing business to major ports in Korea, China and Singapore.[40] Liberalising port services has been found to be very effective in lowering service charges. One study (Fink *et al.*, 2002) estimates that it could reduce prices by an average of 9%, while ending co-operative working agreements and price-fixing arrangements could lower prices by another 25%. In sum, the government should strengthen competitive pressure in the harbour industry, putting a priority on reforming the prior consultation process, actively pursuing deregulation and adopting a more pro-active competition policy. In addition, privatising harbours would boost competition, leading to higher productivity and lower cargo handling costs.[41]

There has also been some regulatory reform in the air transport industry. The permission requirement for changing airfares was relaxed to a prior notification system and the government abolished the demand and supply adjustment scheme in 2000, while the licensing requirement to enter and leave the industry was changed to a permission system. Nevertheless, the OECD indicator of entry barriers in air transport was more than twice as restrictive as the OECD average in 2003. Overall, progress has been relatively modest compared to the electricity and gas sectors, with only a 27% fall in Japan's regulatory index between 1995 and 2005 (Figure 5.11, Panel A). As for the OECD indicator, there has been no change for air transport since 1995, in contrast to the large drop in the OECD average (Panel D). Given the limited progress, consumer surplus gains during the decade to 2005 were small (Table 5.4). The Japanese business sector has complained about the high charges in airports, as well as ports (Keidanren, 2000).

To strengthen its international competitiveness, Narita airport, which serves the Tokyo region, reduced its landing charge by about 20% in 2005, compensating by cutting costs through improving outsourcing activities and increasing non-aeronautical revenue. Nevertheless, charges at Narita and Kansai, the second largest airport in Japan, are still among the highest in the world, in part due to high landing charges (Figure 5.15).[42] In addition, overall operational costs per passenger in Japanese airports are the highest among major airports surveyed, according to the Transport Research Laboratory. The high price for airport services in Japan fundamentally reflects the monopolistic powers of airports in the context of a serious shortage of landing slots, particularly at Narita. Despite the opening of a third major international airport in central Japan in 2005, airport capacity appears inadequate to meet rising traffic. Capacity is limited by the rules set by MLIT that impose strict hourly and daily limits on airport slot numbers.[43] In addition, capacity utilisation is limited by the slot allocation mechanism, which is based on the grandfather principle – granting slots to incumbent operators based on their past usage.[44] The slot allocation scheme needs to be more transparent and to fully utilise airport capacity. Increasing capacity is all the more important as it is a prerequisite for fully realising the benefits of further liberalising air transport services, particularly in the context of the worldwide trend toward liberalisation of this sector.[45]

Figure 5.15. **International comparison of landing and departure charges**
Highest = 100, 2005[1]

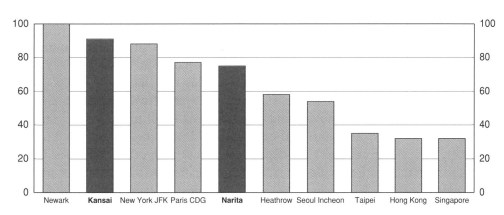

StatLink ⟨ms⟩ http://dx.doi.org/10.1787/278161763230

1. Based on eight different aircraft types.
Source: Transport Research Laboratory (2005).

Improving the mechanism for allocating landing slots is also essential to reduce entry barriers to potential new airlines. The current slot allocation mechanism, in line with IATA guidelines, reserves a pool of slots for new entrants. However, the mechanism does not sufficiently encourage entry as it is based on the grandfather principle. This approach prevents the provision of slots to airlines that value them most and acts as a barrier to changing service patterns. Introducing market mechanisms, such as secondary trading, auction of slots and higher posted prices, would increase the degree of competition by removing important entry barriers for low-cost and competing long-haul services. A carefully-designed market mechanism is important to realise the full benefits of reform in the air transport sector. Finally, competition policy should be strictly enforced in the airline industry, which has two major players.

Another barrier to competition is restrictive airfare pricing and ticket distribution mechanisms for international travel. The prices of tickets sold by airlines directly to consumers are restricted by MLIT, in principle, with a minimum floor set at 30% of the IATA price,[46] which does not reflect actual market prices. Consequently, the ability of airlines to offer competitive fares to and from Japan directly to consumers is limited, making them sell through licensed travel agencies, which account for most of their sales.[47] This restriction is particularly disadvantageous to foreign airlines as it is difficult for them to set up their own travel agencies in Japan (like Japanese airlines do) due to the lack of scale economies. The restriction on setting international airfares should be removed and airlines should be allowed to sell tickets directly to consumers at market prices. The recent government plan to eliminate the restriction will be beneficial.

The government should focus on reducing high landing and departure charges and operating costs of airports through deregulation and measures to increase capacity. Although Narita was corporatised in 2004, it remains 100% government-owned. It should be privatised, while ensuring a good governance structure and appropriate regulation through the introduction of an independent regulatory body. This should be combined with active enforcement of competition policy, given the natural monopoly status of airports. To expand airport capacity, allowing international routes to use regional airports is one option. For example, Haneda Airport, which is closer to Tokyo than Narita Airport, could handle international traffic.[48] Perhaps even more important is improving the slot allocation mechanism at major airports to increase effective capacity.

Business services

The business services sector – which includes activities such as accounting, legal services, consulting, R&D, marketing and advertising – has been growing rapidly in most OECD countries in the context of increased outsourcing and the growing importance of knowledge-intensive service activities, such as R&D and software development. Rapid advances in information technology and the liberalisation of trade and investment in services has increased international competition in business services. Enhanced productivity in business services creates positive spillovers on other industries, enabling firms to focus on their core activities. In Japan, the business services sector expanded at an average annual rate of 3% between 1990 and 2003, boosting its share of GDP from 12% to 15%, while its share of employment increased from 5% to 6%. This reflected high productivity growth in business services, averaging 4% during 1996-2001, one of the highest rates in the OECD area (OECD, 2007a).

However, there is scope for further improvement in the regulatory framework as competition in business services has long been weak compared to other sectors in Japan. Weak competition is a result of pervasive regulations, such as mandatory membership in professional associations, recommended fixed prices by professional associations, the exclusive exercise of certain activities and restrictions on advertising and business structures (OECD, 2000). According to the OECD's indicator, the stringency of product market regulation in Japan in professional services – accounting, architecture, engineering and legal services (which account for the major share of the business service category) – ranks a little above the OECD average (Figure 5.16). As for the openness of business services to inflows of FDI, Japan was more open than the OECD average, although it lagged significantly behind top performers in 2006.[49] There has been progress, notably in the legal services market, which was opened to FDI in 2005. This reform is expected to significantly increase competitive pressures and enhance the quality of service in Japan, which has a relatively low number of lawyers.[50] Given the importance of business services and the

Figure 5.16. **Regulations in professional services**
In 2003

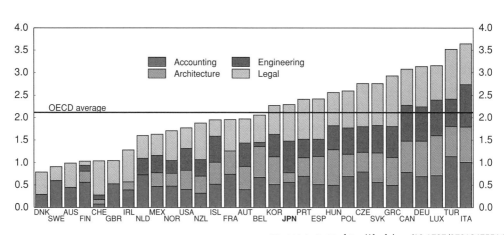

StatLink 🔗 http://dx.doi.org/10.1787/278184755146

Source: Conway et al. (2006b).

potential scope for improvement, the government has implemented various strategies to develop this sector, including it as one of six priority sectors in the recent initiative for the service industry (Box 5.1). The key policy measures include developing human resources by setting skill standards for each individual sector, improving infrastructure to facilitate outsourcing through IT and expanding the scope of outsourcing by the public sector (see below).

As in other areas, there is a negative correlation between the strictness of product market regulations and productivity growth in business services in the OECD area (OECD, 2007a). The government should thus strengthen competitive pressures by liberalising restrictive regulations governing professional services to enhance output growth. Pervasive regulations in professional services are ostensibly intended to improve service quality and prevent market failure arising from information asymmetries and transaction costs. However, there is little empirical evidence to suggest that the regulations imposed on business services in many countries actually improve consumer welfare. Instead, such restrictions have been correlated with higher prices and less innovation (Nguyen-Hong, 2000 and Patterson *et al.*, 2003). For example, the annual target on the number of applicants allowed to pass the bar exam in Japan – around 1 500 in 2006[51] – should be replaced by criteria based on the qualifications needed to be a competent lawyer. Attempts to liberalise restrictions on business services in Japan have been frustrated by the "regulatory conduct doctrine", which exempts anti-competitive behaviour if it is required by regulation (Hoj, 2007). Additionally, the business services market should be opened further to FDI, while expanding the recognition of professional certificates acquired overseas. Finally, OECD principles for high-quality regulation of professional services should be applied:

- Exclusive rights should not be granted where there are other mechanisms available to address market failure directly.

- Entrance requirements for a profession should not be disproportionate to the skills necessary to perform the services competently.

- Regulation should focus on the need to protect small consumers.

- Restrictions on competition between members of a profession should be eliminated while encouraging competition between professional associations.

- Professional associations should not be granted exclusive jurisdiction and should be subject to independent scrutiny in making decisions about entrance requirements, mutual recognition and the boundary of their exclusive rights.

Another priority is to establish an efficient reporting system for intellectual and intangible assets, which are particularly important to business services. Accurate reporting of firms' intangible assets increases their valuations in financial markets, thus facilitating outside funding and the establishment of such firms. This promotes efficient resource allocation and helps to ensure a positive effect of ICT investment on productivity growth. According to one study (Fukao and Miyagawa, 2007), the relatively low level of investment in intangible assets in Japan limits the impact of ICT investment on productivity growth.[52] In addition, setting common industry-wide standards would increase market transparency and competition, thus enabling service providers to realise economies of scale. Finally, the intellectual property rights regime should carefully balance incentives to innovate with adequate access to and sharing of knowledge.

Public services

Public services, such as health and education, have been provided in a non-market environment with limited use of the price mechanism and competition, while relying to a large extent on public funding to promote equity and to ensure national minimum standards. In contrast to the overall decline in regulation in the non-manufacturing sector, there has been limited progress in reducing regulations in health and education, despite some improvement in the early 2000s (Figure 5.17). Moreover, the regulation index for other public services has increased since 1995. Such "government-driven markets" have failed to respond adequately to the changing needs of consumers, resulting in low efficiency and poor service quality. The government's Council on Economic and Fiscal Policy called for "innovation of government-driven markets, especially in the fields characterised by low productivity and failure to satisfy consumers' potential needs".[53] To overcome these problems, as well as to limit government expenditure, the authorities have implemented several initiatives, such as special zones and market testing, to introduce market principles in public services.

The regulation that restricts entry in the education and health sectors to firms that are considered to be "non-profit" has been abolished in some special zones. Under the special zone initiative, 22 private schools for profit, including seven universities, were established by April 2007, but there has been no decision on whether to expand this reform nationwide, partly reflecting problems in the administration of some of these establishments. As for hospitals, only one for-profit institution has been established in a special zone, partly reflecting remaining regulatory barriers. In particular, the incentive to establish for-profit hospitals is limited by a regulation that restricts their activities to advanced medical treatment not covered by National Health Insurance, thus preventing competition with existing hospitals. With only one for-profit hospital in operation, the evaluation of this reform for possible nationwide implementation is difficult. The success of the special zone initiative in the area of public services depends on the removal of the obstacles imposed on the operation of private schools and hospitals for profit so that an adequate number of zones can be established, as well as on the benefits resulting from the operation of for-profit schools and hospitals.

Figure 5.17. **Regulatory reform in public services**

1995 = 100

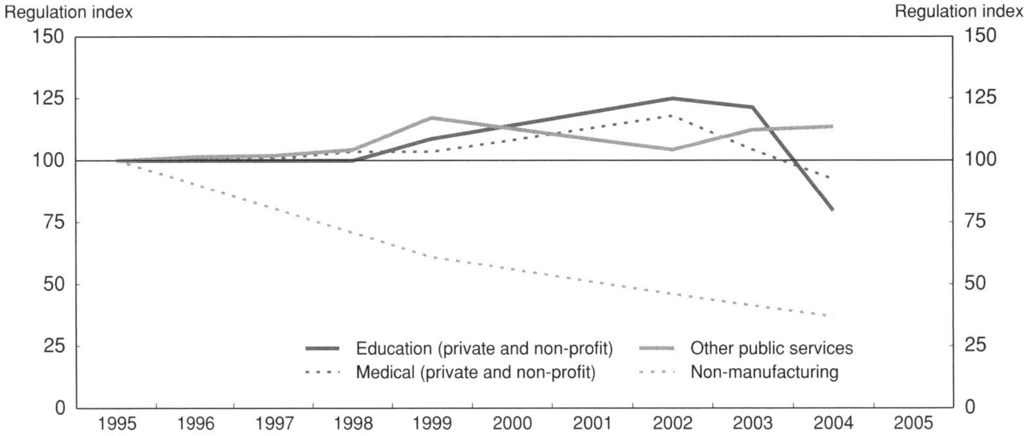

StatLink ⟨⟩ http://dx.doi.org/10.1787/278200806563

Source: Cabinet Office (2006).

Another important initiative is the market testing project, which aims at increasing the efficiency of public services through competitive tendering. Under this scheme, services eligible for market testing are decided by the Cabinet at least once a year. Private companies then bid for contracts to provide those services and the relevant ministry decides the winner of the bidding process. Evaluation of performance takes place three to five years later. The transparency, fairness and neutrality of the process are to be ensured by a third-party watch dog in the Cabinet Office, the "Supervisory commission for public/ private and private/private competitive tendering", which is composed of private-sector experts. Eight pilot projects were implemented in 2005 in three areas – job placement activities, social insurance and prison services. In the evaluation of the market-testing initiative at the end of FY 2006, the monitoring committee gave a C to one ministry (an average grade), while the other 11 ministries received a grade of D for poor performances. The scheme was further expanded to seven areas in 2007.[54] The neutrality and independence of the third-party watch dog is a key to the success of this initiative. In addition, while market testing is mandatory for the central government in the seven areas, it is only optional for local governments, even though they provide some of those public services as well. Public services provided by local governments need to be subject to market testing whenever possible.

Finally, another important reform aimed at increasing the efficiency of the public sector is the privatisation of Japan Post. In October 2007, the government launched the long-awaited privatisation of Japan Post, the largest financial institution in the world with assets of more than 300 trillion yen (60% of GDP and about one-fifth of total household assets) and 240 000 employees (Box 5.3).

Box 5.3. **The privatisation of Japan Post and financial-sector reform**

Japan Post was split into four companies in October 2007, plus a holding company, with all shares initially held by the government, as announced in the 2004 plan.

- The Postal Delivery Service became the **Japan Post Service**, which provides correspondence delivery, packaging and storage services. In addition, it will enter the "international special delivery business", competing with private firms such as FedEx and UPS.

- The Post Office Network became the **Japan Post Network** and offers a wide range of services, including the sale of life and damage insurance and real estate development. However, the new company is required to maintain the existing local network of 24 000 branches to provide services for those living in rural areas, thus making it difficult to increase efficiency through restructuring.

- The Postal Savings System became the **Japan Post Bank** (Yucho Bank) and the Postal Life Insurance System became the **Japan Post Insurance** (Kampo Insurance). Both institutions will be treated as private financial institutions subject to supervision by the Financial Supervisory Agency (FSA), with their initial business scope limited to that under the Japan Post. They need to obtain approval from both the FSA and the Ministry of Internal Affairs and Communications to enter new business areas that they are considering, such as housing loans, credit cards and health insurance.

The two financial companies will be listed on the stock market by the early 2010s and are to be completely privatised by 2017. The holding company will also be listed and will sell shares to private investors. However, even in 2017, the government will hold at least a third of the shares of the holding company, which will in turn hold all of the shares of the Japan Post Service and the Japan Post Network.

Box 5.3. **The privatisation of Japan Post and financial-sector reform** (*cont.*)

The privatisation is expected to bring about a number of benefits. First, it will increase efficiency by improving resource allocation. Indeed, the investment yield from Postal Savings in 2006 was just 1.2% due to its concentration on investment in government bonds, which accounted for around 60% of assets. The privatisation is expected to diversify the asset portfolio by including more high-yielding financial products, including equities, thereby encouraging the flow of funds toward more productive private areas. *Second*, it will develop private financial institutions by ending the preferential treatment of Japan Post. Previously, the insurance payments and savings accounts of Postal Savings and Postal Insurance were guaranteed by the government and both were exempt from major taxes, such as the corporate income tax, and some financial regulations. *Third*, it will provide better service at a lower cost for consumers by increasing efficiency.

However, there are some concerns, particularly on the part of private firms worried about unequal competition with Japan Post as it expands its business operations using its nationwide network, while the government holds all of its shares and allows some preferential treatment. Indeed, the Postal Services Company will receive special treatment for customs clearance and ground transport. Moreover, there is also potential risk that profitable activities, for example the Japan Post Service, with its monopolistic status in correspondence delivery service, may cross-subsidise other businesses or companies during the transitional period before full privatisation. Lastly, the entry of Japan Post in the private lending market, which is already saturated in the context of weak demand from the corporate sector, runs the risk of crowding out existing private players.

The key to the successful privatisation of Japan Post is to foster a business environment conducive to efficiency gains while ensuring a level playing field with private financial institutions. This requires eliminating the remaining preferential treatment for the new companies and privatising them as quickly as possible to minimise distortions during the transitional period. Meanwhile, the independence and neutrality of the government committee overseeing the privatisation process, which provides opinions on allowing the new companies to enter new business lines, must be ensured to avoid conflicts of interest arising while the government still holds all of the shares of the four companies and the holding company. In addition, competition policy should be strictly enforced in areas where these companies are operating.

While the privatisation of Japan Post is a positive step, other measures are necessary to develop Japan's financial markets, which is an important priority to achieve sustainable growth in the context of a globally integrated financial market and an ageing society. The FSA announced a plan in December 2007 to strengthen financial markets by promoting competition and improving the regulatory environment. Concrete action plans to achieve those objectives included:

- Diversifying the range of financial products traded in the exchanges to include various types of derivatives and Exchange-Traded Funds.

- Constructing a tax system that facilitates the shift of resources from savings to investment.

- Easing the firewall regulation in financial companies to maximise the synergy effect between the banking and securities business. This is to be accomplished by lifting the ban on interlocking officers and relaxing the restrictions on sharing information about corporate customers.

- Broadening the scope of business allowed for banking and insurance companies.

- Enhancing the transparency and predictability of financial regulation and supervision through the extensive use of the "No-Action Letter" scheme (see above).

- Developing human resources specialised in finance, law and accounting by supporting specialised graduate schools and encouraging the inflow of foreign experts.

Conclusion

Given its large role in the economy, the service sector is the key to achieving faster economic growth. Accelerating productivity growth in services requires strengthening competition and making Japan more open to international trade and FDI inflows. A summary of specific recommendations to achieve these objectives is presented in Box 5.4. While enhanced productivity in the service sector benefits consumers and improves overall economic performance, structural changes also incur adjustment costs. However, such costs should not prevent reforms to create more open and competitive service markets.

Box 5.4. **Summary of recommendations**

Strengthen the competition framework in general

- Pursue a more pro-active competition policy in the service sector, raising its importance relative to the industry-specific policy objectives pursued by line ministries.
- Increase the transparency and predictability of public administration, notably by enhancing the effectiveness of "Public Comment Procedures", "No-Action Letters" and "Regulatory Impact Analysis".
- Use competition laws more actively to prevent anti-competitive activities by trade associations.
- Further strengthen penalties, such as surcharges and fines for violations of the AMA, to a level that would provide sufficient deterrent effects.
- Reduce the number of explicit exemptions from the AMA, while ending preferential treatment for SMEs, except when necessary to correct clear market failures.
- Ensure the neutrality and independence of the JFTC's hearing procedure while continuing to upgrade the capability of the JFTC in terms of human resources and budgets.
- Strengthen international competition by promoting inward FDI through the elimination of restrictions on FDI and product market regulations that discourage inflows of investment.
- Facilitate trade in services by reducing trade barriers.

Accelerate regulatory reform

- Step up the pace of regulatory reform in the service sector, particularly in ICT-using areas.
- Improve the special zone scheme by focusing its objective on nationwide regulatory reform, removing barriers to the effective implementation of reform measures in the zones and ensuring fair and independent evaluation of the measures to accelerate nationwide adoption of the reforms.
- Focus the government's development plans for the service sector on policies to strengthen competition, while avoiding preferential measures, particularly toward SMEs, that would result in distortions.
- Better co-ordinate government plans to develop the service sector so as to use resources efficiently.
- Remove obstacles discouraging investment in ICT and intangible assets, particularly in services.

Remove restrictions in key service industries

The retail sector

- Pursue further deregulation, in part by enhancing the transparency and predictability of the Large-scale Retail Store Location Law.
- Ensure that other laws, such as the City Planning Law, are not used as entry barriers for large stores.

Box 5.4. **Summary of recommendations** (*cont.*)

The energy sector

- Establish single independent regulators to promote competition in both electricity and gas.
- Further expand the share of consumers allowed to freely choose their suppliers of electricity and gas.
- In the electricity sector, strengthen competitive pressure by expanding the interconnection capacity, facilitating the power exchange and removing remaining obstacles to the operations of new entrants.
- Actively pursue unbundling of vertically-integrated incumbents through formal separation, while ensuring the neutrality and independence of the Electric Power System Council of Japan.
- In the gas sector, strengthen competitive pressures by expanding the network capacity and removing remaining obstacles to the operations of new entrants.

Transport

- In the harbour industry, strengthen competitive pressure by improving the "Prior Consultation" process and relaxing entry barriers, such as the minimum requirement on employment.
- In the air transport industry, expand the capacity of airports, particularly in the Tokyo region, and increase their efficiency through privatisation.
- Introduce market mechanisms in the allocation of landing slots to fully utilise capacity and reduce entry barriers.
- Allow airlines to sell tickets at competitive prices directly to consumers.

Business services

- Further deregulate professional services while preventing negative effects on competition from self-regulatory bodies.
- Encourage international competition through increased inflows of FDI and trade, while expanding the scope of mutual recognition of certificates acquired overseas.

Public services

- Actively use the special zone scheme to promote reforms in areas such as education and healthcare.
- Expand the use of market testing and ensure that it results in outsourcing of activities in which the private sector is more efficient.

Notes

1. The share of employment in services rose from 60% in 1993 to 70% in 2003. In terms of its share of GDP (70%), Japan lags the United States and the United Kingdom, where services accounted for 76% in 2005.

2. Services' share of inputs into manufacturing increased from 20% in 1980 to 30% in 2004 (METI, 2007).

3. In the European Union (the 15 members as of 1999), productivity growth was 2.7% for manufacturing versus 0.9% for services, and in the United Kingdom, it was 2.9% and 1.7%, respectively. In contrast, there was a relatively large gap in the United States: 6.0% for manufacturing and 1.4% for services.

4. The shift-share analysis, shown in Figure 5.1, decomposes aggregate changes in labour productivity into a within-sector effect, a shift effect and a cross-term effect. The within-sector effect measures the impact on total economy productivity growth from productivity growth within each sector, assuming that labour shares are unchanged. The shift effect measures the impact on

total economy productivity resulting from the movement of labour between sectors, assuming that the level of productivity in each sector is unchanged. The cross-term effect measures the change in both labour share and productivity in each sector and accounts for the impact of labour re-allocation between sectors with varying productivity growth rates.

5. Indicators of vertical integration focus on whether competitive activities, such as the generation of electricity, are separated from natural monopoly activities.

6. Japan also had a low score in the area of entrepreneurship and creation of new businesses, according to an indicator calculated by International Management Development (IMD).

7. This estimate is based on a model that makes the increase in productivity growth a function of the gap with the front-running country (Conway *et al.*, 2006b).

8. The 2005 OECD Ministerial (OECD, 2005a) also stressed the importance of improving education and training and upgrading innovation policies (see the 2006 *OECD Economic Survey of Japan*) to develop the service sector.

9. The index is calculated based on both the stringency of a regulation and its administrative classification. For example, a general prohibition receives a weight of 10 000, compared to 10 for a notification requirement. There are four administrative classifications, ranging from law (a weight of four) to a public notice (a weight of one). The series for all industries shown in Figure 5.5 is a weighted sum of the manufacturing and non-manufacturing indices, based on value added.

10. Administrative regulations include reporting, application procedures and burdens on business start-ups that stem from both economy-wide and sector-specific requirements.

11. Under the current system, the JFTC can impose administrative measures, such as a cease and desist order and/or a surcharge payment order, and pursue criminal accusations against serious violations.

12. The surcharge rate can be boosted to 15% for frequent offenders or reduced to 8% for firms that end violations one month before the start of an investigation.

13. The small number of legal actions reflects the use of prior consultations by prospective merging companies with the JFTC on their merger plans before the statutory notification. For example, there were two cases of prior consultation in 2005 in which the JFTC pointed out that the proposed merger would have been harmful to competition, leading to the withdrawal of the merger plans.

14. See JFTC (2004). The study was based on the cartel cases it handled between 1992 and 2003 and bid-rigging cases between 1996 and 2003.

15. In most OECD countries, including the United Kingdom, Germany, France, Sweden, Austria and Spain, financial sanctions can be as high as 10% of total firm turnover, not just of the commerce affected, and there is no time limit in applying the sanctions, except in a few countries, such as the United Kingdom. Moreover, financial sanctions can be up to two times the gain in the United States and up to three times the gain in New Zealand,

16. Between 1990 and 2004, there were only seven criminal cases. While six resulted in fines, prison sentences were always suspended. As a result, no one has ever gone to jail in Japan for violating the AMA (OECD, 2004b).

17. Unfair trade practices accounted for 17.3% of violations of the AMA subject to legal measures between 2000 and 2006, the second highest share after bid-rigging at 69.2%.

18. "Private monopoly of exclusionary type" is an attempt to exclude competitors from the market individually or in collaboration with other firms through unfairly low and discriminatory prices or to monopolise the market by obstructing business activities of new entrants.

19. The surcharge rate for SMEs is 4% in manufacturing, 1.2% in retail and 1% in wholesale compared to 10%, 3% and 2%, respectively, for large firms. The government's rationale for lower rates is that margins are usually smaller for SMEs.

20. At the national level, there are about 3 100 trade associations, compared to around 2 100 in the United States (2004 *OECD Economic Survey of Japan*).

21. Most hearings are entrusted to a hearing examiner in the General Secretariat. The number of hearing examiners increased from five to seven in 2006, four of whom are lawyers. As of December 2005, the JFTC had 138 pending hearing procedures that concerned alleged violations of the AMA (29), surcharge payment orders (103) and allegations of violations of the Premiums and Representations Act (6).

22. The low figure for Japan is partly due to the large size of the Japanese economy, given the inverse relationship between import penetration and the size of an economy. Nevertheless, the import penetration figure for Japan is exceptionally low, even after controlling for the size of the economy.

23. The higher productivity of foreign affiliates may reflect the fact that they tend to concentrate in business lines with higher productivity. However, FDI in services in Japan is rather evenly distributed across the entire sector. At the end of 2001, finance and insurance accounted for 20% of the 13.2 trillion yen of FDI accumulated in the service sector, followed by retail and wholesale trade (15%), business services (11%) and communications (9%). The even distribution between sectors suggests that the higher average productivity of foreign affiliates cannot be attributed to concentration in just a few sectors.

24. In response to the prevalence of unfair trade practices in retailing, the JFTC issued "Designation of Specific Unfair Trade Practices by Large-Scale Retailers Relating to Trade with Suppliers" in 2005. It prohibits large-scale retailers from returning goods without justification, unduly imposing *ex post* price reductions, assigning work tasks to employees of suppliers and requiring suppliers to provide economic benefits.

25. The law applied to two types of stores. Type I was stores larger than 3 000 m^2 (6 000 m^2 in large cities), which had to apply to the Ministry of International Trade and Industry. Type II was stores between 500 m^2 and 3 000 m^2, which applied to local governments.

26. Issues related to traffic congestion and securing sufficient parking space accounted for two-thirds of the comments from local governments, followed by noise and waste issues.

27. Local governments' "presentation of views" have included vague conditions such as: i) "The store opener must show evidence that the parking lot can accommodate the cars of customers to the store and should take additional measures if it cannot provide such evidence"; and ii) "As some parking lots are far from the store, some traffic congestion and accidents are expected. Therefore, the store opener must reconsider the location of those parking lots to avoid such problems."

28. The GEUs establish the tariffs as well as supply terms and conditions for the captive consumers, although any price increases are subject to authorisation by METI and price cuts require only notification.

29. Under the "pancaking" system, power suppliers were obliged to pay tariffs to all network owners on the way from its power plant to the final consumer.

30. Stronger competition also narrowed the price differences between GEUs. The maximum difference among GEUs shank from 3.55 yen/kWh to 1.41 yen/kWh between FY 1994 and FY 2005.

31. Nuclear power plants in Japan are usually located in remote areas due to lower land prices, as well as public concern over building them near urban areas, given the risk of nuclear accidents, thus adding to transmission costs (Beder, 2005).

32. Some customers avoid PPS because of concern about their ability to provide a reliable supply, given that they lack backup capacity in case of emergencies.

33. The OECD indicator of vertical integration in the electricity sector in 2003 was 6.0, the most restrictive score possible, compared to the OECD average of 2.0.

34. The PPS are required to maintain balance between demand and supply in every 30-minute period to ensure reliable supply. Any shortage of supply above 3% by the PPS is filled by large incumbents (GEUs), at a higher fee.

35. This should include expanding the capacity of frequency converters needed for the exchange of electricity between different frequency areas. The GEUs serving the northern part of Japan deliver electricity at a frequency of 50 Hz, while western Japan uses 60 Hz.

36. In order to promote competition in the electricity market, METI and JFTC published "Guidelines for Proper Electric Power Trade" in 1999. In addition, the JFTC published "Issues Concerning the Electricity Market and Competition Policy" in June 2006.

37. Japan's overall ranking in the gas sector reflects a good performance (relatively low scores) for the public ownership and market structure sub-categories. However, the sub-categories for vertical integration and entry barriers (6.0 and 4.3, respectively) are relatively restrictive, as they are well above the OECD averages (3.5 and 2.4, respectively).

38. Thus far, the government has designated six harbours in three areas as super-hub ports: Osaka and Kobe in the Hanshin area, Tokyo and Yokohama in the Keihin area and Nagoya and Yokkaichi in the Isewan area. Government support includes no-interest loans to private-sector firms to build or improve infrastructure. While total government investment in harbours has remained steady at

around 135 billion yen since FY 2004, the proportion allocated to the super-hub ports rose from 27% to 59% in FY 2007.

39. The prior consultation system involving JHTA lacks transparency and effectively gives the JHTA and its members the power to prevent shipping lines from seeking competitive bids for waterfront services (European Business Council in Japan, 2006). The European Union also requested Japan to review the role of the JHTA to encourage competition in the harbour transport business in Japan (European Union, 2006).

40. In terms of the volume of containers handled, Tokyo fell from 16th in the world in 1994 to 22nd in 2004, while Kobe dropped from 6th to 36th and Yokohama from 10th to 27th, according to the Containerisation International Yearbook (Informa UK Limited, 2004). In addition, the transhipment ratio, a major indicator of the international competitiveness of harbours, declined from 20% to 12% for Yokohama between 1990 and 2006, in contrast to an increase from 6% to 43% in Busan over the same period (Jung, 2007).

41. The World Trade Organisation report (2004) of the experience of South American countries in liberalising and privatising port services shows that deregulation and participation of the private sector, including foreign capital, has led to higher productivity and lower cargo-handling costs. It also found that the key to success is the coherence between liberalisation and privatisation measures and other economic policies, such as competition between ports, investment in infrastructure and the flexibility of the labour markets.

42. Before the 2005 reduction, the landing charge at Narita airport was 948 000 yen per aircraft (based on a Boeing 747-400 aircraft) and 825 000 yen at Kansai airport. In contrast, landing charges were only 180 000 yen in Singapore, 283 000 yen in Incheon and 377 000 yen in Hong Kong, China. In 2002, the IATA requested that Narita reduce its landing charge. The 20% reduction in 2005 still leaves landing charges in Japan well above other major airports in Asia.

43. Airport slots are the scheduled time of arrival or departure available for allocation for an aircraft movement at a specific time or date. According to the Japanese authorities, the hourly and daily limits on slot numbers are intended to limit noise pollution for surrounding areas and ensure safety.

44. It leads to the inefficient use of slots due to overbidding, late hand-back of slots and babysitting of slots – maintaining a slot with the smallest aircraft possible in order to preserve its claim for the future (NERA, 2004).

45. The liberalisation of Japan's air transport sector is being advanced by the "Asian Open Skies" strategy, which was included in the *Economic and Fiscal Reform 2007* and in the "Asian Gateway Initiative".

46. These refer to the Instant Purchase Excursion Fares (PEX), as defined by IATA.

47. Furthermore, IATA full economy fares (Y2) are considered as the minimum level for business class fares in an attempt to ensure consistency between service and fare levels.

48. Haneda Airport has handled little international traffic since 1978, when its international traffic was taken over by Narita Airport, based on an agreement between the central government and the prefectures. In addition, the shared use of Yokota Air Force Base for commercial domestic flights and military flights would free up slots at Haneda for international flights.

49. The OECD's FDI restrictiveness index for Japan for business services was 0.063, compared to 0.017 in the United Kingdom, 0.038 in the United States and an average of 0.152 in the OECD area. The index ranges from 0 to 1, with 0 the least restrictive (Golub and Koyama, 2006).

50. The number of lawyers per 100 thousand population was 17 in Japan in 2005, compared to 154 in Germany (2004), 195 in the United Kingdom (2004) and 352 in the United States (2002) (Lee *et al.*, 2007).

51. The annual target has been steadily increased from around 500 in 1990 to 1 000 in 2000 and is planned to rise further to 3 000 by 2010 following the introduction of law schools.

52. The share of intangible investment in GDP was estimated at 7.8% in Japan (1995-2002) compared to 10.9% in the United Kingdom (2004) and 11.7% in the United States (1998-2000).

53. See the CEFP statement, "Program for Enhancing Growth Potential" (April 2007). In the paper prepared by the private members of the Council, it stated that "there are inevitable cases where the government has to be involved (healthcare and education) and hence this requires that regulations remain. However, such excuses do not justify a situation where the choice of consumers is

narrowed, where consumers have to stand in line for these services due to supply shortages, or where those prices are expensive."

54. The seven areas are: 1) statistical research; 2) registration of real estate and corporations; 3) social insurance agencies; 4) job placement activities; 5) independent administrative organisations; 6) local government operations; and 7) collection of fees for public services, such as national health insurance.

Bibliography

Agency for Natural Resources and Energy (2006), "Report by the Subcommittee to Evaluate System Reforms", Tokyo.

Aoki, M., A. Garber, and P. Romer (2000), "Why the Japanese Economy is not Growing: Micro Barriers to Productivity Growth", McKinsey Global Institute, Washington, D.C.

Beder, S. (2005), *Power Play: The Fight to Control the World's Electricity*, Soshisha Publishing, Tokyo (in Japanese).

Bertrand, M. and F. Kramarz (2002), "Does Entry Regulation Hinder Job Creation? Evidence from the French Retail Industry", *Quarterly Journal of Economics*, Vol. 117, No. 4.

Cabinet Office (2006), "On the relationship of recent progress in regulatory reform to productivity", *The Evaluation Report of Structural Reform* No. 6, Tokyo (in Japanese).

Cabinet Office (2007), *Economic Impact of Regulatory Reform*, Tokyo (in Japanese).

Canadian Chamber of Commerce in Japan (2005), "Position Paper on Trade Issues in Selected Sectors of the Japanese Market", Tokyo.

Conway, P., V. Janod, and G. Nicoletti (2005), "Product Market Regulation in OECD Countries: 1998 to 2003", OECD Economics Department Working Paper No. 419, OECD, Paris.

Conway, P. and G. Nicoletti (2006a), "Product Market Regulation in the Non-Manufacturing Sectors of OECD Countries: Measurement and Highlights", OECD Economics Department Working Paper No. 530, OECD, Paris.

Conway, P., D. de Rosa, G. Nicoletti and F. Steiner (2006b), "Regulation, Competition and Productivity Convergence", OECD Economics Department Working Paper No. 509, OECD, Paris.

Council for the Promotion of Regulatory Reform (2007), *Three-year Regulatory Reform Programme*, Tokyo (in Japanese).

European Business Council in Japan (2006), *New Leadership – Renewed Reform: The EBC report on the Japanese Business Environment 2006*, Tokyo.

European Union (2006), *EU Proposals for Regulatory Reform in Japan*, Brussels.

Fink, C., A. Mattoo, and I. Neaugu (2002), "Trade in International Maritime Services: How Much Does Policy Matter?", *World Bank Economic Review*, 16(1), Washington, D.C.

Francois, J., B. Hoekman and J. Woerz (2007), "Does Gravity Apply to Intangibles? Measuring Openness in Services", Paper presented at the conference, "Les Services: Nouveau champ de la mondialisation", 22-23 November 2007, OECD, Paris.

Flath, D. (2002), "The Japanese Distribution Sector in Economic Perspective: The Large Store Law and Retail Density", Columbia University, Center on Japanese Economy and Business, Working Paper Series, New York.

Forsyth, P. (2001), "Airport Price Regulation: Rationales, Issues and Directions for Reform", Submission Paper to the Productivity Commission Inquiry, Canberra, Australia.

Fukao, K. and T. Miyagawa (2007), "Productivity in Japan, the US, and the Major EU Economies: Is Japan Falling Behind?", RIETI Discussion Paper No. 07-E-046, Tokyo.

Golub, S. and T. Koyama (2006), "OECD's FDI Regulatory Restrictiveness Index: Revision and Extension to More Economies", OECD Economics Department Working Paper No. 525, OECD, Paris.

Gonenc, R., M. Maher and G. Nicoletti (2001), "The Implementation and the Effects of Regulatory Reform: Past Experience and Current Issues", *OECD Economics Studies*, No. 32, OECD, Paris.

Hoj, J. (2007), "Competition Law and Policy Indicators for the OECD Countries", OECD Economics Department Working Paper No. 568, OECD, Paris.

Hoj, J., M. Jimenez, M. Maher, G. Nicoletti and M. Wise (2007), "Product Market Competition in the OECD Countries: Taking Stock and Moving Forward", OECD Economics Department Working Paper No. 575, OECD, Paris.

IMF (2006), *Global Financial Stability Report*, Washington, D.C.

Informa UK Limited (2004), *Containerisation International Yearbook 2004*, Essex, United Kingdom.

International Energy Agency (2003), *Energy Policies of IEA Countries: Japan 2003 Review*, IEA, Paris.

JFTC (2004), "JFTC's View on the 2005 AMA Amendment Bill", Tokyo (in Japanese).

Jung, Bongmin (2007), "Reviewing the Comparative Advantage of Major Ports in Korea", *Maritime and Fishery*, Vol. 273, Korea Maritime Institute, Seoul (in Korean).

Keidanren (2000), "Position Paper Concerning Tourism in Japan in the Twenty-first Century", Tokyo.

Kim, Hakso *et al.* (2000), "Financing the Development of New Ports and Encouraging Private Investment", Korea Maritime Institute Research Paper, Seoul (in Korean).

Kox, H. and H. Nordas (2007), "Service Trade and Domestic Regulation", OECD Trade Policy Working Paper No. 49, OECD, Paris.

Lee, Byunghee, Byungik Cho and Youngmin Kim, (2007), "Analysis of Entry Barriers to the Service Industry", Research Paper of the Bank of Korea, August, Seoul (in Korean).

McGuckin, R.H, M. Spiegelman and B. van Ark (2005), "The Retail Revolution: Can Europe Match US Productivity Performance?", *Perspective on a Global Economy*, The Conference Board.

METI (1979-2004), *Census of Commerce*, Tokyo.

METI (2007), "Toward Innovation and Productivity Improvement in Service Industries", April, Tokyo.

National Economic Research Associates (NERA) (2004), *Study to Assess the Effects of Different Slot Allocation Schemes*, Report for the European Commission, London.

Newbery, D. (2002a), "Regulating Unbundled Network Utilities", *Economic and Social Review*, Vol. 33, No. 1.

Newbery, D. (2002b), "Regulatory Challenges to European Electricity Liberalisation", *Swedish Economic Policy Review*, Vol. 9.

Nguyen-Hong, D. (2000), "Restrictions on Trade in Professional Services", Productivity Commission Staff Research Paper, AusInfo, Canberra.

Nicoletti G. (2001), "Regulation in Services: OECD Patterns and Economic Implications", OECD Economics Department Working Paper No. 287, OECD, Paris.

Nicoletti G. and S. Scarpetta (2003), "Regulation, Productivity and Growth: OECD evidence", OECD Economics Department Working Paper No. 347, OECD, Paris.

Nicoletti G. and S. Scarpetta (2005), "Regulation and Economic Performance: Product Market Reforms and Productivity in the OECD", OECD Economics Department Working Paper No. 460, OECD, Paris.

OECD (2000), *Competition in Professional Services*, OECD, Paris.

OECD (2004a), *OECD Economic Survey of Japan*, OECD, Paris.

OECD (2004b), *OECD Reviews of Regulatory Reform: Japan*, OECD, Paris.

OECD (2005a), *Growth in Services: Fostering Employment, Productivity and Innovation*, Report for the meeting of the OECD Council at Ministerial Level, OECD, Paris.

OECD (2005b), *OECD Economic Globalisation Indicators*, OECD, Paris.

OECD (2006a), *Annual Report on Competition Policy Developments in Japan*, Competition Committee, OECD, Paris.

OECD (2006b), *Compendium of Productivity Indicators*, OECD, Paris.

OECD (2006c), *OECD Economic Survey of Japan*, OECD, Paris.

OECD (2007a), *Globalisation and Structural Adjustment: Summary Report of the Study on Globalisation and Innovation in the Business Services Sector*, OECD, Paris.

OECD (2007b), *OECD Economic Survey of Italy*, OECD, Paris.

OECD (2007c), *OECD Economic Survey of Mexico*, OECD, Paris.

Ono, H. (2000), "Restructuring Strategy of Japan's Service Sector in the Twenty-First Century", in S. Masuyama, D. Van den Brink and C.S. Yue (eds.), *Industrial Restructuring in East Asia, Towards the 21st Century*, ISASS, Singapore.

Paterson, I., M. Fink and A. Ogus (2003), "Economic Impact of Regulation in the Field of Liberal Professions in Different Member States", Institute for Advanced Studies, Vienna.

Pollitt, M. (2007), "The arguments for and against ownership unbundling of energy transmission networks", CWPE 0737 and EPRG 0714, Cambridge University.

Tokyo Metropolitan Harbour Bureau (1999), *The 7th Master Plan of the Port of Tokyo*, Tokyo (in Japanese).

Transport Research Laboratory (2005), *Review of Airport Charges 2005*, Berkshire, United Kingdom.

World Bank (2007), *Doing Business 2008*, Washington, D.C.

World Trade Organisation (2004), *World Trade Report 2004*, Geneva.

ISBN 978-92-64-04306-0
OECD Economic Surveys: Japan
© OECD 2008

Chapter 6

Reforming the labour market to cope with increasing dualism and population ageing

The proportion of non-regular workers has risen to one-third of total employment. While non-regular employment provides flexibility and cost reductions for firms, it also creates equity and efficiency concerns. A comprehensive approach that includes relaxing the high degree of employment protection for regular workers and expanding the coverage of non-regular workers by the social security system would help to reverse dualism. Given that non-regular workers receive less firm-based training, it is necessary to expand training outside of firms to support Japan's growth potential, while enhancing the employment prospects of non-regular workers. Reversing the upward trend in non-regular employment may also encourage greater female labour force participation, which is essential given rapid population ageing that is already reducing Japan's working-age population by almost 1% each year. Expanding childcare facilities and paying more attention to work-life balance would also boost female employment, while also raising Japan's exceptionally low birth rate.

Increasing dualism in the labour market is closely linked to Japan's unbalanced recovery, both as a cause and a consequence. The rising proportion of lower-paid non-regular workers is pushing down wages and labour's share of income, thus limiting household income and private consumption, despite record high overall profits in the corporate sector. At the same time, firms, particularly small and medium-sized enterprises (SMEs) in the non-manufacturing sector, have relied on the cost savings generated by hiring non-regular workers to cope with rising input costs and the difficulty of passing on price increases in the context of weak domestic demand. Moreover, increased dualism creates equity concerns, as a large segment of the population is paid substantially lower wages, bears the brunt of cyclical changes in employment and is largely excluded from the social insurance system. In addition, labour market dualism acts as a drag on growth, as non-regular workers do not receive the same amount of training and thus fail to accumulate human capital to the same extent as regular workers. Given the importance of firm-based training in Japan, the growing segment of the labour force that benefits little from enterprise-based training, combined with the marked increase in the incidence of long-term unemployment, creates a need for greater vocational training outside firms. Wages have also been constrained during the past few years by demographic factors, notably the retirement of the baby boom generation born just after the end of the Second World War. Population ageing is reducing the working-age population and increasing the financial burden on the labour force. Measures to raise the labour force participation rate – particularly among women – and immigration are important policies to temper the impact of demographic change. At the same time, policies aimed at boosting female employment also should take account of the low fertility rate in Japan.

This chapter begins by analysing the phenomenon of increasing dualism in the labour market, followed by a discussion of vocational training and the need for a government role in this area. The third section considers the impact of ageing and measures to limit the decline in the labour force. Policy recommendations are summarised in Box 6.1.

Falling wages and labour market dualism

Japan's labour market has shown marked improvement during this economic expansion. Although total employment declined by 3.5% between 1997 and 2002, a majority of firms reported that they still had excess labour when the current expansion began in 2002 and there was only one job offer for every two applicants. The unemployment rate peaked at a record high of 5.5% during 2002 and 2003, 1½ percentage points above its equilibrium (NAIRU) level, as estimated by the OECD (Figure 6.1). During the on-going expansion, in contrast, employment has risen by a cumulative 1%, despite the decline in the working-age population, thus reducing unemployment below its equilibrium rate of 3.9%. The tightness in the labour market is also reflected in the improvement in the job-offer-to-applicant ratio, which remained above one in 2006 and 2007 (on an annual average basis).

Figure 6.1. **Unemployment in Japan**

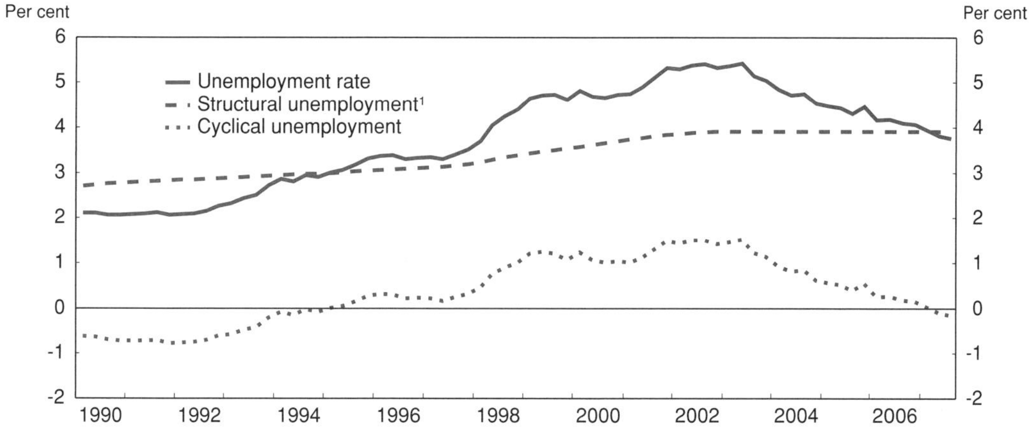

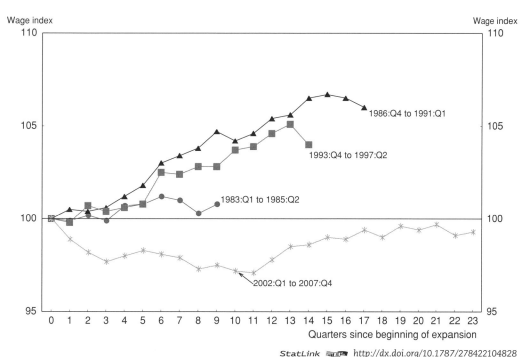

StatLink ⧉ http://dx.doi.org/10.1787/278411072857

1. OECD estimate of the unemployment rate consistent with a non-accelerating rate of inflation (NAIRU).

Source: OECD, Economic Outlook, No. 82 Database, OECD, Paris.

Despite the improvement in labour market conditions in recent years, wages have declined by 1% in real terms since the start of this economic expansion, the longest in Japan's post-war history (Figure 6.2). Although wage growth turned positive in 2005, it

Figure 6.2. **Wage developments in this expansion compared to past upturns**[1]
Wages equal 100 at the start of each expansion[2]

StatLink ⧉ http://dx.doi.org/10.1787/278422104828

1. This figure includes all expansions since 1980 except the aborted recovery of 1999, which only lasted eight quarters.
2. Wage growth per employee in real terms (adjusted by the consumer price index). Wages are total cash earnings per worker at firms with 30 or more workers. The wage is a three-quarter moving average of seasonally-adjusted data.

Source: Ministry of Health, Labour and Welfare, Monthly Labour Survey and OECD calculations.

returned to a downward trend in the second half of 2007. In contrast, previous expansions recorded significant increases in real wages, such as the 6% increase during the upturn that began in 1986. The downward trend in wages during this expansion cannot be explained by weak corporate profitability, as profits per employee have risen more than 80%, far exceeding the increases in previous upturns. Moreover, falling wages are not a result of weak gains in labour productivity, which has increased at a 1.8% annual rate since 2002 (Figure 6.3). Consequently, labour's share of income has fallen significantly, from a peak of 73% in 1999 to less than 65% in 2007 (Panel B). However, there is a marked difference between sectors: labour's share has rebounded in non-manufacturing, where profits and productivity have been weak, in contrast to the decline in the manufacturing sector to a record low.

Real wages declined during this expansion despite a 14% rise in overtime pay between 2002 and 2007 (Figure 6.4), driven by increased output in the manufacturing

Figure 6.3. **Productivity, wages and the labour income share**

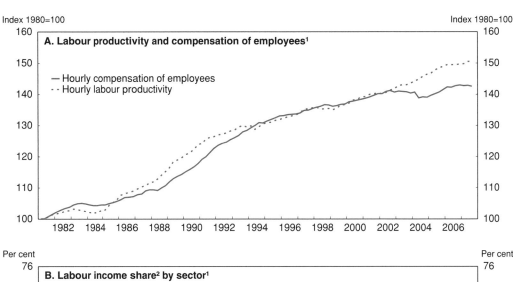

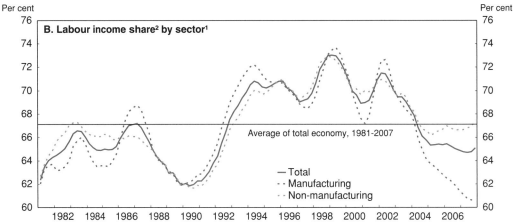

StatLink ᴀᴅˢ⊐ *http://dx.doi.org/10.1787/278474518470*

1. Four-quarter moving average.
2. The labour income share is defined as personnel costs/ (personnel costs + depreciation + business profits).

Source: Cabinet Office, *National Accounts*; Ministry of Internal Affairs and Communications, *Labour Force Survey*; Ministry of Health, Labour and Welfare, *Monthly Labour Survey*; and Ministry of Finance, *Financial Statement Statistics of Corporations by Industry.*

Figure 6.4. **Employee compensation by component**[1]

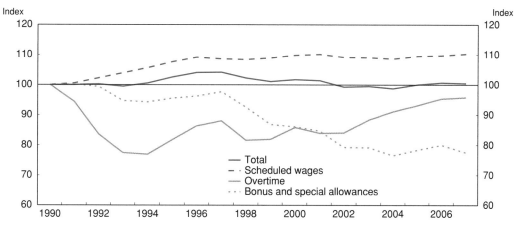

StatLink ⊟ᗑ⅃ *http://dx.doi.org/10.1787/278485736371*

1. Figures are in real terms (deflated by the consumer price index), with 1990 = 100, for establishments with 30 or more workers, in all industries.

Source: Ministry of Health, Labour and Welfare, *Monthly Labour Survey* and OECD calculations.

sector. The sluggishness of overall wages was instead largely explained by weak gains in scheduled earnings, which are negotiated each year. In addition, bonus payments, which have traditionally played a profit-sharing role in the Japanese labour market, dropped by 3% between 2002 and 2007 despite buoyant profits. Bonus payments have become less important in recent years, falling from 27% of employee compensation in the early 1990s to 21% in 2007, due in part to the increasing proportion of non-regular workers, who generally do not receive bonuses.

The increasing proportion of non-regular workers

Despite an increase in 2007, the number of regular workers has declined by almost 3% since the expansion started in 2002, lowering its share of total employees from 71.3% to 66.3% over that period (Table 6.1). Falling regular employment was more than offset by a rise in non-regular employment, which now accounts for more than one-third of total employment. Non-regular employment includes part-time workers, about two-thirds of this category, plus temporary and dispatched workers. By sector, the largest increases in non-regular employment were recorded in "other services" and in medical and nursing care (Table 6.2). Not surprisingly, the proportion of non-regular employment is highest in services, notably restaurants and hotels (65.4% in 2006) and "other services" (49.3%). In contrast, the share of non-regular employment has been relatively low and stable at around 20% in the manufacturing sector, which has benefited from the export-led expansion.

As for the supply side, the non-regular workforce includes young people on temporary contracts, married women working part-time and older persons who are re-hired by their former companies on fixed-term contracts. Table 6.3 summarises the major differences between workers by their employment status:

- Non-regular workers are concentrated among younger and older age categories, with a quarter under the age of 30 and almost a third over the age of 50. Overall, their average age is three to four years older than regular workers (Panel A).

- More than half of female employees are non-regular workers (Panel B). Consequently, two-thirds of non-regular workers are women.

- Non-regular workers tend to be less educated, as only 12.1% have a university degree compared to 31.4% for regular workers (Panel C).

- Nevertheless, the proportion of professional and technical workers among non-regular workers (13%) matches that of regular workers (Panel D).

- As noted above, non-regular workers are most prevalent in the service sector (Panel E).

- Non-regular workers are concentrated in SMEs (Panel F). Indeed, the proportion of non-regular workers is twice as high at firms with five to 29 employees, at 37.9%, as at firms with more than 1 000 workers.

- Most non-regular workers are paid an hourly wage while regular workers are paid on a monthly or annual basis (Panel G).

- The average number of hours worked by non-regular employees is significantly lower (Panel H), reflecting the large number of part-time workers in this category (Table 6.1). However, nearly half work more than 35 hours a week.

- There is a major difference in social insurance coverage: while virtually all regular workers are covered by the social insurance systems, less than half of non-regular workers are covered by employees' pension and health insurance, while two-thirds are covered by employment insurance (Panel I). However, some are covered as second earners in a household.

- Non-regular workers change jobs relatively frequently (Panel J): 21.5% have less than one year of tenure and only 13% have more than ten years, compared to 49.4% in the case of regular workers.

Table 6.1. **Employed persons by status**

Year[1]	Total[2]	Regular workers		Non-regular workers		Of which			
						Part-time workers[3]		Other[4]	
	Million	Million	Per cent	Million	Per cent	Million	Per cent	Million	Per cent
1985	40.0	33.4	83.6	6.6	16.4	5.0	76.2	1.6	23.8
1990	43.7	34.9	79.8	8.8	20.2	7.1	80.6	1.7	19.4
1995	47.8	37.8	79.1	10.0	20.9	8.3	82.4	1.8	17.6
2000	49.0	36.3	74.0	12.7	26.0	10.8	84.7	2.0	15.2
2001	50.0	36.4	72.8	13.6	27.2	11.5	84.7	2.1	15.3
2002	48.9	34.9	71.3	14.1	28.7	10.2	72.8	3.8	27.2
2003	49.4	34.4	69.7	15.0	30.3	10.9	73.0	4.0	27.0
2004	49.3	33.8	68.5	15.6	31.5	11.1	71.1	4.5	28.9
2005	49.2	33.3	67.7	15.9	32.3	11.0	68.8	5.0	31.2
2006	50.0	33.4	66.8	16.6	33.2	11.2	67.4	5.4	32.6
2007	51.2	33.9	66.3	17.3	33.7	11.7	67.5	5.6	32.5

1. Data is as of February until 2001 and as of the first quarter since 2002.
2. Excludes executives.
3. The significant fall in the number of part-time workers in 2002 and rise in the other category is due to a change in the questionnaire. In these surveys, part-time workers are those so defined by their employers.
4. The category "other" includes those working on short-term contracts, dispatched workers (employed by temporary worker agencies), entrusted workers and other types of non-regular workers.

Source: Ministry of Internal Affairs and Communications, *The Special Survey of the Labour Force,* from 1984 to 2001 and the *Labour Force Survey (Detailed Tabulation)* since 2002.

Table 6.2. **Employment by industry and employee status**

	Growth between 2003 and 2006			Composition in 2006
	Total employment[1]	Regular employment	Non-regular employment	Share of non-regular employment
Construction	–8.6	–9.6	–5.4	18.4
Manufacturing	–2.7	–2.2	–4.6	20.7
Transport	–1.4	–3.0	4.7	23.1
Wholesale and retail	0.0	–4.1	5.4	44.3
Restaurants and hotels	–3.7	–8.9	–0.6	65.4
Medical and nursing care	15.0	11.6	23.2	33.0
Other services	17.9	1.6	42.3	49.3
Total	2.8	–1.0	11.5	33.0

1. Excludes executives.
Source: Ministry of Internal Affairs and Communications, *Labour Force Survey* (*Detailed Tabulation*).

Table 6.3. **A comparison of regular and non-regular workers**[1]
In per cent unless indicated otherwise

A. Average age in years	Male	Female	Percentage under age 30
Regular workers	39.6	37.0	23.0
Non-regular workers	43.2	41.0	25.1
B. Gender	Male	Female	Female employees by status
Regular workers	47.3	18.2	44.4
Non-regular workers	11.8	22.7	55.6
C. Education[2]	Lower secondary	Upper secondary	University
Regular workers	2.4	42.2	31.4
Non-regular workers	7.2	55.8	12.1
D. Occupation	Clerical workers	Service workers	Professional/technical workers
Regular workers	44.7	6.2	13.4
Non-regular workers	25.5	24.0	13.2
E. Sector[3]	Manufacturing	Services	Construction
Regular workers	76.7	58.7	85.6
Non-regular workers	23.3	41.3	14.4
F. Size of company[3] (number of employees)	More than 1 000	30 to 999	5 to 29
Regular workers	81.0	66.6	62.1
Non-regular workers	19.0	33.4	37.9
G. Wage payment system	By hour	By day	By month or year
Regular workers	2.3	4.9	89.7
Non-regular workers	66.4	8.7	21.3
H. Working time	Average hours per week	Percentage below 35 hours	Average days per week
Regular workers	40.4	0.6	5.3
Non-regular workers	30.3	53.0	4.8
I. Coverage by social insurance	Employees' pension	Health insurance	Employment insurance
Regular workers	99.3	99.6	99.4
Non-regular workers	47.1	49.1	63.0
J. Tenure	Less than 1 year	1 to 10 years	More than 10 years
Regular workers	3.9	45.8	49.4
Non-regular workers	21.5	65.5	13.0

1. Non-regular workers include part-time workers, temporary workers, dispatched workers, workers on loan from other companies, and contract workers. This survey was based on a random sample of 16 232 firms (with more than five employees) and 35 094 workers engaged in those firms. The response rate was around 70%. The numbers in the table show the sample average of the answers to the survey.
2. Highest level of education attained.
3. Figures show the percentage of regular and non-regular employees in each sector and for each size of company.
Source: Ministry of Health, Labour and Welfare (2003), *General survey on diversified types of employment*, 2003.

According to a 2006 survey of firms, reducing labour costs is the most important reason why firms hire non-regular workers (Table 6.4). Indeed, cutting labour costs was cited by 71% of firms (Panel A) as the major advantage of employing part-time workers (58.4% in the case of other non-regular workers). The proportion was somewhat higher than in a similar 2001 survey, suggesting that the corporate sector is even more focused on cutting costs in this economic expansion than during the 2001 downturn. On an hourly basis, part-time workers were paid only 40% as much as full-time workers in 2006.[1] In addition, hiring non-regular workers reduces firms' payments for bonuses and retirement allowances.[2] Moreover, firms hiring part-time workers benefit from an additional 13% of savings in non-wage costs because employees working less than a certain number of hours are exempted from health insurance, pension contributions and employment insurance, thus eliminating the need for co-payments from employers.[3] Firms justify the difference in wages between regular and part-time workers on a number of grounds: i) part-time workers have more flexibility in working hours (73%); ii) regular workers are expected to contribute more (33%); iii) regular workers are subject to more frequent and longer over-time work (31%); and iv) regular workers are expected to transfer to different workplaces (15%).

The strategy of reducing labour costs through increasing non-regular employment appears to be effective, as there is a strong negative correlation between the increase in part-time employment and wage growth by industry (Figure 6.5). The four service industries with the largest increases in part-timers – retail, restaurants and hotels, medical and nursing care and other services – also experienced the largest wage declines. These four industries alone account for almost half of total employment in Japan.

The survey of firms also reported that employment flexibility is a second important objective for hiring non-regular employees; in 2006, 23.8% hired part-time workers to cope with temporary increases in demand (Column B) and 21.9% did so to facilitate adjustments in their workforce to business fluctuations (Column C). Similar proportions hired other types of non-regular workers for these reasons. The enhanced flexibility afforded by using non-regular workers is important to compensate for the high level of employment protection provided to regular workers. Indeed, Japan is ranked tenth out of 28 OECD countries in terms of the strictness of employment protection for regular workers, including voluntary practices by enterprises (OECD, 2004). The 2003 revision of the Labour Standard Law stated that any dismissal of workers that is not objectively justifiable and that is not considered to be acceptable by society's standards shall be deemed an abuse of power and is therefore invalid. Judicial precedents have set four conditions to judge whether employment adjustments as a result of corporate downsizing can be deemed as an abuse of power by a firm; i) the necessity of the firm reducing its workforce; ii) whether efforts were made to avoid dismissals, such as taking alternative measures that could achieve the necessary reduction; iii) whether the selection of employees for dismissal was reasonable and objective; and iv) whether the overall dismissal procedure was judged to be acceptable.[4] Given these conditions, enterprises cannot fully anticipate beforehand if measures to rationalise their workforce will be accepted by the courts.

In a world of increasing competition, Japanese firms have an incentive to maintain a minimum number of regular workers and to adjust to demand fluctuations by relying on non-regular workers and outsourcing. While employment protection legislation applies to all workers in principle, non-regular workers, who in general are non-unionised, are less protected in practice. Employment protection is thus strongest for regular workers, who are defined as those with indefinite contracts. Moreover, many non-regular workers have

Table 6.4. **Reasons given by firms for hiring non-regular workers**[1]

	Share of firms hiring non-regular workers	To reduce costs	To cope with temporary increases in demand	Facilitate adjustment to business fluctuations	To cope with busy periods in the day	To work on easy tasks	Easy to hire	To hire experienced and skilled workers	To re-employ retired regular workers	Difficulty in finding new graduates for regular jobs	Other answers or unknown
		(A)	(B)	(C)	(D)	(E)	(F)	(G)	(H)	(I)	(J)
2001 survey											
Part-time workers	56.6	65.3	27.3	16.4	39.2	31.4	17.8	12.2	12.4	5.8	6.5
Other non-regular workers[2]	15.3	57.9	17.3	19.6	11.0	15.7	8.1	19.8	16.0	6.4	13.0
2006 survey											
Part-time workers	61.0	71.0	23.8	21.9	39.5	36.3	29.5	18.8	15.5	12.9	7.9
Other non-regular workers[2]	17.3	58.4	18.8	19.0	9.0	18.6	15.0	31.9	29.3	16.1	17.1

1. Firms were allowed to give multiple answers. This survey was based on a random sample of 9 133 firms with more than five employees (the response rate was 72.8%).
2. Includes non-regular workers whose working hours are the same as regular workers or longer and are thus not considered to be part-time workers.

Source: Ministry of Health, Labour and Welfare (2007b), *General research on the condition of part-time workers, 2006.*

fixed-term contracts, making it easy for firms to terminate employment by not renewing the contract. In sum, non-regular employment helps firms achieve the profit-maximising levels of output and employment, while containing adjustment costs.

The survey of firms shown in Table 6.4 suggests a number of other reasons for the growing use of non-regular workers. *First*, a rising number of firms have hired experienced and skilled workers as non-regular employees, suggesting that labour mobility is increasing (Column G). *Second*, demographic factors have also boosted the re-employment of older persons, who retire as regular workers when they reach company retirement ages but continue to work on fixed-term contracts (Column H).[5] *Third*, increasing competition for new graduates has forced some firms to rely on non-regular workers instead.[6] The number of new graduates hired increased by 19% between 2002 and 2006, with the manufacturing sector recording a 32% increase, according to the Tankan Survey by the

Figure 6.5. **The link between wage growth and part-time employment**
Between 2002 and 2006

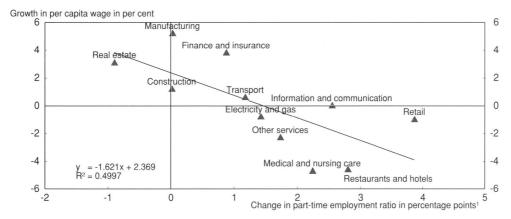

StatLink ᴍʰᴸ *http://dx.doi.org/10.1787/278586610765*

1. Change in the percentage of part-timers in total employment.

Source: Yashiro (2007) based on data from the Ministry of Health, Labour and Welfare.

Bank of Japan. Given the declining pool of young people graduating from school, the number of firms hiring non-regular workers because of difficulty in finding new graduates jumped from around 6% in 2001 to between 12.9% and 16.1% for part-time and other non-regular workers, respectively, in 2006 (Column I).

In addition to part-time workers, other categories of non-regular employment, notably dispatched workers (who are employed by temporary worker agencies) and employees on fixed-term contracts, have increased significantly in recent years (both are included in the "other category" in Table 6.1). The rise in these types of employees was facilitated by changes in labour laws. In 2003, the maximum length of fixed-term contracts was extended from less than one year to three years and to five years in the case of workers who have specialised knowledge or who are over the age of 60. The number of sectors where dispatched workers are permitted has been gradually expanded from 13 specific job categories and now includes manufacturing, although such workers are still prohibited in some areas, notably construction and much of the healthcare sector.

While for some workers, such as second earners in a household, lower pay can be compensated by the opportunity to work in flexible and diverse ways that match their lifestyle, the wide disparities in the treatment of non-regular workers raises a number of equity concerns. *First*, the large gap in wages appears to be too large to be explained by productivity differences, suggesting that there is an element of discrimination in the segmented labour market.[7] *Second*, non-regular workers are poorly covered by the social safety net. *Third*, given that firms hire non-regular workers to enhance employment flexibility, non-regular workers bear the brunt of the adjustment in employment during periods of economic weakness, resulting in their short average tenure compared to regular workers (Table 6.3). *Fourth*, the traditional employment system in Japan, based on long-term employment stability, has encouraged firm-based training of workers, since long tenures make such investment worthwhile. However, given their short average tenure, non-regular workers receive less firm-based training.[8] This has negative implications both for the individual non-regular workers and for Japan's potential growth rate.

The negative consequences of a dualistic labour market are reinforced by the limited mobility between the segments of the labour market. Not surprisingly, for those between the ages of 20 and 35, 76% of the men and 69% of the women who were non-regular workers hoped to become regular workers, according to a 2003 survey by the government.[9] However, another government survey reported that only 23% of part-time workers who changed jobs in 2005 were hired as regular workers, compared to 31% in 1990. In sum, the dualistic labour market traps a large proportion of the labour force in low-paying jobs with little employment security, limited coverage by the social safety net and limited access to training.

Policies to cope with increased labour market dualism

The 1993 Part-time Workers Law was revised in 2007 in an effort to improve the working conditions of part-time workers. The revisions, which were fully implemented in April 2008, are aimed at achieving balanced treatment of all part-time workers relative to regular workers. The key points of the revision include:

- To reduce uncertainty about working conditions, the revision introduced an administrative penalty (up to 100 thousand yen) on employers that fail to explicitly disclose the possibility of wage hikes and whether the employee will receive the retirement allowance and bonus payments.

- The revised law prohibits discriminatory treatment of part-time workers who have the same job description, degree of job rotation, and type of labour contract as regular workers. This provision thus applies only to part-time workers with regular contracts. However, no penalties are imposed on firms that fail to provide such treatment, although the government can issue orders to improve the situation.[10]

- To encourage mobility, the revised law requests employers to implement measures to shift part-time employees to regular employee status through a system of internal promotions and transfers.

- The labour market dispute resolution mechanism that exists in all prefectures can be used by part-time workers.

- Public support for part-time workers is provided through subsidies to employers who provide fair treatment for part-time workers, based on certain criteria, such as introducing a common wage mechanism for regular and part-time workers and health checks. This system is operated by a non-profit organisation created by the government. It appears that a firm would be able to get up to 1.7 million yen (about $16 thousand) from this subsidy scheme.

The direct impact of the provisions against discriminatory treatment may not be so large, as they protect only around 4-5% of part-time workers. However, over time, the provisions against discrimination could have a larger impact to the extent that it encourages employers to change management practice and improve the treatment of part-time workers. In practice, international experience suggests that it is often difficult to determine how much of the wage gap between regular and part-time employees is explained by workers' characteristics (education, experience, etc.) and how much is due to discrimination. Given these uncertainties, enforcing a prohibition on discrimination against part-time employees could subject firms to costly and time-consuming litigation that would discourage the employment of such workers. For example, if non-discrimination were interpreted as wage parity, the total wage bill could increase substantially. The end result could be a reduction in employment of part-time workers and in overall employment. In any event, the anti-discrimination provision will only cover a small fraction of part-time workers, as noted above. In addition, the introduction of subsidies for firms improving their employment practices for part-time workers raises concerns, as these subsidies often result in high deadweight costs.

A second concern is whether requesting employers to introduce schemes for mobility between part-time and regular status will have any effect. Management is already free to shift part-time workers to regular jobs, so it is doubtful whether the government's request will have much impact. Moreover, given that forcing firms to increase the flow of part-time workers to regular worker status could lead to even worse results, the revised law should not be interpreted as an obligation. Instead, the government should address the underlying causes of immobility in the labour market, notably labour costs, employment flexibility and the lack of a secondary market for experienced workers. Enhancing mobility requires removing features that discourage regular workers from moving, for example by abolishing preferential treatment of retirement allowances and shifting firm-based pension and health insurance systems to individual-based systems. As for labour costs, while the government cannot narrow the difference in wages, it should decrease the overall gap in labour costs by increasing the coverage of non-regular workers by the social insurance system. In addition, it should reduce employment protection for regular workers to weaken the incentives to hire non-regular workers. Countries with strict protection for regular workers tend to have a higher incidence of temporary employment (Grubb *et al.*, 2007). While the incentive could be reduced by raising the effective protection for non-regular workers, such an approach would risk reducing overall employment. Finally, the government needs to ensure adequate training for non-regular workers.

Ensuring adequate vocational training in Japan

Traditionally, job training in Japan has been a company responsibility, especially in large enterprises, in a context of long-term employment relations. In contrast, public training programmes were relatively limited compared to other OECD countries. For example, public expenditure on training programmes for the unemployed amounted to only 0.04% of GDP in FY 2005, well below the OECD average of 0.17%. Direct provision of job training by the public sector varies by contents and duration. For example, there are six-month training courses for those who need new skills to be re-employed, weekly training courses for those who wish to improve their skills, and long-term courses for youths who need to master skills and knowledge necessary to be employed. In addition, several training programmes are outsourced to private schools and institutions depending on the speciality. On average, nearly 0.5 million persons (0.6% of the working-age population) participate in programmes per year. Including financial support for employees and employers, total spending amounted to 145 billion yen (0.1% of government spending) in FY 2007.[11]

However, the rising proportion of non-regular workers who benefit little from firm-based training creates a need for a larger government role in this area. The problem is concentrated among the so-called "freeters".[12] The government estimates that there were 1.87 million freeters in 2006, accounting for 5.9% of the 15 to 34 age group and 2.3% of the total working-age population. The problem is most serious among those in the 25 to 34 age group who graduated from school when the hiring of new graduates was sharply reduced and have since moved from one non-regular job to another without gaining much job experience. More generally, Japan has an increasing incidence of long-term unemployment in contrast to the downward trend observed in the OECD area in recent years (Figure 6.6). Indeed, the proportion of unemployed who are out of work for more than one year has almost doubled from 17.5% in 1994 to 33% in 2006, surpassing the OECD average. Long-term unemployment poses a particular challenge as it leads to a deterioration in workers' skills, making it harder for them to find a job.

Job training and job search assistance activities are major themes of the "Challenge Again" plan launched in 2006 to assist those facing unemployment and financial difficulties.[13] This initiative includes new and existing programmes:

● A total of 59 policies,[14] including training, counselling and the creation of employment opportunities, are aimed at freeters. The objective is to reduce the number of freeters, which peaked at 2.17 million persons in 2003, to 1.74 million persons by 2010. Another objective is to ensure permanent worker status for 250 thousand freeters.

● There are 11 policies aimed at non-regular workers, including part-time workers. In addition to training, this includes the revision of the Labour Contract Law to specify rules on labour contracts for all workers, including non-regular workers such as employees on fixed-term labour contracts. Other important elements include the revision of the Part-

Figure 6.6. **An international comparison of long-term unemployment**

As a per cent of total unemployment

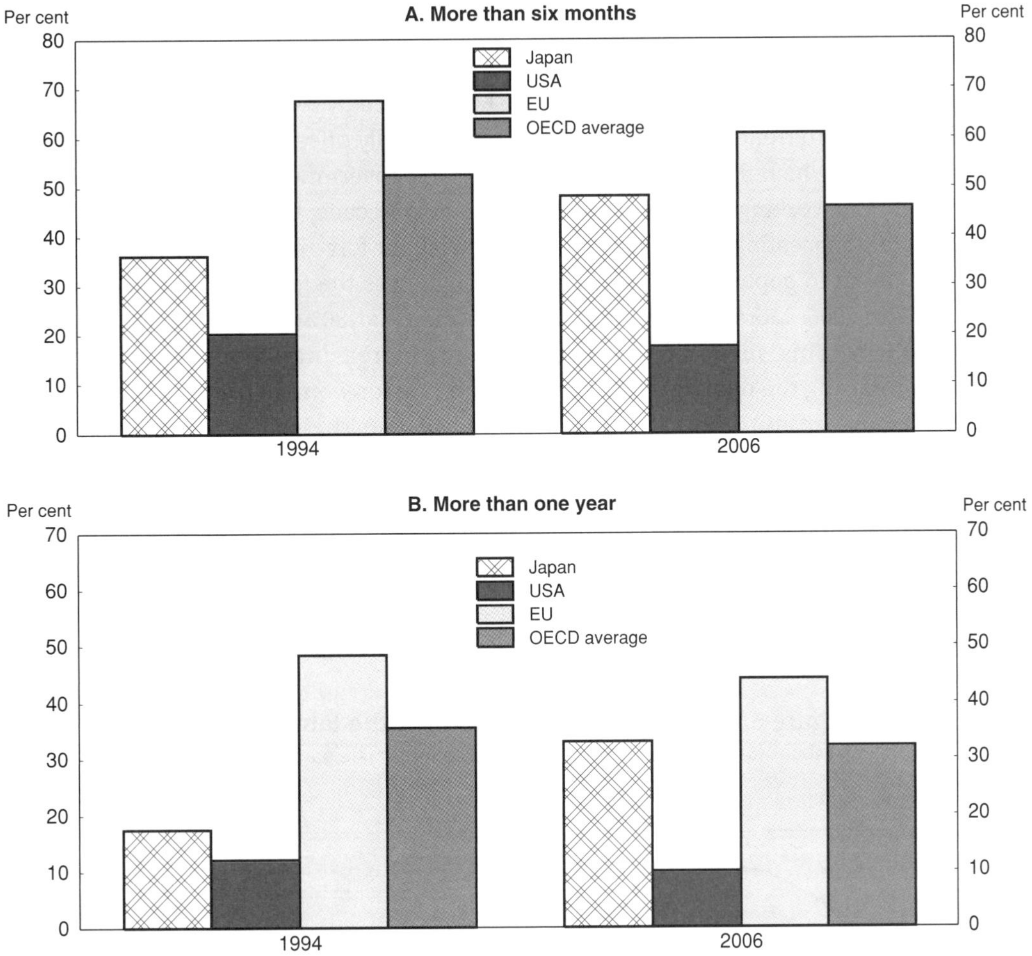

StatLink http://dx.doi.org/10.1787/278587048847

Source: OECD (2007), OECD Employment Outlook, OECD, Paris.

time Workers Law to realise balanced treatment (see above) and the expansion of social security coverage.

● Ten policy actions have been introduced for adult re-education. These measures include the provision of education-related counselling and educational opportunities by the creation of "Challenge Again" education support councils in ten specific areas, and support for the development and implementation of practical education programmes at universities and technical colleges.

As many of the policies were only implemented in FY 2007, it is too early to evaluate their impact. Evidence from OECD countries suggests that appropriate training policies can improve the labour market position of specific targeted groups (OECD, 2004). In addition, higher spending on labour market training is associated with lower unemployment (OECD, 2006a). At a macroeconomic level, it is clear that investment in human capital fosters economic growth and long-term improvements in living standards. The success of training in Japan will depend on the design of the programmes and the extent to which they provide qualifications and expertise that are attractive to firms. It is essential to closely monitor the outcomes of these training initiatives in order to ensure a positive outcome.

Coping with rapid population ageing

Japan's working-age population (ages 15 to 64) declined by 3.4% during the decade 1996 to 2006. The upward trend in the participation rate partially offset the impact on the size of the labour force, which declined by less than 2%. The government projects an additional 9% decline in the working-age population over the next decade, the largest fall expected in the OECD area, suggesting that policies to promote labour force participation are a priority. The employment to population ratio for men, though, was the fourth highest in the OECD area at 81% in 2006. Moreover, the rate for older men – at 80% – is well above the OECD average of 63%. This suggests that the scope for increasing labour inputs depends primarily on raising the relatively low participation rate for women. For prime-age women (the 25 to 54 age group), the rate is the sixth lowest in the OECD area (Figure 4.14). Moreover, the proportion of women who work part-time is one of the highest in the OECD area at 41%.

The size of Japan's labour force depends importantly on female labour force participation. If the rate for each age cohort by gender remains at its 2005 level, the labour force would decline by a fifth by 2030, based on the government's population forecast (Figure 6.7). In contrast, if female participation rates were boosted to the current level for

Figure 6.7. **Long-term projections of the labour force**
Labour force based on different scenarios for female participation[1]

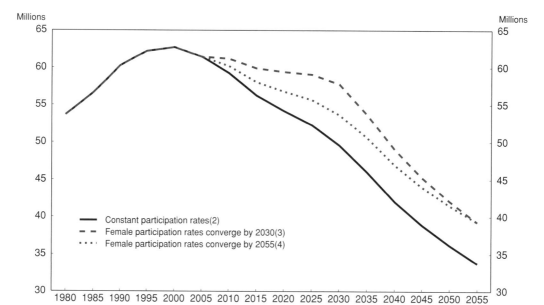

StatLink http://dx.doi.org/10.1787/278621725468

1. The labour force covers the population between the ages of 15 and 64.
2. The participation rates for men and women remain at their current levels for each age group.
3. The female labour participation rates converge by 2030 to the rates for males for each age group.
4. The female labour participation rates converge by 2055 to the rates for males for each age group.

Source: National Institute of Population and Social Security Research, Population Projection for Japan (December 2006 version); Ministry of Internal Affairs and Communications, Labour Force Survey; and OECD calculations.

men by the year 2030 for each age cohort, the decline in the labour force would be limited to 6%, about a third as much in the case of unchanged participation rates, thus easing the burden of population ageing on the labour force. Looking further ahead to mid-century, changes in female participation rate make less of a difference: the labour force would fall by 41% assuming unchanged participation rates compared to 31% if female rates converge to male levels. By that point, the proportion of elderly (over age 65) is projected to reach 72% of the population aged 20 to 64, the second highest rate in the OECD area (Figure 1.7). Coping with the demographic situation over the longer term thus depends on promoting labour force participation, as well as by increasing population growth by raising the fertility rate and allowing more immigration (see the 2006 *OECD Economic Survey Japan*).

Encouraging greater labour force participation by women

The government launched a package of 21 initiatives in 2006 to increase the female labour force by a quarter million by 2015. In particular, these policies are aimed at facilitating the re-employment of mothers, reflecting the fact that around 60% of women withdraw from the labour force when their first child is born. The initiatives include the provision of job counselling and specialised job placement centres for women with children. Despite these efforts, a number of the policy recommendations to boost female labour force participation contained in past *OECD Economic Surveys of Japan* remain important:

- Reducing dualism in the labour market would help expand regular employment, thus enhancing the attractiveness of employment for women. As noted above, women account for about two-thirds of non-regular workers.

- The tax and social security systems should be reformed to reduce disincentives to work by secondary earners, as discussed in Chapter 4.

- Increasing the importance of performance assessment in pay and promotion decisions would reduce the importance of seniority and tenure, thus narrowing wage gaps between genders.

- The availability of childcare facilities should be increased by easing the licensing regulations and encouraging more private-sector firms to enter this sector. There is not sufficient capacity in certified day-care centres in major urban areas. Profit-making companies were allowed to enter this sector in 2000, subject to strict licensing conditions.

The biggest obstacle to greater integration of women in the labour market is probably some workplace practices that are difficult for those with family responsibilities. This problem has been acknowledged by the growing government emphasis on "work-life balance". A 2005 law obliges firms with more than 300 workers to make an action plan to promote work-life balance. By June 2006, nearly all companies had submitted plans and the government is currently helping smaller enterprises develop similar programmes. Companies that introduce policies to help their employees balance work and childcare can receive awards from the government. In addition, it is important to strictly enforce the Labour Standard Law, which sets working time at 40 hours per week, and the guideline limiting overtime work to 15 hours per week, 45 hours per month, 120 hours per quarter and 360 hours per year.

Policies to increase the low birth rate

As noted above, measures to boost the fertility rate would help ease the demographic challenge in Japan. The fall in the birth rate (the total fertility rate), from 2.16 in 1971 to 1.26 in 2005, is a major concern of the government. Although it rebounded to 1.32 in 2006, it remains the lowest in the OECD area after Korea. The declining birth rate is due to delayed marriage and the fall in the number of children per couple. Empirical research (Date and Shimizutani, 2004) suggests that a number of factors influence the birth rate: i) labour force participation of women tends to reduce fertility, with the impact stronger for full-time than part-time workers; ii) a higher wage level for women is negatively correlated with childbearing, reflecting higher opportunity costs, while higher income for men is positively correlated; iii) child support by firms is positively correlated with the childbearing of female employees; and iv) the availability of childcare services promotes employment, marriage and childbearing.

The government implemented several plans to reverse the declining birth rate, such as "The Angel Plan" in 1994 and "The New Angel Plan" in 2000, which focused on improving the environment for childbearing, including reforms in the areas of employment, social welfare and education. Nevertheless, the birth rate continued to fall during this period. More recently, the government has been increasing spending on policies aimed at boosting fertility. Such expenditures rose by 12% in FY 2007 to 1.7 trillion yen (0.3% of GDP). This funded a hike in the child allowance[15] and raised the rate of child-care leave benefits. In addition, preferential tax treatment will be provided to companies that establish a qualified on-site childcare centre. Finally, affirmative labour market policies related to young and non-regular workers will be introduced. To evaluate policies in these areas, the government established a committee, which issued its final report in December 2007. It stated that; i) effective fiscal expenditure is needed to support the social infrastructure for achieving good balance between working and childbearing and this should be regarded as investment rather than consumption; ii) the provision of healthcare and employment insurance, child welfare, and maternal and child healthcare needs to be better co-ordinated; and iii) work-life balance should be decided freely between employers and employees while the government provides the necessary social infrastructure to achieve such a balance.

Efforts to expand the availability of childcare are likely to increase the fertility rate (D'Addio and Mira d'Ercole, 2005), while at the same time encouraging women to work (Jaumotte, 2003). Policies that reduce the direct cost of raising children, such as child allowances, also boost fertility rates in OECD countries. However, such policies have also been found to lower female employment by reducing the need to work (Jaumotte, 2003). Given the more immediate priority of mitigating population ageing through greater female labour force participation, policy measures to increase fertility should focus on those likely to also boost female employment at the same time.

Conclusion

Japan's challenges of rising labour market dualism, weak productivity growth in non-manufacturing sectors, increased income inequality, low female labour force participation and a low fertility rate are inter-related. With Japan's working-age population projected to decline by more than 40% by 2050, it is essential to make efficient use of the country's human resources, including women and young people. Resolving these problems requires a comprehensive approach that is summarised in Box 6.1.

Box 6.1. **Summary of recommendations to reform the labour market**

Reverse the trend toward increasing labour market dualism

- Reduce employment protection for regular workers to reduce the incentive for hiring non-regular workers to enhance employment flexibility.

- Expand the coverage of non-regular workers by social insurance systems based in workplaces, in part by improving compliance, in order to reduce the cost advantages of non-regular workers.

- Increase training to enhance human capital and the employability of non-regular workers, thereby improving Japan's growth potential.

Raise the labour force participation rate of women, while encouraging higher fertility

- Reverse the rising proportion of non-regular workers to provide more attractive employment opportunities to women.

- Reform aspects of the tax and social security system that reduce work incentives for secondary earners.

- Encourage greater use of performance assessment in pay and promotion decisions.

- Expand the availability of childcare, while avoiding generous child-related transfers that may weaken work incentives.

- Encourage better work-life balance, in part by better enforcing the Labour Standards Act.

Notes

1. The difference has been relatively stable since 1993. However, according to the 2006 survey cited in Table 6.4, 40% of firms did not give any pay increase to non-regular workers, while only 20% did not give pay increases to regular workers. This reflects the fact that 34.4% of regular workers get regular promotions compared to only 7.7% of non-regular workers.

2. The 2006 survey cited in Table 6.4 also asked firms why non-regular workers cost less. For part-timers, firms cited wages (70.3%), bonuses (63.5%), retirement allowances (47.9%) and social security payments (35.1%). For other non-regular workers, the responses were bonuses (70.6%), wages (64.2%), retirement allowances (54.8%) and social security payments (18.9%). In addition, around 6% of firms cited lower costs of training for part-time and other non-regular workers.

3. Employees who work less than three-quarters of the hours worked by regular employees in an enterprise (on a daily, weekly or monthly basis) are exempted from employees' pension and health insurance contributions. Employees working less than one year or less than 20 hours a week are exempted from employment insurance.

4. Prior to 2003, the legal code did not specify any legal grounds for dismissing workers in principle. A reform proposed by the government in 2003 stated that corporations have the right, in principle, to dismiss workers. However, this was eliminated from the bill due to resistance from opposition parties and labour unions. The new law states that any dismissal of workers that is not objectively justifiable and that is not considered to be acceptable by social standards shall be deemed an abuse of power and therefore invalid.

5. In fact, the category "To re-employ retired regular workers" includes both older workers and women who leave regular jobs. In 2006, the share of firms rehiring older persons as part-timers or other non-regular workers was 8% and 22%, respectively. As for women, the proportion was around 7% for both categories.

6. Between 1997 and 2003, the number of new graduates hired fell by more than half, sharply raising the unemployment rate for those in the 15 to 24 age group to a double-digit level and boosting the proportion of idle youth who were not in the labour force or in school (the so-called "NEETs").

7. In 2000, female part-time workers earned 55% as much as female regular workers. One study (Onoue, 2003) found that differences in age and tenure accounted for only 5 to 10 percentage points of the difference. In other words, after adjusting for the age and tenure of a part-time female

employee, she earned only 60% to 65% as much as a regular female employee. The results are consistent across sectors. For example, in the service sector, part-time workers make 56% as much as regular employees. Adjusting for age and tenure reduces the gap by only 6 to 9 percentage points.

8. This was shown in Ministry of Health, Labour and Welfare (2007a), which surveyed 6 886 firms and 23 637 employees. According to firms, 72.2% provide "off-the-job" (formal) training for regular workers but only 37.9% provide it for non-regular workers. According to the survey of employees, 58.2% of regular workers said that they had received off-the-job training, compared to only 31% of non-regular workers. This problem is acknowledged in Ministry of Health, Labour and Welfare (2007c), which called for more focus on the lack of opportunities for non-regular workers to develop their human resources. It is necessary, therefore, to develop a system that allows all workers, regardless of their current employment status, to develop their human capital and thereby increase their earnings.

9. This is based on the "Actual conditions survey on the attributes of young people" in 2003 by the Cabinet Office. However, a survey covering all age groups, the "General survey on the actual conditions of diversification in employment styles" in 2003 by the Ministry of Health, Labour and Welfare found that only one-fifth of non-regular workers wished to become regular workers. This indicates that older workers and second earners in households are less concerned about non-regular employment.

10. The Labour Standards Law prohibits discriminatory treatment of employees based on gender, nationality, religion, etc. Violations are subject to fines and imprisonment. In general, though, this law has not been applied to discrimination against non-regular workers, on the grounds that wages are determined freely and independently by firms and workers.

11. For a detailed account of this issue, see Ministry of Health, Labour and Welfare (2006a). The government made a five-year plan to improve such programmes based on the advice of employers, employees and outside experts.

12. "Freeters" are defined as people between the ages of 15 and 34 who have graduated from school (for women, those who have graduated and are unmarried) and who are; i) employed as part-time workers, or as an *arbeit* (refers to a young person working a secondary or temporary job while engaging in some other activity, such as education); ii) unemployed and searching for a part-time job or an *arbeit* position; or iii) out of the labour force and expecting to find a part-time job or an *arbeit* position.

13. This programme is described at *www.kantei.go.jp/jp/saityarenzi/Outline.pdf*.

14. The total includes 15 new programmes, 39 existing programmes and the expansion of five existing programmes.

15. Child allowance is provided for those with a child below 12 years of age, unless previous annual income is above the limit, which varies by the number of dependent family members (for example, 5.7 million yen for a salaried worker with one dependent family member). For households with children less than 3 years old, 10 thousand yen per month is provided. For those with children aged over 3 years old, the first and second children are entitled to receive 5 thousand yen per month and the third and subsequent children are entitled to receive 10 thousand yen per month.

Bibliography

D'Addio, F. and M. Mira d'Ercole (2005), "Trends and Determinants of Fertility Rates in OECD Countries: The Role of Policies", OECD Social, Employment and Migration Working Paper No. 6, OECD, Paris.

Date, Y. and S. Shimizutani (2004), "On analyses of Japan's declining birth rate: A survey of empirical research and an examination of the policy implications", ESRI Discussion Paper No. 94, April, Tokyo (in Japanese).

Grubb, D., J.K. Lee and P. Tergeist (2007), "Addressing Labour Market Duality in Korea". OECD Social, Employment and Migration Working Paper No. 55, OECD, Paris.

Jaumotte, F. (2003), "Labour Force Participation of Women: Empirical Evidence on the Role of Policy and Other Determinants in OECD Countries", *OECD Economic Studies*, No. 37, 2003/2, OECD, Paris.

Ministry of Health, Labour and Welfare (2002), *General research on the condition of part-time workers*, Tokyo (in Japanese).

Ministry of Health, Labour and Welfare (2003), *General survey on diversified types of employment, 2003*, Tokyo (in Japanese).

Ministry of Health, Labour and Welfare (2006a), *Human resources development administration in Japan*, Tokyo (in Japanese).

Ministry of Health, Labour and Welfare (2006b), "Towards implementation of the re-stated OECD Jobs Strategy: The Japanese Experience", A forum on the re-stated OECD Jobs Strategy, Tokyo 30-31 October 2006.

Ministry of Health, Labour and Welfare (2007a), *Basic survey on human resource development, FY 2006*, Tokyo (in Japanese).

Ministry of Health, Labour and Welfare (2007b), *General research on the condition of part-time workers, 2006*, Tokyo (in Japanese).

Ministry of Health, Labour and Welfare (2007c), *White Paper on Labour Economics 2007*, Tokyo (in Japanese).

OECD (2003), *Babies and Bosses: Reconciling Work and Family Life*, Vol. 2, Austria, Ireland and Japan, OECD, Paris.

OECD (2004), *OECD Employment Outlook*, OECD, Paris.

OECD (2006a), *OECD Employment Outlook*, OECD, Paris.

OECD (2006b), *OECD Economic Survey of Japan*, OECD, Paris.

OECD (2007), *OECD Employment Outlook*, OECD, Paris.

Onoue, T. (2003), "On the current state and issues regarding wages of female part-time workers,"*Monthly Report DIO*, No. 172 May, Research Institute for Advancement of Living Standards, Tokyo (in Japanese).

Yamaguchi, M. (2006), "Macroeconomic Factors in the Widening Wage Differential between Regular and Part-time Workers", *Japanese Journal of Labour Studies*, 554, September, Tokyo (in Japanese).

Yashiro, Naomitsu (2007), "Japanese Economy; Challenge toward a Sustainable Growth", Ministry of Economy, Trade and Industry, Tokyo.

OECD PUBLICATIONS, 2, rue André-Pascal, 75775 PARIS CEDEX 16
PRINTED IN FRANCE
(10 2008 04 1 P) ISBN 978-92-64-04306-0 – No. 56037 2008